Born in Russia and educated at Moscow
Boot lectured on English and American lit
KGB, he emigrated in 1973, first to the USA and then, in 1988, to
the UK. His other books include *God and Man According to
Tolstoy*, *The Crisis Behind Our Crisis*, *How the Future Worked*
and *Democracy as a Neocon Trick*. Alexander Boot divides his time
between London and Burgundy, working on his next book and
blogging on alexanderboot.com.

'There are many wise ideas in this book'

Roger Scruton

*'A startlingly clear analysis of why we have become who we are, written with
such admirable clarity and wit that news of humanity's defeat seems almost
bearable. No one who claims to know anything should open their mouth in
public without reading it'*

Fay Weldon

*'Highly original ... an extremely important argument even for those who
have no religious belief, and Alexander Boot puts it more unflinchingly, more
courageously, than anyone else'*

Theodore Dalrymple

*'Those reading Alexander Boot's vigorous and witty assault on the modern
superstitions of progress and science will never see the world in the same way
again. A refreshing and original voice'*

James Le Fanu

*'At last! Someone with the courage to say the unsayable: that one can be
for liberty while detesting many of the means by which liberty is achieved'*

Digby Anderson

*'Alexander Boot puts his finger precisely on the malaise affecting western
societies. His book is the most readable account of the decline of the West
since Spengler, and serenely free from the contamination of academic jargon.
It should be read by politicians, teachers, bishops and anyone who has
anything to do with public administration. We should all read it. Twice'*

Peter Mullen

'We are tickled by [the Barbarian's] irreverence, his comic inversion of our old certitudes and our fixed creeds refreshes us; we laugh. But as we laugh we are watched by large and awful faces from beyond; and on these faces there is no smile.'

(Hilaire Belloc)

HOW THE WEST WAS LOST

ALEXANDER BOOT

With a Foreword by
Dr Theodore Dalrymple

I.B. TAURIS

LONDON · NEW YORK

FOR PENELOPE, THE WESTERN WOMAN

New paperback edition published in 2016 by
I.B.Tauris & Co Ltd
London • New York
www.ibtauris.com

First published in hardback in 2006 by I.B.Tauris & Co Ltd

ISBN: 978 1 78453 460 8
eISBN: 978 0 85772 922 4

A full CIP record for this book is available from the British Library
A full CIP record is available from the Library of Congress

Library of Congress Catalog Card Number: available

Typeset in Sabon by Oxford Publishing Services, Oxford
Printed and bound by CPI Group (UK) Ltd, Croydon, CR0 4YY

CONTENTS

Contents

FOREWORD

However prosperous we grow, however long-lived, there are
certain questions that gnaw at, or just below, our consciousness.
How should we live? What is life for? What is the basis of
morality? The fact that contemporary man has no satisfying
answer to these fundamental questions accounts for the fact that,
material progress notwithstanding, we do not experience life as
any better than our forefathers experienced it.

On the contrary, says the author of this highly original book. It
is not merely our experience but our conduct that has
deteriorated. When mankind loses its belief in a transcendent
authority superior to itself, it begins to worship itself: and no self-
worshipper, whether individual, national or collective, is very
attractive. Indeed, self-worshippers are dangerous, for they
recognize no limits to the power of their reason and will. This is
an extremely important argument even for those who have no
religious belief, and Mr Boot puts it more unflinchingly, more
courageously, than anyone else. It helps to explain the radical
egotism that seems to be so marked a feature of modern society
(an egotism without real individuality), and why people are
unable to tolerate even minor frustrations gracefully or
countenance checks to the satisfaction of their whims.

He tells us that the advent of self-worship happened during the
Enlightenment. Thus the terrible and unprecedented slaughters of

the last century were not a contradiction, but a consummation of the Enlightenment, brought about by people who believed that they could reason their way to utopia. It is one of the great virtues of this book that it seamlessly connects philosophy, politics and psychology. The author understands, as most people do not, that the way people behave is profoundly affected, even determined, by their philosophical outlook and their answer to the fundamental questions of human existence to which I have already referred. This is so even when they do not realize it themselves. In fact, no man can live without a philosophy, whether implicit or explicit.

The author does not confine himself to political or sociological matters. For him, culture – in its traditional sense, which is to say high culture – is the most important of all man's activities. And he points out that the greatest achievement of Western civilization in the arts, certainly in music and painting, preceded the Enlightenment. This is despite the fact that the populations of pre-Enlightenment societies were, by our standards, small, poor, unhealthy and what our current governors would no doubt call 'under-resourced.' (Florence in its heyday had a population considerably smaller than modern Croydon's, and was, moreover, subject to war, famine and epidemic. But few, I suppose, would dissent from the proposition that Florence contributed rather more to our cultural inheritance than has, or will, Croydon.) It is highly unlikely that any of our artistic productions will command much admiration or even antiquarian interest in three hundred years' time.

Mr Boot's explanation for the startling observation that our wealthy, healthy and technologically sophisticated society has produced nothing in the arts that can remotely compare with Shakespeare, Velazquez or Bach, is simple: pre-Enlightenment man's culture (in Europe) was entirely Judeo–Christian not only in origin but in sensibility. This meant that supreme artists such as Bach were not glorifying themselves, as present-day artists usually do, but God.

Not everyone will agree with all of Mr Boot's judgements or

arguments. But he raises very powerfully the fundamental questions of human existence in an age that, despite its manifold shortcomings, is philosophically complacent. We think that the Victorians suffered from shibboleths: Mr Boot demonstrates that we are even more unreflecting. Compared with us, Mr Podsnap was a radical sceptic. Mr Boot rouses us from our philosophical torpor and self-satisfaction.

Dr Theodore Dalrymple

PREFACE
TO THE SECOND EDITION

My publisher's kind offer to bring out a second edition has turned me from the writer of this book into its reader. For in the intervening ten years or so I had hardly opened *How the West was Lost*, a gap I now had to fill in a hurry.

This role reversal caused some trepidation. Will I find my thoughts superseded by subsequent events or indeed a change in my own thinking? What if the West that appeared lost at the time of writing has been found again? Alas, it has not. Nor has my analysis of the situation changed fundamentally. Granted, if I were writing this book anew today, I would probably revise some details at the periphery of the argument. But the argument itself would remain intact. Moreover, subsequent events have reinforced my conviction that any attempt to understand any historical period has to proceed not from politics, economics or sociology but from metaphysics. All else is derivative.

The 2008 financial crisis is a case in point. It was caused, as we know, by promiscuously incontinent borrowing, both private and public. Rather than paying their own way, individuals and governments were busily erecting pyramids resting on the termite-ridden foundations of debt. Sooner or later such flimsy structures are bound to collapse, as they did in 2008 and will predictably do so again before long. Recklessness on this scale is a recent phenomenon. To wit, the last 50 years of the nineteenth century produced a negligible combined inflation of 10 per cent. However, the same indicator for the last 50 years of the twentieth century stood at 2,000 per cent. In other words, both individuals and governments suddenly developed such voracious fiscal appetites that they could only be satisfied by massive infusions of borrowed or freshly printed cash.

Why did people change their fiscal behaviour so drastically? Because, I maintain, they changed the metaphysical premise from which they proceeded. After all, what we think affects what we do, and what we believe affects what we think. The dominant formative belief of modernity is that life lacks any transcendent meaning: it is an accident of birth ending in death. That makes the *process* of life its highest meaning, and the aim then is to squeeze as much as possible out of every moment. Any self-limitation of passions becomes illogical. The polarity of good and bad is replaced by useful and useless. The worst sin stops being sinful if it brings pleasure. And since, contrary to the popular truism, the best things in a life so defined are far from free, we shall have to pursue aggressively the means of acquiring them.

Pursuit of money comes to the forefront of aspirations, and impatience to the forefront of emotions. Taking the waiting out of wanting, as an old advertisement promised, becomes an urgent imperative. An individual feels entitled to gratification now, and if he cannot pay for it he will borrow with little regard for tomorrow. Tomorrow, after all, he may be dead. It is no surprise then that, in the decade preceding the crisis, private spending in America, to cite one example, was three times greater than private income. Similarly, government officials will borrow billions to buy peoples' support, allowing voters to pay for things they have not earned and would otherwise be unable to afford. Hence the growing pyramid of public debt bound to come down on the heads of future generations; and hence also the crises past and future.

Or take science as another example of a metaphysical premise at work. It is only thanks to sound metaphysics that Western civilisation has more or less made science its exclusive property. The greatest philosophers of Hellenic antiquity proceeded from the assumption that the world exists not objectively but subjectively, as a reflection of individual perception. Such a metaphysical premise can encourage philosophical contemplation, and the Greeks did produce a profusion of sublime thinkers. But the meat of Greek philosophy was the poison of science. Natural science cannot succeed, or indeed proceed, without two core assumptions, both metaphysical: first, that the world exists irrespective of our senses; and second, that it is rationally arranged and therefore rationally knowable.

Western civilisation corrected the Hellenic metaphysical error by stating that, because nature was created by a rational law-giver, it functions according to universal rational laws. This made nature a legitimate object of intellectual quest and experimental study. Science was born as a result. You will also notice that those Eastern civilisations that perceive the world as an evil chaos, with only man's inner world possessing any reality or virtue, have also made an understated contribution to science. This realisation of the primacy of metaphysics in the make-up of a civilisation – and culture, as its most visible manifestation – was the starting point of this book. Some of the aspects of life in general and the West in particular that had hitherto left me baffled began to make sense.

One such aspect is the manifest hostility of modernity to the metaphysical and cultural heritage of the West. Empirical evidence of such animosity is easy to find everywhere we look. For example, during their revolution, and in the century following it, the French destroyed 80 per cent of their Romanesque and Gothic buildings (mercifully the remaining 20 per cent is still more than most countries boast in their entirety). People tend to treat their prized possessions with more care. The Modern Frenchmen, however, no longer regarded their cultural possessions as prized or indeed theirs. Those old buildings symbolised something alien and detestable, and swinging a wrecking ball communicates such feelings with eloquent finality.

The same wrecking ball, physical or metaphorical, has been taken to everything that made the West Western in any other than the geographical sense. The underlying assumption seems to have been that we would be able to enjoy the material products of the West's metaphysics while dumping the metaphysics itself. The guns opening up 100 years ago voiced a thunderous objection to this line of thought by heralding the arrival of the twentieth century, in which more people died violent deaths than in all the previous centuries of recorded history combined. The appalling death toll was made so much higher by the technological advances of which modernity is so proud.

Technology is of course a good thing, provided it is wielded by good people. We must never forget that the same company that gave us aspirin also gave us Zyklon B, and that the same energy that heats so many of our houses can also turn them to radioactive dust. Unless scientific and technological progress is accompanied by a similarly vectored cultural, which is to say metaphysical, development, it can become very regressive indeed. My contention is that no such incremental improvement in this faculty is observable. Quite the opposite: physics and metaphysics seem to be heading in opposite directions.

The conclusion I reach is that Modern Man is typologically different from Western Man, and the hostility of the former to the latter is a principal animus of modernity. Contrary to the prevailing view, Western modernity is not so much a development of Western tradition as its corruption. This book was – and still remains – an attempt to record the manifestations of this process in different walks of life, and to understand its origins.

Now a decade is a long time in a writer's life, but it is but an instant in the lifespan of a book. Still, certain conclusions can already be reached even after such a risibly short time. Mindful of Cassandra's fate, I studiously avoided indulging in any prophesies when writing this essay. However, reading the book now I realise that such uncharacteristic reticence did not always succeed. Fully aware that 'I told you so' are among the most despised words in the English language, I still notice with some satisfaction that the intervening decade has done nothing to invalidate some of the predictions that I let slip through. For example, I wrote that 'it is relatively safe to predict that, over the next ten years, more and more people in Western Europe and North America will be sent to prison not for something they have done, but for something they have said'. Any newspaper reader will confirm that this has indeed happened. Also, writing at the time of the euphoria over Russia's perestroika which, according to some unenlightened commentators, spelled the end of history, I observed that little of substance had changed in Russia – another comment lamentably borne out by recent history.

I cannot claim any prophetic talents, but I do suggest that modernity is not that hard to understand if one finds the right vantage point to look at it. I believed 10 years ago that I had found such a vantage point and, having taken a fresh look at this book, I am happy that I still feel that way. You can hear me heave a sigh of relief even as we speak.

PREFACE
TO THE FIRST EDITION

When my son Max was still a boy, he often was on the receiving end of the kind of ideas you will find in this book. Once, no doubt wishing to divert my didactic zeal elsewhere, he said, 'Dad, why don't you just write a book about this?' I promised I would, soon. Little did I know that in the time it would take me to act on my promise Max would grow up and write his own books. Looking back, it is easy to see why. As nothing in life exists in isolation, separate ideas on various outrages of modernity can only enliven a dinner party or, at a pinch, make a reasonable magazine piece. But unless they all come together as a cohesive analysis *ab omnibus*, truth will not emerge. Too many things will remain unexplained; too many questions will go unanswered. So one cannot just sit down and write such a book. It has to be lived – and living takes time.

I have set out to answer – or at least to ask – many of the key questions of modernity. Such as, 'Is the West still Western?' 'Does our present have anything to do with our past?' 'Why do so many people hate tradition even when paying lip service to it?' 'By gaining wealth, have we in the West lost something more important?' The conclusion I reach is that vogue commentators are right: there is such as thing as a clash of civilizations. Where I diverge from the fashion of today is in my belief that, first, the clash has already taken place and the West has lost; and second, that the vanquishing civilization, rather than coming from a remote continent, grew to maturity within the West itself. How did this come about? This question is interlinked with many others, and, as you read this book, the links will come into focus. But, to see them clearly, few intellectual stones could be left unturned, and then a liveable house had to be built out of the stones. The immediate inspiration for this synthetic method comes from Spengler, but its roots go back to Plato who saw links where others did not; for example: 'the forms and rhythms of music never change without also causing a change in the crucial political structures and trends.' Obviously, building a case *ab omnibus* gives one many entries into the core of the issue; and, if the issue is as vast as modernity, breadth is as essential as depth. The disadvantage of this method is that it gives so many more targets to any compulsive sniper. Anticipating every possible cheap shot (no writer will ever admit vulnerability to any other kind) is hard, but at least some will have to be aimed at my peripatetic background.

English is not the only language in which I could have written this book as, apart from England, I have lived in four countries. Two of these, Russia and the USA, are treated in this book as the champions of what I shall describe as, respectively, the 'nihilist' and the 'philistine' wings of modernity. For 12 years or so the Soviet Union shared the nihilist burden with Nazi Germany, a partner as hideous but less influential both in its lasting impact and its geographical and temporal spread. It is for this, and not any personal reason, that I allocate more space to the Soviets than to the Nazis when analysing the nihilist horrors of modernity. This of course runs against the grain of the emotional consensus in the West, where many will happily sport Soviet lapel pins but not, outside the loony fringe and the less mature members of the British Royal family, Nazi insignia.

My book is non-partisan in that I feel loyalty only to the truth and not to any political cause, much less to any party. Thus, I shall often disagree emphatically with iconic figures not only on the left but also on the right. For instance, unlike Hayek, I treat socialism as a natural consequence of liberalism, not its denial; unlike Chesterton, I am not unequivocal in my praise of the scholastics; and unlike Tocqueville's, my admiration for democracy in America is not without some, rather narrow, limits. In short, readers of any persuasion will be exposed to a certain amount of bloody-mindedness which, however, will always relate to the book's central theme.

Truth-seeking can lead one in all sorts of directions. In this case, it made me question not just this or that facet of modernity but its fundamental premises. Communicating this in an anodyne manner that would offend nobody is impossible. Like it or not, modernity has left an imprint on us all, and people do not take lightly to having their axioms rejected. So some will consider this book to be sharply polemical or even deliberately provocative, an effect as inevitable as it is unintended. One can only hope that even those readers will find the book not only infuriating but also stimulating, helping them to ponder their own ideas more deeply even if they ultimately do not change them.

A London *Times* columnist recently pronounced that only people who hold modern views are fit for a public office. Mercifully, I am not running for one; but if I were, this book would disqualify me not just on its content but also on its language. In these pages I shall treat political correctness as a symptom, not the disease. But I, along with many others, find this symptom to be particularly painful. Reading sentences like 'A partner has a right to their share of the estate' sends blood rushing to my head, and if I myself used such grammar no anti-hypertensive would work. So, consistently and unapologetically, I follow singular antecedents with singular pronouns; and if the gender of the antecedent is not specified I apply the ancient law of 'man embraces woman', which, in my view, has never been repealed. Similarly, I use the word 'man' in the compound terms denoting social and cultural types, as in 'Western man' and

'Modern man' (or 'Westman' and 'Modman', the central concepts of this book). I hope that even readers who are less rigorous in these matters will not find such usage offensive.

Books that are radical of approach and melancholy of tone are notoriously hard to publish. So I am forever grateful to Iradj Bagherzade of I.B.Tauris for having seen the merit of my effort, especially since his own ideas are very different from mine. Such fairness is hard to find in our politicized world. Also, Iradj's editorial comments have made the book's style leaner and its content more sound – no writer could have asked for more. Thanks should also go to Dr Theodore Dalrymple, even though I failed to get in a word before him yet again. Many of my illustrative examples are based on his pioneering – and impeccably stylish – social commentary, shared with me both through various publications and privately. And of course I must thank my wife, the wonderful pianist Penelope Blackie, who inspired the book, lived it with me and kept me straight on many important points. Some men have all the luck.

PART 1
EXPOSITION

THE MAKING OF WESTERN MAN

Western man was born in the East. This paradoxical fact alone suggests that, though his geographic habitat was mostly coextensive with Western countries, geography was not what made this type of man Western.

He was brought to life by an earth-shattering event that took place 2000 years ago at the eastern outskirts of *Pax Romana*, in a plain Galilean barn. Whether we believe that event to be the Incarnation, as Christians do, or simply the birth of a remarkable man does not matter in the context of this narrative. What matters is that after the birth of Jesus Christ it was as impossible for the world to remain the same as it had been for the Hebrews to stay pagan after Moses.

The event caught people unawares though it was not exactly unheralded – various Hebrew prophets had shared some vague premonitions with their contemporaries. Yet vague those premonitions were, and they hardly had more than a parochial effect: the Romans neither counted years in a descending order in the run-up to the Nativity nor started from zero after it. Caesar did not foresee the cataclysm awaiting Rome; Tiberius was probably unaware it had occurred.

But once the upheaval arrived, and its true scale became apparent, it could no longer be ignored. People had to come to terms with the idea of a God who, while remaining the infinitely remote deity of the Hebrews, revealed an aspect of himself as a man, showing that absolute good can exist in a man's flesh, not just as an abstract ideal. The words in which the evangelists conveyed his message were simple, so simple that they were destined to remain largely misunderstood. The Christ of the New Testament spoke like God and died suffering like a man, leaving the world to ponder the words he left behind.

People weaned on a steady diet of Hellenic thought found it hard to come to terms with Christianity. Whatever else they may have believed in, at the heart of their being lay belief in reason, the supreme part of Plato's tripartite soul. But the new religion maintained that truth lay so much higher than reason that it was for ever to remain outside its reach. How then was God to be understood? Look within you, said the Gospels. This is where the Kingdom of God is to be found. All else is at best derivative, at worst meaningless. Man was thus beseeched to embark on a lifetime of introspection, intense to the point of being painful. That entreaty came as a shock to Hellenic men brought up to look outwards, to seek truth in civic rectitude and the perfection of both human and man-made form. The shock caused structural damage to the Hellenic world. Cracks appeared and out of them emerged Western man, the sociocultural type that dominated life in the erstwhile *Pax Romana* for the next 16 to 17 centuries. This book will refer to this type as 'Westman' so as to de-emphasize its coincidental geographic aspect.

As any other human type, Westman is defined by a common element shared by a large number of individuals regardless of how different they are in other respects. All successful human types and societies have such a common element, acting as a social and cultural adhesive. If we attempted an exercise in taxonomy, Westman could be classified as 'a unique sociocultural type whose founding animus came from an all-consuming, introspective need to undertand Christ's message, to express this understanding by every means, mostly artistic, and to fashion a society that would encourage and reward a life-long spiritual quest – this ultimately irrespective of the intensity of faith.'

Though eventually Westman's habitat spread over Europe and later to America, it was never limited to those locations. Conversely, not all inhabitants of Western countries could ever be described as Westmen. Indeed, by its very nature this sociocultural type was always in a minority, albeit a dominant one. 'Sociocultural' may not sound very mellifluous, but it does describe the essence of Westman accurately, for it was through culture that Westmen tried to gain and then to express their understanding of God. St Anselm's uniquely Westman definition of culture as 'faith seeking understanding' set the terms and implicitly raised culture to a status it had never enjoyed before.

Westman's culture was multifaceted, and in due course we shall see that at different times he relied on some facets more than on others. Theology came first, with architecture overlapping with it for a while only to take a prominent role later, which role it was to cede to painting and later to music. All of it was underpinned by philosophy and its offshoot, literature, which eventually went its own way. All together they combined to refine – and largely to create – a new way of thinking, feeling and looking at the world. Westman grew to maturity as a direct result.

We shall also see that Westman was a sociocultural, rather than merely cultural, type because he had to create a society that would allow various facets of his culture to cast their illuminating glitter unimpeded by external and internal obstacles. Derivative from this argument is the distinction between culture and civilization that will be drawn later. The argument will go so far as to state that Westman civilization and culture were not as organically intertwined as they had been in the Hellenic world. Westman's civilization, though created to cocoon his culture, ended up having the opposite effect. That goes a long way towards explaining the modern history of the West.

THE METHOD IN THE MADNESS OF MODERNITY

And an explanation is sorely needed for without it things do not make much sense. Unless, of course, we accept the improbable view that in the last two hundred years Westman went mad.

For no apparent reason, he began to lay waste everything it had taken him agonizing centuries to create. The first to go was his religion, for a millennium or so the seat of learning, bedrock of civic virtue, guardian of public morals, inspiration behind great thought and ineffable beauty; then came the turn of his culture, a tireless source of delight and a sure-footed guide to soaring spiritual heights; and then tumbled his civilization that had delivered a society freer of tyranny than ever before or since, produced unprecedented advances in the sciences, begun to bring about widespread prosperity. This too was destroyed.

That such destruction has taken place needs no further proof than the history of our time. Without getting into what might be construed as a matter of opinion, let us just consider that more people, by an order of magnitude, were killed in the twentieth century than in all the other centuries of known history combined. Barring the possibility of a sudden outbreak of pandemic sadism, violence on such a scale can only be a symptom, not the disease. What happened in front of our fathers' eyes was a shredding of the social, political and cultural fabric of Western society, not just a demonstration of advances in killing efficiency.

The disaster was interwoven into a century of what is commonly believed to be the paragon of progress. This is a composite belief, one that encompasses every axiomatic assumption of modernity. Casting a glance around him, a modern man sees progress everywhere he looks. Call him 'progressive' rather than 'modern' and he will accept the new designation as his just due. When the presumption of progress is compromised by the murderous twentieth century, then no smaller modern assumption can be safe. We have to question them all before attempting an exegesis. Nothing short of merciless scepticism will do; complacency will leave too much unexplained.

Quick explanations of the mayhem, especially those based solely on scientific advances or other material factors, are inadequate. Moreover, they trivialize the tragedy by tearing it off its moral underpinnings. The carnage seen in the past 100 years has been so cataclysmic, accounting for over 300 million violent deaths (some historians offer somewhat lower, some much higher estimates), half of them in the Christian world, that it cannot be explained away by better homicidal technology and increasing supply of cannon fodder. After all, many – perhaps as many as half – of those deaths were caused by low-tech executions, torture and artificial famines, expedients long within Westman's reach. But while he often did horrible things in the past, somehow Westman refrained from unrestrained violence on a global scale. The unsavoury Spanish inquisitors, for example, are variously estimated to have carried out between 10,000 and 30,000 executions during the three-and-a-half centuries they were in business, which seems a low figure by the standards of a monthly Cheka quota or the annual output of an Auschwitz. While every unjust death is morally as deplorable as any other, numbers – especially when they creep into hundreds of millions – do matter at the level of political, social and cultural history.

Why did the carnage spin out of control? How, for example, was it possible for the Bolsheviks to cordon off vast areas in the late autumn, take all food away from the people inside the cordon, and then move in with bulldozers in the spring to clear away millions of frozen corpses? How could the Nazis shoot so many people that even the SS men could no longer stomach the ravines flowing with blood and had to switch to gas? The answer may lie in the bias of the mass murders in the twentieth century: whatever the explicit justification was, many of them were carried out neither to pursue a geopolitical interest nor to settle a princely quarrel, but rather to advance an ideology. The targets were often whole groups of people irrespective of any individual wrongdoing. However, what makes the twentieth century unique in this respect is the limitless scale of such murderous activity, its span both in length and in width. It is the scale that cries out for an explanation, not ideological murder as such. For the twentieth century cannot boast exclusive rights to killing large numbers of recalcitrant folk for didactic reasons. In pre-modern times horrific murders were committed, among others, by Albigensian crusaders and Spanish conquistadors, American colonists and British Empire builders. And at its historical début during the French Revolution, modern ideology, armed with the rather basic guillotine, musket, sabre and rope, ran up a score that looks respectable even by the standards of our technologically advanced age.

That ideological massacre, like most subsequent ones, followed a rabid assault on religion, which is a point that has been made many times by many great men: Burke, de Maistre, de Tocqueville and Dostoyevsky spring to mind. Still, the point is worth making in the context of this essay, as the destruction of religion, since then completed, has had a devastating effect on both the culture and civilization of Westman. Religion, for all the misdeeds committed by it or in its name, was the foundation on which Westman culture and civilization had been erected. Destroy the foundation, and down comes the whole structure with a big thud.

A short walk through any great European city will provide sufficient evidence for this observation: Westman, the creator of a great culture, is nowhere in evidence. It is as if he has degenerated in every faculty, except those involved in keeping him fed, clothed and entertained. In fact, ever since the destruction of religion,

Westman's material acumen has been growing in inverse proportion to his ability to maintain his culture and civilization. For example, crime in most Western cities has shot up in the postwar years – at exactly the time when the West has grown rich beyond any level ever imagined in the past. The same period, incidentally, is characterized by a precipitous dip in church attendance. This statistic, like most such data, is interesting primarily for its predictability. We shall delve deeper into this in due course, but for the time being suffice it to say that evidence of Westman's madness is not hard to find. In fact, it more or less finds us wherever we go.

But is it really madness? A spontaneous onslaught of emotional instability, turning the formerly prudent and urbane Westman into a suicidal and homicidal barbarian, is one possible explanation of the mess we see around us. But until scientists provide evidence of a pandemic nature of madness, this explanation will remain improbable. Yet an explanation is needed and the more comprehensive, the better: The last couple of centuries have been too different from the previous dozen to be passed up without some comment on the difference. And there have been many such comments. The problems of the West were anticipated by the giants mentioned earlier; and as the sores festered they were noticed and described by Nietzsche, Spengler, Weber, Ortega y Gasset and James Burnham, to name just a few.

But in describing Westman's collapse, they all overlooked an important fact that has since then become evident: it was not one type undergoing a crisis, but a different breed altogether taking over (only Ortega came close to this conclusion). The situation was even more serious than they thought: at some point in the past Westman had curled up and died. That is, he stopped being the dominant force in the west, having been replaced in that role by a new sociocultural type: modern man. For the sake of brevity, and also to emphasize the sociocultural rather than purely temporal aspect of the new breed, we shall be referring to him as

Modman. If we tried to classify this type in the same way as we previously classified Westman, the definition would run along these lines: 'A sociocultural type whose intuitive two-pronged animus comes from a desire to destroy the spiritual and cultural essence of Westman heritage, while at the same time magnifying the material gains that were incidental to that heritage.'

THE UNFASHIONABLE THINKING BEHIND THIS BOOK

'Le coeur a ses raisons que la raison ne connaît point.'
(B. Pascal)

the heart has its reasons which reason does not know

In this book I attempt to support the validity of the above definition by describing and analysing Modman. Even though this type, in rapidly growing numbers, has been with us for at least a quarter of a millennium, Modman – as opposed to modern Westman – has largely escaped the nets cast by taxonomists and sociologists, who have so far failed to classify him and trace his evolution back to the time when he first joined life's fauna. In a way they are not to blame for this oversight. Modman's natural habitat is roughly coextensive with Western countries and, as he resembles his predecessor Westman in many superficial character- istics, the two are mixed up as a matter of course. Thus scholars such as Ortega y Gasset may have thought they were commenting on Westman gone awry, while their object was in fact his conqueror. Ortega described the difference between the traditional society and one run by what he called 'the mass man'. But he saw a continuum, however lamentable – overlooking the fact that the emerging society and the one it had emerged from had nothing in common whatsoever.

Through no fault of his own Ortega was suffering from limited hindsight: Modmen may have existed for two centuries by the time *The Revolt of the Masses* was published in 1930, but they had not yet won their final victory. They still had to be coy, stress- ing their similarities with Westmen and trying to mask the differences. As a result, both Spengler and Ortega – and certainly the thinkers who preceded them – had to rely on prophecy to describe what hindsight has by now turned into a topic for reportage: Modman as conqueror. For it was in the second half of the twentieth century that the new species succeeded in mopping up the last vestiges of Westman's resistance.

Indeed, unlike Westman and his own predecessor, Hellenic man, the two species have nothing in common. As the book unfolds, we shall see that, if anything, they are mutually exclusive opposites, with the Modman sociocultural type born out of a widespread urge to do away with Westman and everything he stood for. In that task Modman has succeeded so thoroughly that Westman is now dead as a social and cultural force. His sociocultural loins have gone dry.

Since in Westman the balance of good and evil generally – though far from always – swung towards the former, he created more than he destroyed. He was not so much an iconoclast as a synthesizer, one not only ready to discard what he deemed useless in other cultures, but also willing to keep what he found useful. Modman, however, found nothing worth keeping in Westman's world. All of it was equally abhorrent to him.

Though Westman is now dead as a driving force, isolated throwback specimens of the breed still can be found here and there, usually trying to stay out of harm's way by impersonating Modmen. But deep down they are aware of the short distance separating them from the taxidermist's good offices. As these holdouts cast furtive looks at the scattered fragments of their existence, their eyes mist over, and they drop a tear for the grandeur they once created but are no longer able to reproduce or even to protect. It is indeed worth lamenting: possibly no other civilization, and certainly no other culture, has produced such a record of sustained achievement in every area of man's spiritual life. However, a lament would be misplaced unless we agree that (a) the people who have taken over Westman's world are not themselves new Westmen, or at least that (b) Westman may still be alive physically but dead in some other, more important, ways.

These ways can be traced back to the soul, an aspect of man that Darwin never quite got around to describing, one responsible for the part of life that has nothing to do with physical survival or the passing on of genes. Even though the soul is a somewhat nebulous concept that does not pass the positivist test of being either provable or disprovable, people of most religions or none have always accepted its existence in some form. The forms of course differ, so Plato, St Augustine, Rousseau and a New Age guru would not have accepted one another's definitions. But for the purposes of this essay the broadest of definitions would suffice: the soul is man's inner metaphysical self.

It is by his soul that Westman is circumscribed. This statement is not at odds with the philosophy of Hegel who saw history as a dialectical self-expression of Absolute Spirit, for which we can use the warmer term 'soul'. Whatever the terminology, the system of thought on which this book is based attaches little importance to the corporeality of Westman, his physical shell, his geographic location or his race, toys he played with, ways in which he fed or treated himself. All these are variously interesting only as an antithesis, a backdrop of what Westman was not that gives a blinding prominence to what he was. It is not the outer trappings of his life that distinguish Westman from, say, Eastern man. In fact, Asia has shown that the West can no longer claim exclusive possession of comfort made possible by a semblance of democracy. What sets Westman apart from other historical types, such as his predecessor Hellenic man and his nemesis Modman, is not his body but his soul. That soul has been destroyed or at least marginalized. And, for many reasons we shall discuss later, Westman cannot live at the margins of society.

An essay on Westman has to have the Judaeo-Christian religion as a frame of reference. However, religion will be here treated as a matter of fact rather than an article of faith. For even atheists cannot deny that the God of Israel, Abraham and Jacob has had a demonstrable influence on Westman's life. We may doubt at a weak moment that God exists, but that does not matter, for enough people in history have believed in him with sufficient fervour to do many great, and quite a few rotten, deeds in his name. By the same token, enough people throughout history have undone those great deeds, and outdone the rotten ones, by illogically attacking God who according to them does not exist. In either case, religion has shaped Western culture and, as a consequence, civilization. It is thus a fact of Western life whether we like it or not. Religion can take its rightful place as the first bead in the string of other facts that move an argument along – even if it does not act as the whole argument in itself.

Other frames of reference have to be based on Westman culture, born largely out of his religion, and his civilization that in turn came out of the culture the way Eve came out of Adam's rib. All these shared a common destiny: together they lived and together they died. For they, just like human nature, had in them the seeds of both grandeur and paucity, and there was death always implicit in their lives. Their life and death are again demonstrable physical facts, and thankfully so: these days it is difficult to argue a point on rhetoric alone.

Reliance on physical fact rather than metaphysical inspiration parallels the victory Modman's rational mind has won over Westman's intuitive soul, leaving Westman dead on the battle-field. But it was a hollow victory, akin to an insect causing its own death by stinging a foe. Without the warmth of a metaphysical soul, reason is a cold-spermed warlock, capable of destruction but unable to procreate. Or perhaps the reason that defeated the Western soul was not real reason at all but an awful mask used to disguise evil. Anyone who does not think reason can be falsified so thoroughly must believe that Marx was above all interested in economics, Lenin in agrarian reform and Hitler in improving the lot of the Germans.

Inspiration relates to reason as philosophy relates to double-entry accounting. The latter is useful, but it is the former that is capable of approaching the truth. Inspiration is linked to what Burke called prejudice and what we today are more likely to call intuition. In cultural matters, as in faith, intuition is a more productive epistemological tool than reason. Reason is limited by coherently enunciated thought that in turn is limited by language, our tool for coherent enunciation. Intuition, on the other hand, can perhaps be described as non-verbal thought. As such, it is – in any human terms – limitless.

Contrary to the modern view of education, knowledge has more to do with recognition than with accumulation. Because of the danger of producing what Berkeley called 'a mind ... debauched by learning', intuitive knowledge must set limits to learning, accepting whatever rings true, rejecting anything that does not. Real knowledge is thus more about reduction than expansion – the narrowing rather than broadening of one's horizons. Of course, to make it knowledge, as opposed to obscurantism, one must first study a multitude of options and only then, following Michelangelo's advice, chip away everything extraneous. This does not change the basic assumption that, unless ruthless discrimination is applied to information and ideas, no knowledge will emerge from simple accumulation of data. And discrimination has to come from both verbal and non-verbal thought, reason and intuition.

Since the early Middle Ages theologians and philosophers have been struggling with the role reason plays in acquiring the ultimate knowledge, the realization that God exists. The most direct route to such knowledge starts with revelation, and faith thus arrived at is both purer and surer than any other. But revelation does not come from within. It is a gift in the literal sense: something presented by an external donor. Most religious thinkers realized this, as they were aware of the dim future awaiting Christianity had it had to rely only on such gifted communicants to swell its ranks. In addition, many of those thinkers were not beneficiaries of the revelatory largesse themselves. Naturally, they had to look for other paths leading to the ultimate knowledge, and hence their belief that reason could take one almost all the way.

Reason can indeed go far on the road to the truth – once intuition compels one to embark on the right journey. Reason can lead us in all kinds of directions, not all of them praiseworthy. An intelligent pervert, for instance, can easily chart a plausible course to justifying necrophilia (for example, being victimless, it increases the amount of joy in the world), but to want to do so he has to be a pervert to begin with. The rational mechanism has to be set off by intuitive predisposition. On a different plane, a man can arrive at accepting God by reason, but only if his mind is pushed that way by intuitive need. He has to want to become a believer irrespective of reason, for reason to do its job.

The same applies to other forms of knowledge as well. It is possible, for example, to learn the intellectual aspects of music. But to start making the required effort one has to like music, respond to it emotionally, consider it important. Again intuition comes first. Intellect is at its best when justifying a conviction that already resides in the realm of intuition. In that sense, perhaps one can say that, wittingly or unwittingly, any rationalization is post-rationalization.

All intellectual attitudes may have been latently political to Thomas Mann, but we can delve deeper to find that all cultural, as well as political and intellectual, attitudes are latently intuitive. Reason, of course, has to move in later to claim its slice of the epistemological pie, but it only gets crumbs off intuition's table. Thus, in common with Westman's faith, his culture is inspiration made flesh by post-rationalization. Or, to repeat St Anselm, culture is faith looking for understanding. Without the foundation of intuition, reason is nothing but a weather vane sensitive to the way the wind is blowing. That is why changing one's opinions is an easy matter; and even convictions can be remodelled with relative ease, as shown by all those ex-communist conservatives.

Intuitive assumptions are the building blocks of culture, which in turn is the most reliable – or at any rate the most visible – manifestation of the soul. It is in the realm of intuition, and not necessarily enunciated ideas, that Westman differs culturally from other human types. Western music, for example, appeals mainly to intuitive perception. It could not have become the most significant expression of Western culture unless most listeners had similar, or at any rate compatible, intuitive assumptions. Western music caters to this predisposition by conveying the dramatic inner tension of our soul. In the absence of such drama, our music would be meaningless, as it sounds meaningless to oriental people who tend to look for harmony and serenity in their music, not soul-wrenching drama. Spengler observes that all Western music appears to be marching tunes to the Chinese. Conversely, Westerners cannot tell apart the sad and merry bits in Chinese music.

Exactly where intuition comes from is difficult to say. Both nature and nurture must act as tributaries, but which delivers what into the mainstream is unclear. Nature contributes through intelligence and temperament, one suspects mostly the latter. Nurture acts, again to use Burkean terms, through prescription, which is truth passed on by previous generations; and presumption, which is inference from the common experience of mankind. When intuition and reason are in harmony they can create an ability to distinguish between virtuous and evil, right and wrong, good and bad. When they clash the two can only destroy. The conflict between them, with reason emerging victorious, did occur and it was a curious combination of parricide and suicide. It was the former, for reason had been once a child of intuition and formed a familial unity with it. It was the latter, for Westman died as a result.

Even though religion is crucial, for the purposes of this essay it is a process, not the result. It is the foundation of the pre-Enlightenment, morally absolutist system of thought used throughout this book. Such thinking has to trespass upon religion's property and must be reconciled with it, if only to apply for right of way. And property it is, for science, having first played a part in the development of the Western soul and then in its demise, has lost interest in it. Though it too often starts with an intuitive hypothesis, modern science is ultimately concerned with things that are describable by physical facts, and the soul is not one of them. This clear signposting of its intellectual holdings is a laudable aspect of science, and it would be even more welcome if for the last couple of centuries so many scientists had not been trying to convince us that no territory beyond those signposts exists. Since in doing so science became linked with some methods, not all of them strictly academic, that are associated with the more unsavoury political practices of Modman, it is hard not to feel some antipathy towards the type that will be described later as the 'totalitarian scientist'. Indeed, for those who cherish Westman heritage this antipathy tends to extend to post-Enlightenment modernity in general, both in its cultural and temporal meanings. In the latter meaning, modernity is the time when Westman died; in the former, it is the cause of his death. In the absence of a comparable spiritual attainment, it is difficult to view modernity solely with admiration for the trinket-laden riches it has delivered.

The pre-Enlightenment system of thought mentioned earlier is based on the belief that most things in life are reducible to the underlying moral choice, which is mostly intuitive and has little to do with a rational weighing of pros and cons. This system is quite a versatile tool, lending itself to thinking on such diverse subjects as music, literature, painting, education, politics, philosophy, foreign policy, history, education, architecture, theology. That the same system of thought can be applied, in however a rudimentary way, to all these fields should mean that they have an element on which they all overlap. And so they have: they are all glints on various facets of moral choice. The facets refract moral choice, distorting it and sometimes obscuring its presence at the core of everything that happens in the world. But it is there all right, shining through.

However arcane the object of study, if we ponder human behaviour with the benefit of pre-Enlightenment, which is to say Judaeo–Christian, thought, then it must be reducible to the dichotomy of good and evil implanted into human nature from without – and the choice between the two that comes from within. Even in the middle of a drawn-out enquiry into, say, a revolution of centuries ago, it should be possible to stop and remind oneself that history is made by people who are similar to us, irrespective of the differences in the outer trappings of our lives. Just like us, they faced moral choices every day. Just like us, they got some of them right and most of them wrong. The difference lay in their ability to attenuate the consequences of the bad decisions, while enhancing the effect of the good ones. A peek into the human soul can remove some of the veil of mystery that time has draped around history. This never-ending reference to the moral traits of human character as it is, rather than as we may think it ought to be, is the basis of the taxonomy in which 'Westman' and 'Modman' are all-important definitions.

Applying absolute standards of good and evil to human behaviour was common fare before the Enlightenment, as was a general distrust of reason or, at any rate, of rationalism. Supra-rational tools were in the popular domain then, but they have since been discarded. Previous title to them has thus been rendered invalid, and so anyone can pick them up, dust them off and claim them for his own. But he would do so at his peril. For using pre-Enlightenment thinking to analyse the post-Enlightenment world is a risky undertaking. A superior system can comprehend an inferior one, but not vice versa. If a cognitive methodology based on intuitive assumptions fails to produce the desired result, with no understanding emerging at the other end, the explanation may lie in a faulty set of premises. If one is led into too many blind alleys, it is not just one's conclusions that are in danger, but one's whole set of assumptions. And Nietzsche, for one, showed through his own tragic life that unresolved contradictions can destroy even a great man. He thus issued a grave warning to us mere mortals. Still, seeking truth is impossible without taking risks, so even a coward takes them, especially if he likes the odds.

This book is one such risky endeavour. The underlying methodology will be tested against various aspects of history and modern life, as many as are necessary and a reader can stand, to see if it is adequate to achieve clarity. If it is, then the prize can be glittering, a theory of modernity explaining most of the key events and personages. If it is not, then both the methodology and its wielder will die in the attempt – the latter one hopes only figuratively.

A willingness to apply the same way of thinking to every aspect of life has to have at its foundation the belief that most things are interlinked. They are, although the connections are seldom as straightforward as chain links clasped together in sequence. That this is so can be demonstrated using any starting point at all. Let us say we wish to consider how traffic congestion in London could be eased. We start from the observation that London traffic is bearable during school holidays and impossible at other times, a situation that did not exist a generation ago. Obviously, more parents drive their children to school these days, whereas before they must have sent their offspring to their daily ordeals by public transport. Why have they stopped doing so? It is partly because modernity has spread affluence so wide that most people can own cars. It is partly because this wealth has encouraged sybaritic tendencies in both children and parents. And it is partly because it is no longer safe for children to travel alone. So before we can begin to solve traffic congestion we must first consider a whole raft of problems encroaching on the issues of legality and punishment, public duty and personal responsibility. And, should we wish to follow the thread further, we shall reach the domain of morality, its relation to religion, politics, economics, philosophy and – ultimately – human nature. *En route*, few parts of our existence will be bypassed as we continue a meandering journey that started with a small step: trying to do something about London's traffic.

Tugging at another string, we observe that modern life brings about centralization run riot. For example, Britain's commercial activity and consequently jobs are concentrated in the Greater London area, attracting almost a third of the country's workforce, a situation that is not uncommon in Europe. Within the capital, commercial, political and financial activities are disproportionately concentrated within a three-mile radius from the centre, again not an unusual setup. The demise of small local government, small local businesses and small local shops under the onslaught of corporatist megalomania thus makes the traffic problem in central London much worse, with congestion charges offering at best a temporary relief.

Then again, road works seem to be extremely widespread in London. In the last 27 years, for example, the entire 2.5-mile length of the King's Road, one of London's important thoroughfares, seems not to have been free from road works for a single day. Last year there were over 150 road works in London, with some other western European capitals not far behind. A cynic may not believe that every one of those jobs was strictly necessary. A realist would suspect that the local council's budget is in need of spending, the unions are in need of mollifying and, spiced up with a dollop of corruption, a 'jobs for the boys' mindset may emerge that is expressed via the endless rat-tat-tat of pneumatic drills.

So far we have unravelled only a few strings of, to repeat, a trivial problem, yet these slippery threads have already led us to a point where we begin to question the conventions, institutions and fashions of modernity – a point where we try to understand how people who are normally good at solving practical problems can be prepared to override that ability for the sake of silly incidentals. Thus we have allowed London transport to carry us to the destination that is human nature.

And so every aspect of life should be reducible in such a manner. For at the core of the infinite relativities of outside life lies the finite dichotomy of absolute good and evil inside us. The world reflects the clash between them, with the good struggling to create reminders of the beauty of life, and the evil trying to destroy every such reminder. When one is alert to their existence, telling them apart is seldom difficult; telling which practical manifestation comes from which is easier still. The balance of good and evil within a man's soul pushes him towards choices that can be right or wrong – in the same way in which his hormonal balance can push him towards either aggression or docility. His innate qualities thus have to give a bias to his life. But they do not determine it: the will to make the right choice remains free. Even though exercising it is sometimes difficult, it is never impossible.

History, too, gives bias to human behaviour. His time has to influence a man's thoughts and actions – but not nearly so much as a man's thoughts and actions influence his time. It is people who make history, not vice versa; no matter how much pressure history may exert, free will is capable of overcoming it. This belief in biased as opposed to determined choice can be extended to society, an aggregate of men and women. Society too has what Durkheim, a founding father of sociology, called 'collective consciousness', largely the sum of its parts. That is why societies, like individuals, tend to respond to certain provocations in a certain way. However, belief in causality is a far cry from determinism, a desire to aver that because things happen they were bound to happen. This can more accurately be stated in a different way: because things happen, there is something in human nature that made them likely to happen under the circumstances. But there could also have been enough in human nature to prevent

them from happening. As, one hopes, there still is enough left
there to undo them.

THE BIRTH OF WESTMAN

'Credibile quia ineptum, certum quia impossibile.'
(Tertullian)

The soul is a religious, or in any case metaphysical, concept.
When religion is treated only as a matter of fact, it would be
illogical to hang an argument on the peg of a concept seen as an
article of faith. Putting its faith-related immortality aside for the
time being, let us note that the soul is a fact to observant people
simply because the products of the soul are there for all to see, and
these cannot be attributed to any other source.

Sherlock Holmes pointed out to the hapless Dr Watson that
when he had exhausted all possibilities but one then the remaining
possibility, no matter how absurd, had to be the answer. Using
this logic, Chartres cathedral, Zurbarán's St Francis and Bach's
fugues could only have come from the metaphysical soul, as the
inspiration behind them cannot be traced back to any other
source. Simply a combination of a well-trained mind and well-
practised technique would not explain the startling difference
between our three examples and, say, Westminster Abbey,
Murillo's self-portrait and Handel's Messiah. Yet they were all
created at roughly the same times by similarly competent men.

Philosophers from Plato and Aristotle to Kant pondered the
relationship between the inner essence of a thing, 'thing in itself',
and its outer, visible properties, those that make it a physical fact.
The soul as a 'thing in itself' is too vast a subject to live as a
subsidiary theme in this book. However, setting a more modest
task, it is possible to talk about the visible properties of the soul,
describing it not as the sum of what it is but the totality of what it
does. When such an approach is adopted to describe anything, the

most succinct description would be one that concentrates on the exclusive properties of the thing, omitting those it shares with many others. Thus an aeroplane is a manmade object that flies, not a means of transporting large numbers of people; and a football is a leather balloon kicked in a popular game, not a hermetically sealed sphere. In both cases, the second part of the description is true but unnecessary. It could also be misleading if we fail to make the first part clear to begin with.

The most visible part of Westman's soul is its ability to produce culture. Some hidden, but doubtless real, tectonic plates smash together with astounding force, and tremors of sublime creations are sent out into the universe: a Bach chorale shaking the rickety house of philistine complacency to its foundation, a Dürer portrait knocking the roof off, a Shakespeare sonnet scattering the now useless stones. We may not know what the tectonic plates are, how or why they have clapped together, but we can see the signs of the devastation, with the shadow of the soul soaring over the ruins. There may be other ways to describe the soul, for example by its quest for God, which is a more seminal property. But the urgent and universal need to perceive God, whether gratefully acknowledged or regrettably denied, is not a property of the soul. It is the soul as a thing in itself, or almost that. As such, it lies too deep for this essay to dig. The ability to create culture, on the other hand, is on the surface, visible to the naked eye. For all practical purposes, this can suffice.

If we arbitrarily reduce the soul to its demonstrable aspect we can equate it with culture. Sandwiched in history between Hellenic and Modern men, Westman is defined by his soul revealed through culture. A simple equation then leads to a workable conclusion: Westman equals Western soul, which in turn equals Western culture, the centrepiece of a triptych preceded by religion and followed by civilization. Therefore, in practical terms, Westman equals Western culture. Logically imperfect as this conclusion is, it is good enough to act as a working hypothesis since it lends itself to empirical proof. Thus a cursory comparison of Westman's culture and that of his immediate predecessor, Hellenic man, gives us a few insights that go beyond mere aesthetics.

The first insight can be triggered by a simple question. Was the Venus de Milo beautiful? The statue of her is perfect, but what about the model? What was she like as a woman? Flirtatious or detached? Brilliant or stupid? Profound or flighty? Did she light up every room she was in or turn it into a chamber of sorrow? We do not know. All we can do is admire the perfect marble form of the statue's body. If we tried to peek into the substance beyond the form, our eyes would limply slide off the polished stone. There is no substance. The form is all there is.

Or look at the sightless busts of ancient Greeks and Romans, as Spengler suggested. Presumably, all the models had eyes, the window to the soul. Then why are we looking at the solidly filled eye sockets? Even assuming that the eyes were originally painted onto the stone and then lost to the erosion of time, or were made up of implanted jewels eventually lost to theft, we still have to wonder why the artists selected such a flimsy medium. Donatello and Michelangelo did demonstrate that it was possible to sculpt eyes in eternally durable stone. So why did their Hellenic ancestors merely apply some dye as an afterthought? It could be that Hellenic artists were not interested in the soul and therefore did not need to show windows through which it could be seen. It even could be that Hellenic man had no soul to look into, which is more or less the view taken by J. Jaynes in his *Bicameral Mind*. More likely, the artists were interested in the form only because their culture did not call for introspection. Their idea of beauty was skin deep.

The concept of the soul was neither alien nor central to Hellenic antiquity. Immortality was important only to some philosophy, Plato's and Aristotle's most prominently, but neither thinker saw the soul as an exclusively human property. Even before Plato,

Orphic mysteries had involved immortality of the soul as the foundation of belief in life after death. 'The souls of all are immortal; those of the virtuous are divine' became a widespread notion in the Hellenic world, even though it was opposed by the Stoics. But there, particularly in Rome, it led not to the genesis of a new culture but to the doctrine of consecration whereby the souls of all dead emperors were declared divine. In some ways consecration eased the subsequent transition to Western religion – it anticipated the idea of God-man. In other ways it led to the Romans seeing Christianity as a threat, since it deified a man other than the emperor.

Plato and especially Aristotle went on to have a greater impact in our times than in their own. For it was not so much theoretical philosophy as practical ethics that lay at the core of the Hellenic world, the Socratic belief that virtue is the source of happiness, defined as joyous life in this world. Happiness was one reward for virtue; health and physical perfection, another. Hence all those immaculate discus throwers whose sound bodies bespoke sound minds. Westman's suffering soul was not just incomprehensible but abhorrent to Hellenic men. On the other hand, their insistence on sending ethical messages mostly through formal perfection and harmony is alien to us.

It is with the disappointment of Westman throwbacks that we look at, say, the busts of Roman emperors, trying in vain to find a flicker of expression beyond their chiselled features. Had we not read Tacitus, Pliny or Gibbon, we would not realize that Tiberius was a greater man than Titus, Claudius a kinder one than Caligula, or Vespasian the only straight one among the lot of them. By contrast, let us look at Zurbarán's St Francis or St Catherine, any of Velázquez's portraits of Philip IV, any late Rembrandt self-portrait or, if we stay with sculpture, Michelangelo's slaves. No contemporary of these artists would have looked merely at the combinations of colours and shapes. Their first glance would have captured, respectively, mystic transport, sagacity growing with age, tragic depth and fury. Their second would perhaps have revealed despair, diminishing sensuality, fear of death, resignation. Glance by glance, Western viewers would have unveiled what the Western artists really depicted: their subjects' souls.

This points at one critical distinction between the Hellenic and Western cultures, one that goes far beyond art. The former treats form in a what-you-see-is-what-you-get way. For the latter, the form is only a shell that contains the real meaning. The Hellenic body that held no secrets was replaced by the Western soul that was not only a mystery, but an unsolvable one at that. Thus, the streamlined façade of a Greek temple is the whole book, while the elaborate façade of a Gothic cathedral is only the table of contents. This points at a crucial paradox: conveying the soul in any genre of art requires a more intricate technique than it takes to convey formal beauty alone. That is why Western artists with the greatest souls, such as Bach, Velázquez or Shakespeare, also commanded the greatest technique. If an artist is given the ability to approach the truth, he also is given the means of doing so – and, usually, the other way around. Hindsight often helps us to reassess the significance of artists who used to be acclaimed as simple-minded virtuosos in their lifetime. Applying this optically perfect instrument, we realize that either those artists were not as simple-minded as all that, or not so virtuosic. For example, many musicians will now agree that Chopin explored greater depths of piano technique than Liszt, the less intricate spirit but in their time the more celebrated technician. Chopin needed the greater means for he was out to achieve a higher purpose.

Born at the time of Christ, Westman began to grow up towards the beginning of the second millennium AD. The time between Tiberius and a century or two after Constantine was what it took to get rid of most vestiges of Hellenic polytheism and get accustomed to the idea of a god in whose image man was believed to be made. Westman also used that time to come to terms with the idea of reaching out to his soul by artistic means, something that had not been encouraged before. To do so, he had to mitigate his rigid monotheism that was at odds with such expression, and this could only be achieved by reconciling himself to some aspects of Hellenic creativity. This process must have been as painful as it was long, for during that time the Western soul, if not exactly silent, was often as incoherent as befitted a child. It was, however, a self-assertive infant, aggressive and cruel in a childish sort of way.

Expansive self-assertiveness is another feature that distinguishes Westman from his predecessor. Hellenic man may not have looked inwards very much, but neither did he look too far outwards. His politics was contained within one city, often within the agora, one square within the city. The concept of a world outside his own was alien to him; he was sometimes an acquisitive conqueror but seldom an inquisitive explorer. The Caesarean idea of a country, as opposed to the polis, came to Hellenic man only in his old age when he was already too feeble to enforce it with sustained vigour.

His narrow view was applied not only to space but also to time. A Hellenic man was not exactly ignorant of history; he simply did not see how it affected his life. He would not have understood a Buddhist arguing that any human life is but a link connecting the generations past and present, a view that would not unduly upset a Westman. Hannibal's exploits would have meant less to, say, Caesar than they do to a modern historian who is two millennia further away. This Hellenic synchrophilia was best expressed by Thucydides who began his history of the Peloponnesian War by saying that nothing of any interest whatsoever had occurred before his time (circa 400 BC): '*after looking back into it as far as I can, all the evidence leads me to conclude that these periods were not great periods either in warfare or in anything else,*' was how Thucydides put it. Thus, he leapfrogged some civilizations (Egypt, Babylon and Persia to name just a few, not to mention

Judaea) that any Western historian would have deemed worthy of at least a cursory mention.

All this is not to pass judgement. What is important here is not that Westman was better than any previous human type but that he was different. As a matter of fact, Hellenic man had many endearing characteristics that went missing in Westman. His emphasis on ethics as the crux of philosophy and theology made Hellenic man selective in his methods. For him the end did not always justify the means, and there was no heavenly redemption for beastliness in this life. That is why Hellenic societies achieved arguably a greater civic virtue than Westman ever did. For civic virtue has to be based on tolerance, which was not always Westman's most obvious characteristic.

Hellenic men respected the gods of strangers as much as they venerated their own multiple gods, and anyone who offended any god was their enemy. At the same time, anyone who respected any god was their friend, and Hellenic men felt no compulsion to proselytize. As they proved in the Punic Wars, they were ready to die defending their city from those whose ways were unacceptable to them. But they would not fight merely to impose their ways on those who were happy with their own. Hellenic thinkers were not bashful in sharing their views with others, but they did not really care if others got to share their views. Socrates, if Plato is to be believed, spent more time teaching his disciples a cognitive methodology than leading them to any conclusions. He taught them how, not what, to think, which proved to be his undoing. For, left to think for themselves, his pupils went astray, and their mentor had to take the blame. But Socrates did not create Socratism, and Plato would have been astonished to find that centuries after his death people began to talk about Neo-Platonism. Hellenic men seldom saw schools of thought for individual thinkers; the Academy and the Lyceum were schools in the purely educational sense of the word.

Not so Westman. His newly acquired monotheism was becoming fused with a new expansiveness. Good and evil were to him absolute, as were truth and falsehood: his truth, the other man's falsehood. If there was only one God, then those who believed in other gods (not believing in any was not mooted as a possibility at the time) had to be persuaded otherwise for their own good. In that sense, St Paul was the first Westman, which may explain the violence of his clash with James and other apostles who were Hellenic men by residual culture, if already not by conviction. Monotheism alone does not explain Paul's outward mobility, for the Jews were as monotheistic as he was, and yet they were more concerned with shielding their God from outsiders than helping outsiders see the light. They were not Westmen.

Judaism did attract proselytes but most of them had not been actively encouraged to join any of the broad networks of Jewish communities. Usually they joined of their own accord, attracted perhaps not so much by the Jews' God as by their social stability. Proselytes often wavered in their religious beliefs, as converts tend to do after the initial outburst of neophyte zeal. Later it was those Jewish proselytes who were drawn to Christianity in droves, not so much the ethnic Hebrews of Judaea among whom the apostles made little headway. This partly explains why Paul's mission was so much more successful than James's. The former operated at the soft periphery of Judaism, the latter tried to strike at the centre and died in the attempt.

Christianity is a complex religion, and it is hard to agree with Spengler who maintained that the apostolic and crusading versions of it were two different religions, similarities of dogma and ritual notwithstanding. More plausible seems to be the view that the crusaders acted upon their exaggerated sensitivity to one strain in Christianity, perhaps to the detriment of others. But they did not invent the strain; it was there to begin with. Expansiveness was to Westman what insularity was to Hellenic man: not so much a matter of self-acknowledged belief as a vague yet powerful longing. It subsisted not on reason but on intuition.

WESTMAN'S YOUTH

Starting from the first millennium AD Western culture was demanding that God be sought at increasingly remote distances. Westman still did not possess a concept of infinity, but felt an intuitive need to find a spatial expression of his understanding of God – hence the apostles' peregrinations and, later, the Crusades. The Gothic cathedral, with its towers pointing at a fathomless sky, was an expression of the same need by different means. The height reached by the Gothic tower played the same role as Corinth converted by Paul, the Saracen lands conquered by the mediaeval crusader or the new lands discovered by the Elizabethan explorer. Though working towards their goal in the company of others, the builder, the warrior and the adventurer were each making an individual statement. The statement made by Hellenic men was collective; the former came from a restless soul, the latter from a satisfied mind. The former was theological, the latter ethical.

Hellenic men found safety in numbers; conformity was to them the highest civic and intellectual virtue. Their 'I' was part of a 'we', meaningless if made to fend for itself. In that sense, it is Oriental man rather than Westman who is today's heir to Hellenic heritage. This, of course, is another paradox. Western religion whose ethics are defined by the Golden Rule and love of not only the neighbour but even of the enemy, produces individualism; whereas the selfish agnosticism of Oriental man produces collectivism. Collectivism is a virtue to the Orient but not to the Occident. That is why it never would have crossed a Westman's mind to admire the communal spirit behind today's industrial practices in the east, as many Modmen profess to admire it. A wry smile would have been a Westman's sole reaction to the sight of Japanese workers starting the day by collective aerobics and a rendition of the company song. A Westman would have sensed that he was looking at something alien, and a thought of emulation would never have crossed his mind – regardless of the success of the oriental economy. Modmen, having suppressed Westman within their domain, have no such compunctions. They would try anything for material gain and, if they could enforce it, Detroit and Dagenham assembly workers would be saluting the Ford flag even as we speak. Mercifully, Modmen cannot enforce anything quite so ludicrous yet.

For Westmen, perdition could sometimes be collective but salvation was always individual. It was inevitable that, as Westmen were beginning to feel not just in their mind but in their bone marrow that they had a free choice between good and evil, that choices made by their free will could either save or destroy their soul, they would become even more introspective. Their respect for themselves and others like them continued to grow until they reached the logical apex of believing in the sovereignty of the individual, his supremacy over collective aspirations.

While we are piling up paradoxes, here is another. Because Westmen's individualism leads to respect for the individuality of others, and because at the core of their individuality lies belief in a power that is beyond man, they are political pluralists. They will neither attempt to impose nor agree to accept the political tyranny of a giant omnipotent state. Modmen, on the other hand, are not metaphysical individualists but materialistic egotists. That is why they think it desirable that all individual beings be rolled into one, that of a state. Thus loss of respect for the individual soul is spiritually reductionist. The collective is smaller than the individual.

Free individual choice between good and bad is the basis of Western culture as much as the choice between good and evil is the bedrock of Western religion. The two fused together to define – and refine – Westman's soul, while sovereignty of the individual became the backbone of his body politic, his civilization. But, unlike those perfect Greek statues, this body contained the very human soul of Westman, and so it reflected not only its grandeur but also its foibles. As time has shown, these were in fact congenital defects.

The foibles reflected human nature with its dual potential for good and evil. Westmen tried in vain to exorcise the evil within them, externalizing it in the shape of the variously named Satan, the Devil, Beelzebub or Lucifer. But evil has a life-long lease in the human soul, which it never quite forfeits no matter to what lengths we go to push it outside. Here is yet another paradox: while good and evil live overlapping lives in the soul, the latter is naturally gregarious, while the former is a born loner. Good is often happy to forgo the physical in favour of the metaphysical; evil demands its pound of physical flesh no matter what. Good tends to see the outside, if it sees it at all, as an arena for self-expression. For evil it is an opportunity for conquest.

It was mostly, though not exclusively, evil that made Westmen expansive; it was mostly, though not exclusively, good that made them introspective. The Scripture points at this conclusion: Christ, the externalized good of Westmen's beliefs, states unequivocally that his kingdom is not of this world, relinquishing the worldly crown to Satan, described elsewhere as the prince of this world. Could it be that, in this sense, Christ's statement that the meek would inherit the earth was also a prophecy of gloom? This prophecy is widely seen as establishing the supremacy of faith over reason, or even as a political attack on the Pharisees. But few things in the Scripture are clear-cut, and a different reading is often possible. Meekness, of the spiritual kind that is, can indeed produce worldly riches, and it is certainly not an obstacle in the way of their acquisition – as a strong spirit can be, and almost invariably is.

LOOKING OUT BY LOOKING IN

'Inquietum est cor nostrum, donec requiescat in Te, Domine.'
(St Augustine)

'The kingdom of God is within you'. If one had to express the essence of Westman in a sentence, no other set of words would come close. It explains why, as Westmen grew more introspective, their culture grew

more intricate. They knew intuitively that God lived inside them. No other proof was necessary until much later, when the existence of God became a point of debate. But at any time in history a Westman could have agreed, though not without reservations, with Kant's statement that the starry sky above him and the moral law inside him were all the proof he needed: God without and his kingdom within.

Westmen accepted this idea because they had to mitigate the externalized God of the Old Testament, an attempt that led to an inevitable compromise with Hellenic man. Kant borrowed this thought from Aristotle who was the first to search for God by contemplating the subjective feeling within his soul and the objective stars whose glitter reflected eternity. What for Aristotle, and later for the Stoics who developed this thought, was prophetic longing for a higher God than their contemporaneous deities was for Kant an attempt to deny the supremacy of Westman's God over human morality. God, to Kant, was a function of morality, not vice versa. Kant's meiotic humanism was characteristic of his time, whereas Aristotle's similar idea was ahead of his own. Westmen who lived between the two men went further than either. Their certitude of God's existence had room for the Aristotelian–Kantian idea only as shorthand for something much greater. But, for all practical purposes, it was useful shorthand.

Certitude requires expression, for it is in our nature to hold understanding to the test of criticism. It is also in human nature to think out loud, making sure an idea can survive articulation. That is why, though culture may have grown out of Westman's desire to express his understanding of God, it – in the manner of a bright child opening his parents' eyes to new twists of fancy – also refined that understanding. This means that at every stage in Westman's life his culture had to be adequate to expressing his current understanding. As the substance of the culture developed, so did the form.

At the beginning, Westmen's understanding of God was simple and so it required only elementary forms. Westman still had not travelled sufficiently far in time from the Scripture whose idea was simplicity itself. 'The kingdom of God is within you' was a thought so simple that it required a genius to understand. Moreover, no genius other than the Jesus of the Gospels has ever managed to find such unaffected words. The rest of mankind had to encumber the message until the words lost any link with the original truth and began to live a life of their own.

The Scripture exhausted the divine capacity of language in the same way in which Bach later exhausted the divine capacity of contrapuntal music. St John tells us that 'In the beginning was the Word'. However, he omits to tell us that the original Word rendered all subsequent words woefully inadequate: in a brightly lit room, the light cast by a match is unnoticeable. It was precisely because of the omnipotent Word that was at the beginning, not in spite of it, that music rather than literature has become the ultimate expression of Westman. There were men after Christ who found beautiful words to express God, as there were men after Bach who wrote beautiful counterpoint. But in spite of the success – more accurately, because of the ultimate failure – of such men, the need for new forms became ever so more pressing.

Because of the near divine role assumed by culture in Westman's world, we cannot regard Western culture as a self-contained repast stewed in its own juice and served separately from other aspects of life. Before such a view could become utterable, Westman had to die and be replaced by Modman. Had a sci-fi time machine made it possible for Stravinsky to share his pet view of music expressing nothing but music itself with the likes of Palestrina, Lasso or Schütz, never mind Bach, the older artists would have thought they were dealing with a madman. Had Wilde tried to convince Dr Johnson that there is no such thing as moral or immoral art, he would have been told he knew not what he was talking about. And even Ortega would have got in hot water had Velázquez been able to read Ortega's purely formal analysis of him and Goya.

The culture of Westmen was intertwined with the way they viewed the world, and at no moment was it inadequate to their spiritual needs. That is why it is wrong to describe the pre-Renaissance centuries as culturally backward simply because Westmen had not yet got around to painting pictures of plump babies sucking rosy-cheeked breasts. God within Westmen was at that time most clearly expressed through architecture, and he was still a new God, one who had not yet escaped into infinity. He was contained within the space of high, but not infinitely high, vaults propped up by flying buttresses, and the sacrifice of his son was symbolized by cruciform transepts. The Romanesque or Gothic cathedral was not only an aesthetic expression of God, but it was also a place where God lived so he could stay close to man. The beauty and grandeur of the cathedral, its perfect proportions and rich adornment were thus meant to reflect the perfection of God. Both painting and music were at the time mere aspects of architecture, with the former acting as interior decoration, and the latter as accompaniment to words of devotion. But then the house became too small; God was running out of space. Architecture had gone as high as it could go, so now it had to step down and give way to new forms more conducive to new understanding. Once the summit has been reached, down is the only way to go, and no post-Gothic architecture has ever achieved the same grandeur and technical mastery. This in spite of all those computer-generated models behind which our contemporary architects hide the salient truth: the genre has been exhausted. Epigones like Pugin tried – more in form than in substance – to go back to the Gothic summit from time to time, to find it is only climbable once. At best they have succeeded in creating witty pastiches, such as Gaudi's *Sagrada Familia* in Barcelona.

Apart from a natural desire to seek new forms, there were more fundamental impulses that later drove Modmen away from Gothic architecture and, especially, what it represented. Correctly under-standing that the old style was merely a shell containing the old content, Modmen transferred onto the shell their venomous feelings about the content – with predictable results. In the eighteenth and nineteenth centuries, the time when Modman was finding his feet, thousands of Romanesque and Gothic buildings were defaced or destroyed in Europe, and more than half of all Paris churches. Some were later restored at a time when Modmen no longer perceived Western culture as dangerous and could safely relegate it to the level of tourist attraction. Most were lost forever, and many of those that survive still bear the stigmata of Modmen's fury: empty niches stripped of statues, smashed stained glass, scarred façades.

As with all falls, artistic decline has gravity-assisted acceleration built in. The greater the distance travelled from the peak, the more visible is the decline. Having fallen from the Gothic summit, it took several centuries of incremental plummeting before architecture crashed into the dung heap of the Canary Wharf, Centre Pompidou or Tribeca, buildings that fail not only in aesthetics and spirituality but also in functionality, being devilishly hard to heat, ventilate and indeed navigate. It is testimony to the height of the peak that the decline took so long.

After architecture had been found wanting, painting got its chance. This is, of course, a crude way of describing that transition, and it survives here only for brevity's sake. Whenever one talks about history, it is important to remember that periods do not replace one another the way images pop up in the slots of a one-armed bandit. The moment one begins to look upon historical continuity in a mechanistic way, something Bergson, Whitehead and Spengler (not to mention assorted Marxists) were guilty of, one forfeits a measure of credibility. A telltale sign of such a mechanistic approach is an author's preoccupation with chronological tables in which different epochs are juxtaposed so as to demonstrate parallel trends. Whenever we see such tables, a warning signal should go off inside our heads, telling us to be on guard. History may have its winners and losers but it is not a knockout contest. The losers do not just drop out never to be heard from again. If a cultural trend is dominant in a certain period, other trends cannot be automatically presumed to be non-existent at the same time. Thus, although Modman replaced Westman as the dominant social force, as the latter had replaced Hellenic man, each replacement took centuries, with much overlapping in between. Modman overlapped with Westman for roughly a quarter of a millennium, which is how long it took for his victory to become irreversible. Westman overlapped with Hellenic man for even longer than that and only eventually achieved historical dominance by reaching a compromise with his predecessor. In our example, painting, too, overlapped with architecture and took two centuries, the fourteenth and fifteenth, to come to the fore.

Expanded use of perspective gave Westmen a link between their individualism and the urge to look outwards – a marriage between the keenly felt living God in their souls and the disembodied Old Testament God who was drifting farther and farther away. Perspective placed the artist at the vantage point of individual vision and created an illusion of endlessness. At the same time, the newly refined art of portraiture added another illusion, that of an ability not just to feel but also to see the God within. But illusions they were, at least to some extent, for the physicality of the painting was getting in the way. It took too much suspension of disbelief to perceive the painter's vision as infinite, to forget that the seemingly endless perspective had to end at the wall behind the canvas. And the human face merely hinted at God, stating that a mystery existed without attempting to solve it. Physics interfered with metaphysics in the same way in which the body has to interfere with the soul. This interference pointed at a conflict already existing and presaged the cataclysmic conflict yet to come.

For perspective is not reality but make-believe. It is not so much the ultimate, scientific arrangement of space as a statement of belief in the exclusive truth of a scientific arrangement. In other words, perspective fakes reality to make it agree with a set of scientific principles that, as Westman was growing feebler, were taking on an ever-greater importance. Extended use of perspective also reflected an increasing shift from theocentrism to anthropocentrism. Westman's introspection at some point began to overstep the line separating God as the starting point of vision, giving rise to the arrogance of believing that man himself was at the centre of the visual – and therefore philosophical – universe.

To believe that the 'invention' of perspective represented progress compared with mediaeval art is naïve. More accurate would be an understanding that acceptance, rather than invention, of perspective reflected Westmen's growing anthropocentric arrogance. For, by the time the Renaissance arrived, perspective was old hat. Dürer acknowledged as much by stating in the introduction to his book that a reader familiar with Euclidean geometry needed to read no further. Quite apart from Euclid, we must not think that Hellenic and mediaeval artists could have failed to notice that lines of vision converged as they travelled away from the eye. They were perfectly aware of this, and acted on that knowledge extensively – but not in high art. Perspective was known in ancient Greece, but there it was used in applied arts only. For example, the stage sets for Aeschylus's plays in the fifth century BC were executed in perspective. The Greeks accepted this: unlike real art, theatre to them was frivolous. The truth lay elsewhere, so why not accept the self-evident falsehood of perspective in the backdrop?

Mediaeval painters also knew perspective and yet chose not to use it. They saw perspective as a fake that was unworthy of their higher purpose. Instead, mediaeval, particularly Byzantine, paintings relied extensively on reverse perspective wherein parallel lines drifted further apart as they moved away – or else converged as they moved towards the artist. Thus the farther from the artist's eye a figure was, the larger it got, especially if it was a divine personage. This corresponded to the perception of the figure of

God as the most remote and yet by far the largest of all – large beyond any human understanding. Mediaeval artists did not regard themselves as God-surrogates. Their paintings were an exercise in prostrate humility, not arrogant self-assertion. When that began to change, the use of perspective grew. Characteristically, it was mostly mediocre painters who were the first to rely on perspective dogmatically. The real ones, while acknowledging the existence of perspective, often complemented this plane of vision with others, where the rules of conventional single-point perspective no longer applied.

Even if we look at the evolution of just one artist, some interesting observations can be made. For example, Giotto, widely seen as the first 'modern' painter, started life as an agnostic wag, a Whistler of the late Middle Age. During that period, Giotto used perspective extensively, though not with the same unswerving devotion that characterized most Renaissance painters. As he grew older, however, Giotto became a deeper, more spiritual man. Amusing his friend Dante by bawdy epigrams was no longer enough; more and more he searched for the meaning of life. In the process, Giotto's use of perspective began to decline; his vision was no longer that of a self-satisfied man. He was now attempting to understand how God might view man rather than the other way around.

The Renaissance and the period immediately after it was the swan song of painting, and it was so because of the growing secularization of art – hinted at by the universal use of perspective. As often happens with swan songs, the sound was so much more beautiful for being a dirge: painting was on the way out as the principal expression of Westman's soul. However, the greatest artists of the Renaissance and post-Renaissance periods, such as Michelangelo and Rembrandt, continued to defy the soulless, scientific constraints of perspective. Their vision would not be squeezed into a proto-Modman straightjacket.

The Spanish masters, particularly El Greco and Zurbarán, treated perspective as they treated a colour in their palettes: one of

many. Walking through the Prado, one is transfixed by a
Zurbarán painting depicting the artist as a minor saint struck by a
vision of St Peter nailed to the cross upside down. Despite being in
the background, Peter is noticeably larger than the saint who is in
the foreground. To emphasize the hagiographic pecking order, the
artist shows the minor saint in three-quarters from the back. Yet,
not just his praying figure, but the barely shown face, convey the
impression of passionate spirituality. At the same time, the cruci-
fied St Peter dominates the canvas not just by being its centrepiece
but also by 'violating' every known law of perspective.

Rational arguments in favour of the scientific and therefore
more 'realistic' nature of perspective compared with the vision of
the mediaeval masters are as misplaced as arguments in favour of
atheism. 'Obviously,' clamours a Modman convinced of his scientific rectitude, 'when a Sienese master, such as Duccio, shows
three walls of a palace at the same time, he demonstrates his
ignorance of the laws of perspective. It is impossible to see three
walls at the same time.' The answer may be that, yes, naturally it
is impossible to see three walls at once. But likewise it is
impossible to see two walls at once, or even one. What is possible
to see at once is a tiny fragment of one facet, and arguably even
that fragment is not seen 'at once'. What Duccio is thus showing
is not a naturalistic depiction of a building, but the image of it
that the artist sees in his mind's eye. The painter seems to hint that
God would see the building this way, and it would be blas-
phemous for a mere mortal to argue. Since Duccio is a greater
artist than, say, Canaletto, his vision of a Sienese palazzo
presenting three facets at once is in the higher sense of the word
more real than Canaletto's picture-book depictions of Venetian
palaces. A Westman's vision is spiritual, not just optic.

Verticality in music is a rough parallel of perspective in painting. One dominant voice, presumably the composer's, relegating
all others into the background again may be a misrepresentation
of the workings of the higher inner voice. The assumption is that,

just as it is self-evidently impossible for the human eye to see both covers of a closed book at the same time, so it is impossible for the human ear to hear several voices at once. The counter-argument could run along the same lines as above: of course it is impossible. What is possible, however, is for an artist to weave multiple voices into the fabric of a seemingly horizontal aural canvas of spiritual infinity. And, as with painting, one can learn a lot by contemplating great artists who find themselves at the watershed of two different visions of the world, one inspired by faith from the start, the other initially driven by humanism. What Giotto was in painting Bach was in music. But, although both were straddling the line of demarcation between the old and the new, Giotto looked mostly ahead, while Bach looked mostly backwards. At the beginning of his career, Giotto was thus the first modern, which is to say humanist, artist. On the other hand, Bach was the last of the great composers who subjugated their personality to God's and their art to God's glory. Giotto was the beginning, Bach the end. And just as a tree bears fruit after its seasonal peak, so did Westman deliver ultimate greatness towards the end of his life.

Painting reached its peak in the seventeenth century when the art of Spanish, Flemish and Dutch baroque had taken over from the Italian Renaissance, having first learned from it. The painting of that period was largely a response to the pseudoreligiosity of the Renaissance. For most of the Renaissance painters, religious subjects were merely an excuse to paint bodies, faces or land-scapes. However, not any young woman breast-feeding a baby is the Virgin, and not any three men or two men and a bird are the Trinity. The more human did divine figures appear to be, the nearer was God moving to man. Towards the end of the Renaissance, the distance had got so short as to be imperceptible, a relationship familiar to students of Hellenic antiquity but abhorrent to men of faith who were still not extinct.

The Reformation, with its steadfast rejection of graven images, had increased the visible distance between God and man. God's likeness could no longer be depicted but only suggested. Man may have been created in God's image, but it was only the soul and not the body whose divine lineage could be expressed pictorially. The Reformation had thus set new terms, and art had to respond. The response could be positive, as in Holland, or negative, as in the Spain of the Counter-Reformation. One way or the other, the cultural terms of the Reformation now were universally accepted even by those who fought it every step of the way.

Culture, still linked with theology, was helped in its understanding of God by the mathematics of Newton and Leibnitz, who saw their work as an extension of faith. After their discovery of calculus relegated the geometry of Euclid to the status of museum exhibit, artists could no longer proceed without an aspect of infinity in their work. The great Dutchmen and Spaniards of the seventeenth century took on the task, attacked Euclidean perspective whenever they could and elevated painting as high as it could go. But the collapse painting suffered in the very next century proved that the distance from the peak to the ground was not as great as in the case of architecture. Yet the effect of the fall even from the lower height was shattering. A walk through any museum shows this instantly. Wandering, for example, through the National Gallery in London, we leave Vermeer's women, Rembrandt's self-portraits, Velázquez's king and Zurbarán's saints only to immerse ourselves in the tepid spittle of Boucher and Greuze. And even the better Chardin, Fragonard and Watteau still appear small next to the giants we left behind. The sage, sad eyes of Philip IV follow us as we walk away; and is it a dirge we hear coming out of Vermeer's virginals?

Growing to maturity during the greatest age of painting was its successor, contrapuntal music. After Gothic architecture had tried to conquer one dimension of God's creation, space, music tried to conquer the other, time. And music was at least as successful although time seems to be more difficult to tame.

Just as a Gothic cathedral achieves its spiritual purpose by an aesthetic arrangement of space, music is an aesthetic ordering of time. Unlike architecture, European music is Westman's exclusive property, the musical exploits of both Hellenic man before and Modman after him presenting an anthropological more than cultural interest. It is telling that, though Guido d'Arezzo had introduced universal musical notation centuries before music came to the fore, this happened at a time when Westman began to realize that in the long run music would serve him better spiritually than any other medium – and when music was therefore becoming more intricate than scoreless singing of single thematic lines could handle. Cometh the hour, cometh the man.

Until Aristotle, Hellenic men simply had not come to grips with time; they had not even had the concept of an hour and told the time of day by the length of shadows. Naturally, they could not find the confidence to try to conquer what they had so recently learned. If we take the theological view, God was jealous in granting access to time, his most mysterious creation outside man himself. It was as if God realized that mastery of this dimension would lead man to more understanding than was good for him. Even when God did reveal time he insisted on keeping the control of it firmly in his own hands, only ever offering short leases to great composers.

So far we have not discussed language and the rich literary culture it has produced in Westman's domain. The reason for this omission is simple: when we want to describe an entity that is different from others, we concentrate on the characteristics peculiar to it. If one were asked to describe a bird, for example, the description would focus on the bird's ability to fly, not on it having two legs. Language is a key formative factor in the history of man, but not specifically of Westman. Were a more ambitious writer to undertake the task of composing the formative history of man, language would merit the longest chapter. It is conceivable that the gift of verbal, which is to say abstract, thinking was what instantly turned beast into man. Language, spoken, written or even poetic, is the ultimate instrument of reason, so closely intertwined with it that to all intents and purposes they are difficult to tell apart. But the aim of this essay is more modest: it is simply to show why and how Modman stepped over Westman's body on the way to his victory. And he did so – at least initially – mostly by attacking the indigenous properties of Western culture, of which language is not one.

Westman is unique, but not in every respect. Not only biologically but also in many cultural and social aspects he is no different from his predecessor, Hellenic man. The way he uses language is one such aspect. It is not his reason that makes Westman unique, it is his soul. And for the soul, reason is a ground-floor employee – it is certainly not what makes it Western. That is why literature and language can here function only in a subsidiary capacity, mainly as support points. It is not the particular but the cosmic in man that made him Western. It is not language but music that is his exclusive property.

Poetry, the only art besides music that by controlling rhythm tries to control time, finds its task even more difficult because it is weighed down by the ever-present semantic anchor of language. The same particularizing anchor inexorably pulls poetry back to its Hellenic antecedents. For Hellenic men poetry was a perfect art, able to convey the ethical wisdom of philosophers with the formal excellence of sculptors. And so it was they rather than Westmen who set the standards. Sculpture and poetry are both more Hellenic than Western arts, and no Western poet can become a real master without studying, and widely emulating, classical models. Western poetry owes Virgil, Horace and Ovid so much as to owe them almost everything, sculpture's debt to classicism is only marginally smaller, architecture's smaller still, painting's minimal, and music's practically non-existent. Listing these arts in reverse order, we get a descending scale of Westman's ownership. Trying to 'Westernize' poetry, modernist poets such as

Valéry, Cummings and Khlebnikov attempted to rid it of its semantic, and Hellenic, chains. Though their efforts were interesting, they were not successful, flying as they did in the face of their genre's inherent limitations. Literature is there to say things succinctly and out loud. However hard it tries not to do so, it has to impose the writer's view and hold back a great deal of the reader's own imagination. Our perception of even poetry cannot be completely divorced from reason, even though the more esoteric verse gets, the more likely is the reader to read his own imagination into it, thus approaching – though never quite reaching – the height he has to scale to perceive music.

Music, on the other hand, guides by suggesting. Like faith, it is not without, but within us, waiting to be released. A performance can therefore unshackle the inner resources of a listener's imagination and lead him towards an intuitive, non-verbal understanding that is his own and not necessarily the artist's. In fact, one can say that music lives in the same compartment of the soul as faith, while literature bypasses this area either wholly, as does prose, or at least to a large extent, as does even great poetry. If we are seeking the kingdom of God within us, then a physical stimulus without us can act not just as a help but also as a distraction. Paintings, sculptures or books are all such distractions in that they exist objectively, quite apart from the site where the ultimate kingdom is located. Music, on the other hand, not just appeals to man's inner self but also actually lives there. That is why, whatever their explicit intent, even secular music is always implicitly metaphysical, while literature is implicitly materialistic – even when dealing with metaphysical subjects. No great composer would have countenanced Thomas Mann's view of all intellectual attitudes being latently political (which is to say transient), a view that even Goethe and Dostoyevsky might have accepted.

Since the Word that was in the beginning was to overshadow any subsequent word, man had to search for a prophet who could illuminate a non-verbal path to intuitive understanding. Palestrina and Monteverdi, along with Dutch and Flemish polyphonists like Lasso and Sweelinck, and England's Byrd, Gibbon and Tallis, were showing throughout the sixteenth and early seventeenth centuries the possibilities resident in vocal polyphony. At the same time, their beautiful music also showed the limitations of vocal polyphony in achieving the underlying aim of music as felt by Westmen; indeed, the limitations of all vocal compositions in which words demand equal time with music. The presence, solo or accompanied, of the human voice – in the capacity of enunciator of words and not merely as the original and perhaps perfect musical instrument – had a restricting effect. It was the crutch of anthropomorphism on which Westmen were no longer able to lean, an attempt to contain the uncontainable God of his beliefs within rational limits.

'Westmen' is the operative word here; for Hellenic men, as exemplified by Socrates and Plato, had different thoughts on this matter. For those thinkers, music appealed to the baser passions of man, not to the higher faculty that they regarded reason to be. To become a high art, music therefore needed the ennobling effect of words in the same way in which man's Eros needed the mitigating effect of philosophy. Consistent as that view was with the ethos of Hellenic man, for Westmen it was unacceptable. That is why throughout the seventeenth century, Western composers, such as Schütz, tried to break away from the voice, to think exclusively in instrumental terms. But Schütz's music was more accomplished than sublime; he was hardly the prophet Westman was seeking. And then the search was over. In 1685 Bach was born.

THE ULTIMATE HEIGHT OF WESTMAN'S SOUL

Prophets become truly appreciated only when their prophecies begin to come true. Bach was no exception. Working as he did in the eighteenth century, this greatest of Westmen was initially pushed aside by juvenile Modman pounding his way onto the world's stage. Everything about Bach was hostile to the new breed, and he could even be regarded as dangerous at a time when Modmen still had not gained total control. That is why Bach had to be neutralized.

As his technical mastery was unassailable, the only option open to Modmen was to stigmatize Bach as an anachronism. While culture in general and music in particular had long since become something appreciated only by few, Bach's music had to be shown up by the adolescent Modmen as strictly esoteric, a how-to guide for musicians. Though Bach's music was studied, for a century after his death it was seldom played. That Modmen were beginning to run the show is evident from the fact that Bach's sons, composers of modest inspiration, were in the late eighteenth century regarded as his musical superiors by the general public. To Modmen, who swear by progress, newer means better. The syllogism applied by Modmen ran as follows: Bach's sons wrote in a new idiom while their father used musical forms as he found them (though revolutionizing them in the process). Ergo, the progressive sons were better. In fact, only one of them, Wilhelm Friedemann, was sensitive enough to know what his father was.

This is not to diminish the significance of C. P. E. and J. C. Bach as conduits between their father and Haydn, and as important contributors to the development of the sonata form (or forms, as Charles Rosen would have it). But it was Haydn, Mozart and particularly Beethoven who breathed inspiration into the form, not C. P. E. or any of his brothers. In general, it is hard to think of a single example of genius sprouting in two con-secutive generations of the same family; whoever allots greatness tries not to be too unfair. Biologists describe this tendency as 'regression to the mean', which makes it sound more scientific but no less just.

Modmen, with their congenital egalitarianism, have to see genius as a quirk of nature or, worse still, a product of the environment. They cannot accept that some people can be superior to them in every respect. Pushkin pointed out this trend when commenting on the sly gossip about Byron making the rounds in St Petersburg:

> The crowd greedily reads confessions, memoirs, etc., because in its baseness it rejoices at the abasement of the high, at the weakness of the strong. It is in rapture at the disclosure of anything loathsome. 'He is small like us; he is loathsome like us!' You are lying, you scoundrels: he's small and he's loathsome, but not the way you are - differently.

Modmen routinely depict geniuses as idiot savants, chaps who, though no smarter than anyone, just happen to have this unconscious knack for mastering the techniques required to create things. Allegedly limited in every way other than in their narrow area of expertise, stupid geniuses are not even supposed to be aware of how they do what they do, or why.

Nothing can be further from the truth. Men like Bach, in as much as there ever have been men like Bach, know exactly what they are and what they are doing. Sometimes, however, they have to hide this for tactical reasons, as an attempt to survive in a hostile world run by belligerent mediocrities. Mozart in particular was a past master of such deception, catering to philistines' preconceptions at every turn. Even though he was, apart from his music, one of the brightest men in Vienna (as any reader of his letters will confirm), Mozart often would try to appear less threatening by playing the buffoon. In that subterfuge he failed with his contemporaries: the adolescent Modmen still had not been so completely blinded by their own smugness as to fail to see through Mozart's ploy. It is only after their final victory that Modmen lost the shrewdness needed to flush out their enemies. They have become too complacent to doubt they are at least equal to anybody. That is why someone like the author of *Amadeus* is ready to swallow the bait Mozart tossed to him over two centuries, and why the better wool-pullers among Westman hold-outs still manage to avoid forcible re-education.

Bach did not stoop to diversionary tactics, apart from writing fawning letters to aristocratic patrons, and even there he might have been genuinely eager to render unto Caesar that which is Caesar's. He was too busy writing his music, with many scores carrying the disclaimer that 'the glory is God's'. More than just a disclaimer, it was a statement of intent. Bach clearly saw his music as a means of breaking through the barriers blocking man's path to God, even such symbolic ones as instrumentation or words. He created the greatest vocal music ever written by treating the voice as just another instrument and using words as building blocks of musical phrasing more than carriers of semantic meaning.

Albert Schweitzer showed that for Bach certain musical devices always corresponded to the same emotions and were sufficient for expressing them. That is why a Bach cantata will always sound better in German than in English even to those who have no German at all. After all, if Bach used words primarily for musical phrasing, then surely they depend on the cadences of the original language more than they do on the inconsequential semantics. Schweitzer, a great scholar of Bach's music, makes this observation but fails to arrive at the logical conclusion that Bach did not need words at all. If he could convey the same meaning by sheer musical phrasing, then words were redundant. This conclusion was reached by Philipp Spitta, another important Bach scholar. He shows how even in the recitatives *the musical spirit predominated in Bach over the dramatic'* and that words were *'only the medium of utterance: the instrument best fitted to the purpose here aimed at'*. Bach's urge was to go forward to musical self-sufficiency, not back to music as accompaniment to words.

He strove to elevate instrumental music so that it would be able to soar not only above words but also beyond specific instruments. String, hammer or vocal chords were to Bach mere incidentals, things he happened to have handy when music came to him and he had to put it into a form that others could comprehend. That is why one cringes every time yet another modern critic carries on about the impurity of playing Bach on the piano. It is typical of Modmen that they should miss the mighty forest of music for the puny tree of an instrument. The medium may be the message to McLuhan, but to Bach his media were almost incidental. He used them much in the same way we use cars, as a means of getting to a destination. To be sure, he revolutionized the writing for just about every instrument that existed at the time, and some that did not, such as the modern piano. But what Bach was after transcended mechanical devices.

It also transcended sectarian boundaries. A devout Lutheran in his private life, Bach was ecumenical in his music, as likely to express his devotion in a Catholic mass as in Protestant liturgical music. Of course, as Schweitzer observes with his sterling erudition, Bach's musical ecumenicalism was facilitated by Luther. Luther, an artist himself, saw something that Calvin missed: that an abrupt and total transition from Latin to the vernacular would destroy the aesthetics of liturgy and by doing so would damage the sacred meaning of it. Schweitzer uses this observation to score a few points for Lutheranism. It also could have been possible to suggest that both the aesthetic and spiritual success of Protestantism were in inverse relationship to its remoteness from Catholicism. The more elements of Westman's tradition were allowed to survive, the better – which is why so many people fail at the childish game of trying to name ten great Swiss. No such problem with the Germans.

As if to prove that instruments did not matter, Bach would transcribe the same pieces for keyboard today, violin tomorrow, flute the day after. And his crowning achievement, *The Art of Fugue*, the only work in which he encoded his own name B-A-C-H, mysteriously was written for no instrument in particular, being playable by a string ensemble, orchestra, organ, harpsichord or piano. By way of an aside, it is not surprising that the glory of

God, as reflected through history's greatest composer, inspired possibly the greatest instrumentalist. Being a true disciple of Bach, Glenn Gould always evaded answers to interviewers' questions about piano technique. I have never been interested in the piano as such, the great pianist would say (slightly tongue in cheek), much to his listeners' consternation. Modmen, after all, have reverted to Hellenic formalism – but without the Hellenic ability to make the form divinely beautiful. 'How' again has become more important than 'what', but this time with neither succeeding.

One can observe how, after Bach, vocal music becomes more and more trivialized. For example, it is partly because of his use of a vocal element that the finale of Beethoven's Ninth Symphony never quite succeeds in being entirely convincing. Powerful vocal pieces by Schubert, Brahms, Mahler and perhaps a few others were offset by a massive outpouring of operatic, and increasingly more operettic, banality so popular with the neonatal Modmen. Opera in general and Italian opera in particular is closer to operetta than to serious music. It is more in the nature of music's PR department than of music itself. Even though we may want to exempt bits and pieces of Mozart's and Wagner's operas from this observation, deep down it is hard to argue either with Gould, who believed that Mozart's affection for opera was a millstone around his musical neck, or with the wit who described Wagner as 'the Puccini of music'.

Music already possesses enough drama of its own not to have to rely on the verbal drama of a libretto. The dramatic potential of the spirit is better revealed in the slow movement of Mozart's Piano Concerto, K488, than in all his operas combined. If we accept this, then words – when they are more than just sounds – subtract from music rather than add anything to it. As if to emphasize the incompatibility of the two genres, great vocal pieces seldom use great poetry.* Schubert's *Winterreise*, perhaps the greatest vocal cycle this side of Bach's *Passions*, remains music of

---

* Bach used the Gospels, but then normal rules cannot be applied to him.

genius even if one does not understand the German words. But any attempt to read Müller's cheesy verses without the music is likely to disappoint. Conversely, whenever Schubert uses Goethe's poems, the results are not always so sublime. Likewise, Tchaikovsky's extensive use of Pushkin's words often has the effect of drowning superb poetry in banal music. Interestingly, whenever someone tried to draw Liszt into an argument about Wagner, he would simply sit down at the piano and play his arrangements of Wagner's music. However, he did not sing along as he played.

Spengler argued that all modern music came out of the first chord of *Tristan*, the formal part of modern music at any rate, and one can see his point. But seeing the point does not necessarily mean agreeing with it. For Wagner, with his larger than life Modman personality and ability to shock with both musical and extramusical statements, started a fashion that was still going strong at Spengler's time. And fashion tends to throw a fog around things, thus sometimes making them appear bigger than they are. Subsequent writers on musical matters, such as Rosen, have been able to see Wagner with more detachment. Now he tends to be regarded not so much as the starting point as a stage along the way. His own indebtedness to composers such as Chopin and – specifically in that *Tristan* chord – Liszt has been noted, as was his insignificant influence on such giants of the twentieth century as Prokofiev and Bartók.

Wagner's music was modern, which is not in these pages a term of praise. Modern means, among other things, politicized, for Modmen think that most things, from the food we eat to the transportation we use, from the books we read to the type of fuel we favour, have a political dimension. Science, for example, has been seen largely as an extension of politics for at least a century and a half, with such celebrated figures as Darwin and Einstein adding much impetus to this trend. Characteristically, Bertrand Russell would apply political metaphors to science: 'In Newton's theory of the solar system,' he wrote, 'the sun seems like a monarch whose behests the planets have to obey. In Einstein's world there is more individualism and less government than in Newton's.' Wagner was an early proponent of pagan ideas communicated by musical means. So, even without reading much of his philosophy, one could deduce what it was simply by listening not only to Wagner's operas but to his instrumental music as well. Wagner was aware of this and did not mind it at all. Tellingly, he described himself as a dramatist first and a musician a distant second, something that Mozart, much as he loved opera, would never have said about himself. Therefore, while Mozart's extra-musical views, interesting though they are, can be dismissed as irrelevant, Wagner's cannot be. There is undeniably more (or less, depending on one's point of view) to Wagner's music than music, and certainly more than an attempt to show how far tonality can be bent without breaking. Good or bad, its provenance in Western culture is more debatable than its technical links with the music before and after. Jumping backwards, Wagner leapfrogged Western culture, landing in the middle of Germany's pagan past.* This could not go unpunished musically, as it did not go unpunished philosophically. In our search for formative influences in Western music, we could do better looking to Bach than to Wagner.

Unshackled by Bach, instrumental music soared and, thanks to the height of the peak he had scaled, took longer than any other art to come down to earth. Great music was written throughout the nineteenth century, and even the first half of the twentieth produced composers of genius. Apart from Austria, these mostly came from Russia and Eastern Europe where musical development was retarded, and a lot of lost ground had to be gained. However, the fact that Prokofiev and Shostakovich were savagely persecuted in one core modern country (Russia) and Bartók almost starved to death in the other (the USA) is a useful illustration of the low

---

* 'No true German can be a Christian,' according to General Ludendorff, who was attuned to the latent paganism of his contemporaneous Germany of the early twentieth century.

esteem in which Modmen hold spiritual elevation. Having said that, Prokofiev and Shostakovich may have died before their time because of inhuman political stress, but at least they did not perish scratching a frozen garbage heap in search of food like Mandelstam; dangling off a hook like Tsvetayeva; of hunger like Rozanov; or from a Cheka bullet like Gumilyov, Babel, Pilniak and many others. Being more esoteric than literature, music finds it easier to protest its innocence. Interestingly, it is hard to think offhand of a single great composer who died a violent death. This is not coincidental: music is too closely linked with things that are not of this world to be subject to the same worldly tendencies. For a related reason, music managed to survive for a while the demise of faith and the attendant subsidence in the foundations of culture. Since the divine message of instrumental music is suggested rather than articulated, it reaches only the few remaining Westmen, and they are unlikely to take umbrage. Music can thus hide behind the camouflage of secular entertainment at a time when any overt link with God would assign it to the same bin into which all other uncool things are discarded. But truth to tell, music can be either secular or great, but never both. Whatever its manifest intent, great music ineluctably follows the path charted by Bach.

MODERN CIVILIZATION AGAINST WESTERN CULTURE

Westman culture demanded a civilization in which it could thrive. Civilization is the opposite of militarization not just linguistically but also in essence. It is a method of running civic affairs without any group having to resort to arbitrary force. All lasting human societies need some semblance of civilization, and they generally end up acquiring one, if not without at first having to overcome certain difficulties and to dispose of some bloody-minded elements. In creating his civilization, however, Westman ran into the kind of difficulties that were inherently his. By their very nature his culture and the civilization derived from it were like two electrodes. Sparks were bound to fly where they abutted. The danger of a brush fire was always there.

While Western culture thrives on esoteric exclusivity, a civilization cannot last unless it includes all, or at least most, members of society. Some may drive it, some may sleep in the back seat, but they all must be inside. Consequently, since culture is – uniquely – the engine of Westman civilization, the two have to be equally gregarious to stay in sync, as culture's exclusivity can reduce those excluded to the role of resentful pariahs seeking revenge. Since Western culture cannot help being exclusive, and Western civilization being the opposite of that, the two are a contradiction in more than just terms.

Because Westman civilization had no option but to reflect culture faithfully, this civilization more or less had to mirror the culture's pattern of disfranchisement. Unfortunately, culture's meat is civilization's poison and vice versa. Carrying Western culture to the masses was impossible as this was bound to corrupt both, something that even most of the political egalitarians realized back in the seventeenth and eighteenth centuries. Keeping the two separate was the only way. But since the masses are by definition more numerous, their exclusion could be sustained only by concentrating political, financial and military power in the same few hands that moulded culture. This amounts to a working definition of an aristocratic society, which – whatever we may think of its fairness – was the only social arrangement able to provide the fertile soil in which Westman culture could grow and, consequently, Westman could live.

An aristocratic civilization is indeed a prerequisite for Western culture. However, this observation must be qualified as aristocracy never has been undiluted. No political arrangement can exist in its pure form without degenerating into something unsavoury. Following Aristotle, Machiavelli argued in his *Discourses* that, when their purity is intransigently maintained, a principality turns into a tyranny, an aristocracy into an oligarchy and a democracy into anarchy. For a political arrangement to last, and for liberty to thrive, a state must combine the elements of all three known forms of government. That is why the synthetic constitution of Lycurgus in Sparta lasted longer than the purely democratic constitution of Solon in Athens. A division of power, in which none of the estates feels the need to usurp the total power, is thus a proven guarantor of social longevity.

But it does not guarantee the longevity of culture, something Machiavelli forgot to mention. Though he gave us many political insights, he suffered from the disadvantage of never having met Modman. In Machiavelli's time, a just political system could promote lasting cooperation among the estates, for they were all united in their desire to make the system work. The aristocracy led the way, but none of the estates felt collective enmity towards another until the balance was upset, making one of the estates feel hard done by. But Modman, born some three centuries after the Florentine, is a unique historical type. Dislike of estates other than his own is not something Modman developed as a result of a provocation but something he was born with, indeed the force behind his birth. Modman is programmed to negate every other culture and human type. Therefore a constitutional balance can only go so far in our times. In such a balance, while Westmen would keep their end of the bargain, Modmen would constantly seek a strategic advantage. Thus the English constitution, which came closer than any other to the Aristotelian and Machiavellian ideal of political balance, was doomed the moment Modman made his entry. The democratic part of the triad was becoming disproportionately strong as Modmen correctly singled it out as one they could own. The power of the aristocracy was waning *pari passu*, with culture following suit.

This is not to say it was primarily aristocrats who created Western culture. Nearer the truth would be an observation that the hierarchical structure of Western society made both a functional aristocracy and a creative elite possible. Sensing this, the latter did not mind paying obsequious tribute to the former. Looking backwards from the vantage point of modernity, we may think that, say, Bach must have felt humiliated by having to write self-deprecating letters to Teutonic chieftains whose names mean nothing to us now. He probably did not. On the contrary, he was affirming the natural order of things, the only one under which the *St Matthew Passion* could have been created. Bach's letters were more self-asserting than they were self-effacing.

'In the deepest devotion,' writes Bach, 'I lay before your Kingly Majesty the accompanying trifling work, proof of the science I have attained in music, with the very humble petition that you will graciously regard it not according to the poorness of the composition, but according to your world-renowned clemency.' Considering that the 'trifling work' in question was the *B Minor Mass*, we today find it hard not to cringe at either Bach's obsequiousness or the social conditions that made it necessary. However, we ought to remind ourselves that our own, supposedly more advanced, social conditions have so far failed to produce anything approaching such an achievement. Egalitarian democracy is more likely to deliver itself of something like *Jesus Christ Superstar*.

Quite apart from any spiritual considerations, one reason for this is the way culture is financed. However much some may deplore this, true Westman culture is created for few by fewer. Consequently, it cannot be sustained by box-office receipts. If it is, culture has to possess more mass appeal than it can afford to have without selling its soul to the highest bidder, who inevitably turns out to be the devil. In this sense, culture is like a commercial product: the higher the volume, the cheaper it gets. Today's classical music scene is a prime example of a Faustian transaction. Record companies are cutting back on classical recordings, a development only partly masked by an abundance of 'easy listening' releases of things like *Eine Kleine Nachtmusik* arranged for electric instruments, which also fall into the rubric of classical music. The situation is every bit as dire as described by the influential critic Norman Lebrecht in his book *Who Killed Classical Music?* 'Ticket sales have tumbled, record revenue has shrivelled, major players have lost their independence, state and business funds have dried up and artists who might formerly have looked forward to an independent career have gone begging for wage packets in the ranks of orchestras, themselves threatened with extinction.' Add to this the preponderance of baroque orchestras playing their original instruments with the opposite of originality, and finally consider the domination of the concert scene by jet-lagged, mass-produced, mechanically proficient automatons, and it becomes clear what kind of trouble we are in. Even a mere half a century ago, such soulless musicianship would have been met by stony silence punctuated by a few perfunctory claps. Today it elicits hysterical ovations whose decibel level is unaffected by, for example, the player having an off day, with even his technique not working properly.

But let us not be beastly to today's audiences. Instead, let us go down on our knees and worship them. For these are the last audiences ever. The history of classical music, the quintessence of Western culture, is at an end. This is not doom saying, but merely an observation. To make it, we need to see the percentage of children at a typical classical concert in the West. That percentage, in round numbers, is nought. Without using focus-group research, one can, more reliably, resort to an empirical observation of the age breakdown at any recital: old and middle-aged people about 50 per cent, those in their thirties and forties 30 per cent, musicians and music students 20 per cent, children next to zero. This observation is amply supported by statistics. For example, a comprehensive study by the US National Endowment for Arts shows that for those born between 1946 and 1965 attendance at classical concerts was significantly lower than for older generations. And the next younger generation attended such concerts even less frequently than the 'baby boomers'. Moreover, their attendance did not increase as they grew older.

Naturally, most concert goers acquire the habit early in life, having been dragged kicking and screaming away from footie and into concert halls by parents with Western cultural ambitions. That is why, even one paltry generation ago, children were amply represented in any concert hall. Most grown-ups one sees in the halls today are the erstwhile babes who gradually stopped kicking and screaming and started listening. Since most music lovers begin to love music as children, and since children these days demonstrably do not love music, few are going to flock to Wigmore Hall or Salle Pleyel when the old people depart for that great Green Room in the sky. So next time we find ourselves at a concert sitting next to a mature gentleman who is about to clap between sonata movements, let us shake his hand. As a practical measure, this will save him from embarrassment. As a gesture, it will be our way of saying goodbye to moribund grandeur.

The whole scene is a reminder of the kind of culture a box office can finance. When it comes to opera and ballet, it cannot finance even that – witness the plight of London's Covent Garden that at the time of this writing is unable to make ends meet even with lavish infusions of public money and ticket prices reaching £200 or more. Literature is another example. While the aristocratic time of Elizabeth I produced many forgotten and forgettable writers, it also gave us Shakespeare, Marlowe and Sidney, something the modern time of Elizabeth II has so far failed to deliver, as if trying to prove that great literature cannot be written for the express purpose of making millions. Given the inadequacy of the free-market option, aristocratic patronage is the only answer. This can be direct, as in the case of Bach, Haydn or Mozart, or indirect, as in the case of Alexandr Pushkin. Coming from an impoverished aristocratic family, the poet financed a lavish lifestyle by the sales of his books, thus becoming the first professional writer in Russia. Yet not one of Pushkin's books ever sold more than 500 copies in his lifetime. A simple calculation will show that in today's terms the books must have been priced at an equivalent of at least £500 each for his royalties to amount to a serious income. Each sale thus represented not a free-market transaction but veiled patronage, in the same sense in which the price of admission to a £1000 dinner has little to do with the cost of the food. This is yet another demonstration of the benefit West-man culture derives from an aristocratic society in which those who are capable of appreciating real culture also happen to be by and large the same people who can afford to pay for it.

That is why, for Westman to survive, it is not enough to have a cultured elite – this elite must be able to finance culture. The elite also has to have plenty of leisure time on its hands, for successful patronage relies on this commodity as much as on money. To remain rich and idle at the same time, the elite has to have the political power to keep the internal barbarian at bay, and the military power to bring to bear should he ever get out of hand. All this adds up to a sketchy but usable description of aristocratic society.

Of course, rationally speaking, there is nothing wrong with aristocracy. The noblemen of the past often showed a greater ability, or at least willingness, to act in society's interests than do the bureaucratic democrats of today. However, we are not always, and never merely, rational. We are as likely, more so if you take the Christian view, to act out of instinctive envy and spite as out of forgiveness and humility. Evil pours naturally out of us but we need to make an effort to bring good out, which is why hatred is more common than love. By the same token, remaining in a state of internal barbarism was the easy option for most people. The opposite of that would have required a life-long effort, which alone could buy access to Westman culture for someone who did not imbibe it from birth. Although this difficult option was always available even in the most exclusive of times, the social return for such Herculean labour always was uncertain. That is why it usually was undertaken only by those for whom ascending to

Western culture was a labour of love: people who would catch a glimpse of the West across a castle moat or hear an echo of it through a concert-hall door. Those chosen few would be moved enough to want to belong, a desire springing not from hubris but from a latent spiritual need. Alas, no generation has ever been able to boast more than a handful of such people. Today, now Westman has been routed and his values are regarded as risibly obsolete, it would not be an exaggeration to say that few are making a serious effort to become culturally Western. Social pressure these days is vectored downwards, not upwards.

As the individual became more sovereign in religious matters, especially with the advent of the Reformation, an increasing number of individuals became dissatisfied with secular exclusion. They were no longer happy to accept on faith that the aristocrats were acting in their interests. They wanted to uphold their own interests, and those had to be strictly materialistic, what with metaphysical culture being off-limits for most. The people were becoming restless, and sooner or later their greater numbers would tell. Thus the coexistence of Westman culture and civilization was never destined to remain peaceful for ever. The potential for conflict was there from the start as the aristocracy could protect its cultural domain only by relying on coercion, thereby militarizing its civilization. This contradiction was more than just an oxymoron. It was the guillotine waiting to happen.

By contrast, Hellenic man knew no contradiction between culture and civilization. The two were roughly coextensive, covering more or less the same groups of people. The nature of Hellenic culture was such that it held few secrets. All Athenian Greeks were equally able to admire a statue, even if they were not equally capable of appreciating the fine technical points. Aristophanes's satires or Euripides's tragedies seemed neither enigmatic nor irrelevant to any Athenian citizen of average intelligence. Hellenic artistic creations often were breathtakingly beautiful and devilishly clever, but both their beauty and cleverness lay not far beneath the surface. To Westmen this does not necessarily appear to be so. Many have felt that the beauty of, say, the Acropolis is divine in origin, appealing directly to the Western God within us. However, the Acropolis did not have such an effect on the good citizens of Athens who to the last had an Olympus full of gods busily copulating with women. And those gods, even when on the verge of being reduced to a single God, did not have a direct spiritual link with the people. So Westmen must be looking at Hellenic beauty through the prism of their own notions. This is why a good grain of salt is a useful accompaniment to any art course in which the Renaissance, neo-classicism, or any other Western trend is depicted as a direct borrowing from the Hellenic world. Western artists and architects took from Hellenic man what they needed so as to be Western at the time – and ignored the rest. Donatello and Michelangelo did not give sightless eyes to their sculptures; as far as Palladio was concerned the Ionic column might never have existed; Raphael may have used advanced technique to humanize his Sistine Madonna along neo-classicist lines, but she still remained his vision of the Western mother of Christ.

COMETH THE NEW MAN

Since the religion of Hellenic man did not exclude anyone, neither his civilization nor his culture could fail to be all-inclusive. Whatever distinctions of class, learning or intelligence existed among Hellenic men paled into insignificance when compared with the parity inherent in citizenship. Outlanders were a different matter; they were barbarians, those from the vast elsewhere beyond the polis. That is precisely what the term meant; it was more descriptive than pejorative. But all citizens of a polis could be presumed to have a cultural commonality, and their views were expected to be compatible, if not necessarily the same. As long as they remained loyal citizens, they could hold any opinions they chose or pray to any Gods they fancied – society did not feel in the least threatened. There was, however, an important proviso, as Socrates and some others had to find out the hard way.

Diversity was tolerated, indeed encouraged, as long as it stayed within a broad but by no means endless band. In that respect Hellenic society resembled a pack of wolves. Wolves can treat other species with violence but they never attack other wolves. Fights among them are ceremonial, lacking the sanguinary outcome one normally expects in a battle between men. However, the situation changes instantly when one of them contracts a contagious disease that threatens the whole pack. The pack then unites against the carrier and dispatches it to kingdom come.

By asserting the supremacy of the individual over the mob, the proto-Westman Socrates and his disciple Alcibiades suffered a similar fate. The mob felt threatened, and rightly so. Westmen, wittingly or unwittingly, are hostile to both Hellenic and Modman values, however hard they profess to be reviving the former or upholding the latter. Socrates, the first and surely best-known victim of democracy, drank his hemlock while Alcibiades had to run for his life from Athens to an ostensibly less tolerant Sparta. Plato's most legendary disciple Aristotle also had to flee Athens one step ahead of the hemlock cup. But such niggling irritations apart, Hellenic society, like a pack of wolves, had to fear the threat of extinction only from outsiders. No internal threat was present, or certainly none that those Hellenic men could not stamp out faster than they could say hemlock. The only internal danger, one that eventually brought Hellenic man down, was ageing accompanied by the slackening of will and erosion of the resolve needed to resist an outside threat. But the threat did come from the outside.

Not so the threat to Westman. His culture was such that most citizens of his own 'polis' were automatically cast in the role of internal barbarians. Westman's Attilas and Alarics were just as much out to get him as the nemesis of Hellenic man, but they were wrapped in an equivalent of togas rather than animal skins. That is why their hostility was more difficult to detect, although ultimately as impossible to resist.

Western religion, in its pre-Reformation shape, was esoteric as well. Its universality was owed to the emotional power of its message to the world; reason was excommunicated. The Neo-Platonist and Aristotelian infusions of the Middle Ages partly rehabilitated reason, but that affected an average Christian only indirectly, through subtle changes in liturgical rhetoric. The Scripture was inaccessible to most Christians, if for no other than linguistic reasons, what with the teaching of Hebrew, Greek and Latin being controlled by the very priests who had a vested interest in particularism. A moat was dug around the clerical estate with its secrets, and trespassers were prosecuted with relentless firmness. Although vernacular Gospels had circulated in tiny numbers before, a serious attempt to produce and disseminate a vernacular Bible was a burning offence in England as recently as the sixteenth century. This should emphasize that the Church had no intention of engaging people's minds and removing its own mediation between man and God. In view of later events, this reluctance was nothing short of prescient.

Reason is an inadequate tool to apply to the mystery of God. That even Aquinas ultimately failed in his attempt to reconcile reason with faith testifies to the parallel but never quite intersecting nature of the two planes. Perhaps some revision is in order of the role played by the pagan infusions Christianity received in the thirteenth century courtesy of St Thomas and others. Later we shall approach this from another angle; for now let us acknowledge that in the Middle Ages Plato and especially Aristotle, using Aquinas as an axe, carved a niche for themselves in the history of Western thought. Had they remained in the niche, Westman would possibly have died in infancy or else developed into a species not even remotely resembling Westman as we know him. But that species might have ended up being less self-destructive than Westman, more resilient spiritually in the face of the barbarian threat.

St Anselm's ontological argument and Aquinas's similar five 'ways', his attempt to prove God's existence by applying sequential Aristotelian logic, are examples of reason impressive in itself but misapplied, like a square of chocolate dipped into a glass of Meursault to ruin both. The two were best kept separate, and then perhaps fewer people today would believe that reason and faith are enemies. For all the grandeur of St Thomas, one can argue that his has not been an unequivocally positive influence, and neither is it certain that Hellenic thought in general ought to have any other than antiquarian value for Westmen. Hellenic creativity is a different matter altogether, and later chapters will argue that the greatest achievement of the Middle Ages was to reconcile this creativity with Judaeo–Christian monotheism, thus opening the floodgates of Western culture. While St Thomas's inchoate rationalism may have widened, or perhaps even created, the invisible cracks in the religious foundations of Western culture, this is offset – in some minds at any rate – by his very visible contribution to the culture itself. That Aquinas's influence was at the same time life-giving and destructive is a paradox, but then the history of Westman is full of them.

Any sociocultural type is a biological organism going through the same phases as any other: birth, infancy, childhood, adolescence, maturity, middle age, old age and then death. If so, then Westman would have died sooner or later anyway, even if St Thomas had not pushed the button for a six-century life cycle. Without him, however, they would not have been such glorious six centuries. Aquinas may have given Westman a way of trading a little longevity for a lot of intensity, and if we acknowledge this, then our assessment of St Thomas should depend on the relative importance we attach to these two aspects of human life. In a way, Aquinas demystified God by shortening the distance between the ineffable and the perceivable. Thanks largely to him, Westmen were encouraged in their efforts to find God through daily spiritual toil. The toil gave us the glory that is Western culture. But in the end it may have cost Western God his life, in the Nietzschean sense.

Because of the contribution made by scholastic thinkers in general and Aquinas in particular, Chesterton regards the thirteenth century as more pivotal than even the eighteenth. On his own, unflinchingly Catholic, terms he is right: it is hard to deny that as a result of the thirteenth century culture assumed its central role in the history of the West and went on to blossom into testimony to the greatness of Westman. On the other hand, we must not forget that the thirteenth century also was an admission of failure. It is religion and not culture that ideally should lead the way. Culture gravitates towards the humanistic middle ground, away from the extremes at which man looks for either God or the devil. Culture may symbolize these extremes or even reflect them credibly (witness Bach). But it never quite overlaps with them. Religion in general, and certainly Westman's religion, is both ontological and eschatological. Culture is neither. Unlike religion, culture demands a cocoon of civilization, for without it culture cannot survive. On the other hand, Westman's creed not only does not have a burning need for civilization but is doctrinally contemptuous of it as civilization is all about making life on earth more palatable. Religion, however, codifies a kingdom that is not of this world. The post-Thomistic prominence of culture and civilization thus equates a failure of religion. Had Christianity been able to satisfy the cravings of Westman's spirit by itself, culture would have been superfluous – there would have been no vacuum to fill. We do not know if Aquinas realized this at the time but, titan that he was, he possibly did. If so, we should admire him for admitting defeat but negotiating passable terms of surrender.

St Francis also borrowed some aspects of Aristotle, striking an unwitting blow from which Westman never quite recovered. It was logical for the pagan Aristotle to believe that plants and animals also had both a physical and metaphysical aspect. Monistic unity of man and nature follows from polytheistic beliefs. But Westman is a theocentric and anthropocentric type; to remain Western he has to believe that man's position in God's design is unique. St Francis's preaching to animals that were, according to him, as much God's creatures as man was not Western. In the eyes of the Church it was also heretical, and it was a miracle comparable to St Francis's stigmata that he (though not many of his less fortunate followers) was spared a walk to the pyre. That he was canonized at all shows how unsure of itself the Church was becoming.

When the mind begins to act as the principal conduit of God or, more perilously, his judge, religion has no chance of surviving as a social force. For, while it can withstand enquiry, it cannot survive vulgarization. And the mind with its verbal tools always becomes vulgar when it overreaches. If someone has never heard a Bach fugue, no amount of commentary will ever approach the effect the music would have in its normal context. Even something as trivial as, say, the taste of avocado is inexplicable in words. Anyone trying to apply words to the task of explaining either the fugue or the fruit, having first sampled them properly, will see how vulgar language can become out of its natural sphere. It is logical that the most complex feeling of all, faith, should suffer from obsessive reasoning to the greatest extent. When, a few centuries after Aquinas, Westman realized he was no longer prepared to keep reason at a respectful distance from God, he became a vulgarian. That is another way of saying that he stopped being Westman.

The culture Western religion produced was one contiguous secret, inaccessible to neophyte and infidel alike. That this particularism was mostly unwitting, Gnostic substrands notwithstanding, did not make it any less real or, to those excluded, any less infuriating. People, even when they are generally good, do not like to be excluded and hate to be patronized. When they are generally not good, when the evil within them has overcome the good, they tend to express such negative feelings in the form of revenge. Desire for revenge seethes under the surface, growing in intensity and only waiting for the physical strength to catch up; the more people are excluded and the stronger they get, the more certain the revenge and the more sanguinary its form. Nietzsche described this craving as 'slave morality'. While Westman (or 'master', to use Nietzsche's term) asserts himself by creation, his slavish opponent seeks fulfilment in destruction. Westman becomes what he is by shouting a resounding 'Yes' to the glory of God within him. Modman becomes what he is by hissing a vindictive 'No' at everything Western, beginning with God.

This leads to yet another seeming paradox: as the culture of Westman grew more sublime and consequently more exclusive, he himself became more vulnerable and his existence ever more precarious. But if we agree that culture had become by default the essence of Westman, the source of his historical strength, then the paradox becomes almost impossible to bear: as Westman grew stronger, he was growing weaker.

PART 2
DEVELOPMENT

THE BATTLE PLAN OF MODMAN

The words 'battle plan' evoke an image of generals stooped over a map that shows arrows converging on the strategic objective. The implication is of a small number of individuals rationally devising the most expeditious way of achieving their aim. Understood that way, any sociocultural type, a collective embodiment of the intuitive and conscious urges of a multitude, can have a 'battle plan' only in the metaphorical sense. But it is a useful metaphor, particularly if we accept the argument (put forth earlier) that what really forms a socio-cultural type is not so much rational as intuitive commonality. Thus no international Modmen conspiracy was necessary for them to iden-tify their adversaries and find the best ways to oust them. Their 'battle plan' lived in the realm of intuition, and it was a long-term strategy.

In general, whenever one sociocultural type replaces another as the dominant force, it is usually a confluence of factors that effect such a development, not a single one. The most widespread con-fluence brings together the growing frailty of the established type and the burgeoning increase in the passion of the upcoming breed. For it takes an impassioned group to throw its weight on the wheel of history so as to make it turn. But passion alone is not enough: the weight itself must be great enough to move the wheel beyond the squeaking stage, and there must be particularly impassioned leaders who alone can figure out how the weight must be applied. No matter how loudly *Zeitgeist* talks, it must have interpreters to make itself understood. The will of a small vociferous elite is thus essential – but merely as a way of channelling the dormant collective will. For instance, there had been powerful reformers before Luther (Wyclif and Hus to name just two); yet, they did not bring about the Reformation, for the collective will was not quite there in their time. While their long-term strategy was similar to Luther's, the tactics could not keep pace with it. And tactics springing from expediency, not just strategy, are what greases the wheel of history when a new human type tries to turn it.

Most people within Westman's domain may have been thrust into the role of internal barbarians, but they could not have brought Westman down the same way in which Alaric sacked Rome. The will to do so was close to the surface all along but the ways were in short supply. The will mostly sprang from an understandable response to the tight grip Westmen had to apply to power. Also present were the constituents of human evil, envy being the most obvious one, but pride and greed not lagging far behind. Westmen, to preserve their culture, had to keep it away from the masses yearning to rule. Since, as we have seen, to do so Westmen also had to pull the political and financial strings, the unshackling of the masses always was going to be dangerous to Westman society.

We can envy only what is close enough for us to understand. Until internal barbarians became prosperous, it was not the aristocrat's ability to understand Dante they envied; it was his house, carriage, clothes and food. The belief that it is possible to become rich only at the expense of the poor comes as easily to the human breast as the readiness to pounce at those seen as oppressors. That destroying privilege was impossible without also demolishing the culture produced by privilege was of little concern to the internal barbarians. The culture was not theirs anyway. As far as they were concerned, it might as well never have existed.

Apart from the gifted individuals able to join Westman culture and thus improve their social standing, most people living in the society built by Westman did not feel they were welcome in that dwelling and so were naturally inclined to pull it down. This may not have been a conscious urge in most; it was more of a dormant giant waiting to be awakened. And awakeners never have been in short supply: destructive men with enough sensitivity to the latent feelings of the masses to use them for their own nefarious ends. Not that mass sentiments of this type are ever hard to grasp. The evil in human nature is easier to understand than the good, for the same reason that an animal is easier to understand than a human. The latter's readiness to die for what he feels to be a better way of worshipping the same God beggars belief, while the former's readiness to satisfy its appetite by devouring a weaker creature is understandable to the point of being obvious. Manipulating people's insecurities is also an easy enough task, as any advertising man will tell you. Succinct articulation usually does the trick, and the terser the better.

Words may be inadequate to the task of expressing the divine quest of man, but they are perfect for expressing his simpler aspirations. A slogan like 'from each according to his ability, to each according to his needs' is instantly understandable even to the dimmest people. But even the brightest Westman would fail to express the spiritual needs of his own ilk with a catchy phrase. He would be equally hard-pressed to counteract a subversive slogan without having to take the internal barbarian out of his depth, thereby losing him as an audience. For example, in order to argue with the slogan above, a Westman would have to explain that for this idea to be applied in practice there would have to exist an authority empowered to decide what constituted both 'ability' and 'need'. Such an authority would have no margin for human frailty and would inevitably become not just authoritarian but downright tyrannical. It would have to be in a position to have total control over both ability and need, which means at least an approximation of concentration camps. As far as catchy counter-slogans go, this cannot work.

Still, regardless of how many slogans of liberation reached the internal barbarian, there was precious little he could do to act upon them as long as Westman's house was sturdy enough for the structural defects not to show. And whenever they did show, it would take time for the cracks to do real damage even with outside help. Attrition was the only way. In other words, to become the omnipotent Modman of today the downtrodden internal barbarian of the past had to bide his time, rapping on the walls in the hope of hearing a hollow sound.

Polarized thinking comes naturally to unsubtle minds. With an unsubtle task like destruction, the natural works best. Powered by the heart-felt collective urge to destroy the society of Westman, internal barbarians and their leaders only had to identify its cornerstones and strike at them with their opposites of greater weight. If Westman lived by faith, it had to be undermined by scepticism first, atheism second. If Westman culture was introspective, accentuating substance rather than form, then it had to be dragged from its shell onto the formal surface. If free choice between good and evil, right and wrong, good and bad drove Westman's morals, ethics and aesthetics to a civilizing union, individual choice had to be knocked out by a collective ukase. If links among the cornerstones made all three stronger, the links had to be loosened and the very belief in their existence ridiculed.

This list easily could be continued *ad infinitum* from the general to the particular: if Western economics accentuated individual risk, it had to be replaced by collective security; if Western music relied on the composer as a messenger of divine revelation, it had to be replaced by the adulation of the performer as a conduit of secular vanity; if Western painting used technique as a means of conveying the soul, it had to be replaced by the elevation of technique itself to God-like status – followed by its certain demise.

Such an extension of the list would show that the internal barbarian faced no mean task. In fact, had all these building blocks of Western society been more independent of one another, and had they had to be attacked one by one, the barbarian's task would have been endless. But they were not independent. They all rested on the same foundation, Western religion. And it proved to be vulnerable.

MODMAN TAKES ON GOD

Now Jesus Christ has become a superstar, he is enjoying the kind of commercial success the homeless carpenter could never have dreamed of in his lifetime. Long since in the public domain, his estate is not entitled to royalties, which keeps down the overhead of West End and Hollywood productions, making them ever more profitable. Mass vulgarity thus has succeeded where the Crucifixion failed: Christ is now dead, at least as a social force, and his house has been converted into luxury condominiums for the whole family, while supply lasts. The question is was it strictly murder that achieved this deed or was there an element of suicide as well? What if, even as Christ may have instigated Judas's betrayal, Christianity contributed to its own downfall?

Christianity became Westman's founding institution largely because of its ability to attract converts. But to acquire this ability, Westman's religion had to carry from birth the seeds of collectivism inside its body. The seeds sprouted and destroyed the body: that which lives by mass appeal will perish by mass appeal. Yet mass appeal is crucial to Christianity because, while the doctrinal essence of this religion is emphasis on metaphysical salvation, it was its worldly promise that enabled Christianity to proselytize successfully so as to triumph over other religions, including Judaism, its monotheistic precursor and rival.

This in-built compulsion to proselytize (more pronounced in the apostles than in Jesus who expressly strove to appeal to Jews only) is not just collective but also rationalist. Christian missionaries had to preach to the uninitiated, those who had had no intuitive experience of Christ. Some of the time, the missionaries achieved success by relying on simple things like performing miracles or frightening people with divine retribution. But the more intelligent pagans did not scare easily. So the missionaries had to explain their creed to the people weaned on Hellenic rationalism and used to arguing logically. To convert them, one had to out-argue them, which is part of what St Paul was doing in his *Epistles*. Thus an act of successful conversion equalled in a way a debate won by superior reason and rhetoric. But reason always shares living quarters with uncertainty. An invitation to a debate is an invitation to doubt. The Old Testament God, on the other hand, was so far removed from man that he was outside the range of doubt. Christ brought God back to earth and suddenly God felt exposed. That is why Christianity had the sword of Damocles hanging over its head: Thomas was not going to remain the only doubter for long.

In that sense, Judaism benefited from its self-contained exclusivity, which became unequivocal after the Bar Kochba revolt. By the time a Jew was old enough to engage his brain he already was a Jew and had no choice in the matter. He could then venture on a life-long intellectual search in the confidence that the foundations of his faith would survive erosion, if any. Talmudic scholarship thus served the purpose of enriching religion without exposing it to supra-intuitive destruction.

Judaism is an introvert religion, which is why it has survived against odds and, on its own limited terms, is doing passably well. Christianity, however, is extrovert, which is why it succeeded in becoming the universal creed of Westman. But even as there is death in life, there also may be failure in success. Christianity, meaning not just the New Testament but the whole synthesis of belief, mythology, culture, theology, philosophy, social and political organization, is so voluminous that it can console people good and bad, animate greatness and accommodate baseness, encourage virtue and forgive sin. Christianity is infinite – and therein lie both its strength and its weakness. Indeed, one can argue that its strength and weakness are more or less fused into one.

This is suggested by the duality of Christ who is believed to be at the same time God and man. The word 'Christianity' accommodates both in a way. It means, of course, the teaching of Christ epitomized by the Sermon on the Mount, sanctified by the Incarnation, Crucifixion and Resurrection, and accepted as infallible by the faithful. But it also means the Christian Church, a manmade institution that is *ipso facto* prone to human folly. That is where duality starts and whence it grows into every aspect of the Christian creed, to a point where it turns into downright ambivalence, often residing in the same Western breast. Let us look at Christian ethics for example. A man like Chesterton could in his theological writings approach the sensibility of *Summa Theologiae* while sometimes echoing, in his political essays, the sensibility of *Der Stürmer*. If such a subtle and sincere Christian mind does not immunize its possessor against a thinly veiled longing for genocide, what effect can Christian ethics be expected to have on the internal barbarian? Precious little, as a cursory look at Christianity even in its peak will reveal. An interesting titbit: at the time of Magna Carta, six centuries after St Augustine baptized England, the courts accepted an Englishman's oath only when corroborated by 11 witnesses. By contrast, a Jew's testimony was accepted without any further validation – this at a less than Judophile time when pogroms were raging in York and elsewhere in England.

This brings us to the ultimate ambivalence of Christianity: the conflict between its elitist core and populist periphery. The core, its sublime beauty, could have played only an insignificant role in the worldly success of Christianity, as it was to all intents and purposes inaccessible to any but extremely subtle minds and refined souls, the likes of which have never been thick on the ground. In addition, at the time Christianity scored its first public triumphs, its theology was not only inaccessible but also linguistically incomprehensible to most converts.*

But even now, when the Bible adorns bestseller lists, how many Christians even purport to understand such fundamental concepts as the Trinity, consubstantiality, God-man, Resurrection, Immaculate Conception, transfiguration, prefiguration or why the poor in spirit will inherit the kingdom of heaven? All these are explained by the Fathers and Doctors of the Church, yet even they found it difficult to be lucid on the subject of the Trinity, and especially the Holy Spirit, as any reader of Aquinas will confirm. But how many Christians over centuries, and especially today, have read *Summa Theologiae* or *The City of God*? They have never added more than a trickle to the vigorous flood of Christianity that engulfed the Western world. That is why, had Christianity relied exclusively on what is beautiful in it, say the Sermon on the Mount, it would be known today, if at all, merely as an attempt to reform Judaism during the reign of Tiberius. What enabled it, in a mere three centuries, to become the universal religion of the Roman world? It was not so much its explicit doctrine as its implicit appeal to neo-pagan collectivism. In due course, this has led to the present-day belief that Christianity has much in common with socialism, usually held by those who love the latter and hate the former. If they understood Christianity, they would realize that its essence is not just different

* As a dominant social force Christianity survived for more than 1000 years before the appearance of the first vernacular Bible, and for only about two centuries thereafter. Whether one regards this as a coincidence or causality is a matter of opinion.

from socialism but opposite to it. Socialism is all about achieving happiness, as defined by Modmen who understand it as universal prosperity and social equality on earth. So defined, happiness lacks a spiritual dimension and, consequently, precludes inner freedom, for such freedom is compatible with neither universal prosperity nor social equality. Christianity, on the other hand, is nothing if not spiritual. It presupposes freedom and not only accepts but positively encourages the suffering inherent in it.

But it is easy to see how a misapprehension could arise. To be sure, there is enough in Christ's teaching, and indeed in the subsequent apostolic theology, to justify free will, individual salvation, personal responsibility, thrift, hard work, freedom of choice and other unsocialist things. There can also be found, however, quite a few other things in 'outer' Christianity that appeal to the innately modern instincts of the internal barbarian – yet another demonstration of the often ambivalent breadth of Westman's faith.

This ambivalence proved to be the undoing of Christianity. The first serious blow, once all the heresies had been sorted out, paradoxically came from the success Christianity achieved by approaching the status of state religion in the Roman Empire. Until Constantine, Christianity had been a matter of individual conscience. People practised it out of a sincerely held belief in salvation achievable through Christ, and various emperors displayed more or less tolerance towards it. Once Christianity had become the state religion, however, many people began to pretend to be believers for pragmatic reasons. Suddenly it paid to be a Christian, which quickly secularized the religion and injected an unhealthy dose of hypocrisy into it. After the institutional disintegration of the Western Roman Empire, the Church also acquired the kind of secular power it was not designed to wield, thus finding itself in a perilous position. It was no longer to be judged just on the basis of the solace it offered believers. It could now live or die by its ability to handle secular matters. Sooner or later things had to go wrong, for no manmade institution can get everything right all the time. And when things did go wrong, the effect proved devastating not only for the Church's secular power, but also for its core business.

Another corollary to Constantine's revelatory conversion was his belief that it was not he, the emperor, who had chosen Christ, but Christ who had chosen him. That gave rise to the belief, shared by most subsequent monarchs, that a king's reign is anointed by God, and that he therefore rules by divine right. This doctrine was not sustainable in perpetuity, as it exposed monarchy to the dangers arising from religion losing currency. Eventually God and his Church failed to keep up their control over minds and souls. When that began to slip, divine right began to totter. Since absolute monarchies could not offer another equally compelling claim to legitimacy, their power started to dwindle.

All these developments had a detrimental effect not just on Westman's religion but indeed on Westman himself, for he was a product of his culture, which in turn was a product of Christianity, or a reaction to it. The sluices of Western religion were flung wide open and the masses began to pour in. When that happened, the Church was doomed, although it took the Reformation to drive the point home. Once the Reformation made the Scripture available to the hitherto marginalized masses, they were free to read into it whatever they wished. And what they wished more than anything else was to have a justification for their attack on Westman.

Indeed, it is not hard to demonstrate that the mass appeal of Christianity relies on the same basic promise and, even more important, activates the same mechanisms of human behavioural response as Modman politics. As an experiment, we can list various impulses that trigger off such mechanisms and juxtapose them with what the internal barbarian could find in the Scripture, once it was made available to him.

Derisory attitude to tradition

As a rule, internal barbarians blame tradition for keeping them, well, barbaric. This was as true in the past as it is these days. Hatred of the past comes as naturally to Modmen as does their belief in a shining future. Modmen are progress-happy and they are innately anomic, a quality that transcends reason. That is why a Modman can never be a conservative, though he may join the Conservative or some such party out of his belief in the virtue of free enterprise. A Modman's anomie is such that he will not merely reject, but become extremely agitated at the sound of any argument that appeals to tradition. The past has no value for Modmen, ever the intuitive Cartesians. As far as they are concerned, the dial is reset for every generation. That is why history is perhaps the sharpest burr under Modmen's blanket, for history is by definition aristocratic: tracing back the life of man is close to studying the lineage of a family. Modmen will have none of that. They are not only atheistic enough to believe that there is nothing after their death, but also self-centred enough to think there had been nothing before their birth. A Modman will see red if you make even a gentle suggestion that perhaps he would be well-advised to think twice before initiating irreversible changes to the institutions that have been in existence for centuries or even millennia. He will pretend not to understand what you are talking about, even as you may feign disbelief that someone can be so reckless. In fact, at a more basic level you understand each other perfectly. Your explicit respect for the past is an implicit declaration of the superiority of Westman over Modman. His explicit anomie is implicit hatred of Westman based on the genetic memory of envy. These days Modmen are no longer athirst, so their envy has shifted from the physical to the cultural aspects of Westman's life. Modern Englishmen, for example, will talk your ear off on the subject of the vile class system that they correctly see as having little to do with money. It is not uncommon for modern Englishmen drawing six-figure salaries plus bonuses to describe as 'those bastards' people who live on modest incomes but speak with cultured accents.

Christianity is the religion of Westman, who is by definition alien not only to Modman but to Hellenic man as well. Roughly at the time the fourth Gospel was written, Tacitus expressed the dominant attitude of the time:

> Nero ... punished with every refinement the notoriously depraved Christians (as they were popularly called). Their originator, Christ, had been executed in Tiberius's reign by the governor of Judaea, Pontius Pilatus. But in spite of this temporary setback the deadly superstition had broken out afresh, not only in Judaea, where the mischief had started, but even in Rome. All degraded and shameful practices collect and flourish in the capital.

Given the religious tolerance of the Hellenic world in general and Rome in particular, this is strong stuff indeed. Clearly, the Romans saw Christianity as a subversive threat, and this attitude did not spring from their objection to all-encompassing charity. It is conceivable that those Romans who did not know better detested not so much the Christians' beliefs, about which they could not have known much, as their clandestine meetings, which were in themselves punishable offences in Rome. But why did those meetings have to be clandestine? Possibly because the Romans sensed that a new, dangerous breed was making its historical début, a breed to be nipped in the bud out of self-preservation.

The Jews did not have to rely on intuition. They had a clear-cut grievance: the very foundations of their religion were under attack. Here we touch upon an unclear area, as it is often claimed that Christ himself never planned to start a new religion. His aim was to purify the old one: 'Think not that I am come to destroy the law, or the prophets: I am not come to destroy but to fulfil. For verily I say unto you, Till heaven and earth pass, one jot or one tittle shall in no wise pass from the law, till all be fulfilled' (Matthew 5:17–18).

Subsequent history seems to support this statement of intent: the first 15 bishops of Jerusalem were circumcised Jews who swore by the Law of Moses. But the bishops of Jerusalem, of whom the first was 'the Lord's brother' James, did not create a new religion. Paul did; and his relations with James and the other apostles were about as cordial as those between Trotsky and Stalin or Hitler and Strasser: none so hostile as diverging exponents of the same creed. Yet Paul too could have found inspiration in Christ's words. For, immediately after assuring his audience that he was not going to encroach upon 'one jot or one tittle' of the Mosaic Law, Christ proceeded to do just that:

> Ye have heard that it was said by them of old time, Thou shalt not kill. ... But I say unto you, That whosoever is angry with his brother without a cause shall be in danger of the judgement ... but whosoever shall say, Thou fool, shall be in danger of hell fire. ... Ye have heard that it was said by them of old time, Thou shalt not commit adultery: But I say unto you, That whosoever looketh on a woman to lust after her hath committed adultery with her already in his heart.
>
> (Matthew 5:21–8)

This theme appears in the Sermon on the Mount and elsewhere. For example, when Christ's disciples went out to pluck ears of corn on the Sabbath day, the Pharisees took exception: 'Behold, why do they on the Sabbath day that which is not lawful? ... And he said unto them, The Sabbath was made for man, and not the man for the Sabbath' (Mark 2:23–7). In short, every tenet of the Law, including the immutable Decalogue, was being revised in what believers could only see as a cavalier fashion. A millennium and a half later, Ridley and Cranmer were immolated for less.

Paul, rightly or wrongly, pushed Christianity further along the radical path than Christ himself ever did: 'Knowing that a man is not justified by the works of the law, but by the faith of Jesus Christ, even we have believed in Jesus Christ, that we might be justified by the faith of Christ, and not by the works of the law' (Galatians 2:16). And later, 'But that no man is justified by the law in the sight of God, it is evident: for, The just shall live by faith. And the law is not of faith' (Galatians 3:11). In other words, do observe the Law by all means, but from the standpoint of salvation it does not matter one way or the other. Pauline severing of the Jewish roots of Christianity has a lot to answer for in the subsequent growth of Modman's anomie.

But what were, in addition to unlawful assembly, the 'degraded and shameful practices' that fed the Romans' hostility towards the Christians? One of them had to be another proto-Modman element in Christianity:

An attack on the family

The attack on this pivotal unit of Roman society was doctrinal in that Christ preached a loyalty that was to supersede loyalty to family. The attack was also physical in that youngsters were yanked out of their families and shipped to the family-like communes of catacomb Christianity, even as in later years they were bound to monasteries and convents. Christ himself was explicit on the subject: 'For I am come to set a man at variance against his father, and the daughter against her mother, and the daughter-in-law against her mother-in-law. ... He that loveth father or mother more than me is not worthy of me: and he that loveth son and daughter more than me is not worthy of me' (Matthew 10:35–7). Even that statement, outrageous as it was by Roman standards, was not deemed sufficient: 'If any man come to me, and hate not his father, and mother, and wife, and children, and brethren, and sisters, yea, and his life also, he cannot be my disciple' (Luke 14:26).

What Christ preached for the higher purpose that the internal barbarian could not grasp, Rousseau, Marx, Lenin, Hitler, Stalin and other Modman prophets preached out of their more common evil-mindedness. But the erosive effect on the family was similar. In fact, Christianity encouraged not family but celibacy, and it was not until the thirteenth century that marriage was deemed worthy of sacramental status in the Christian Church. 'Even married sex, adorned with all the honourableness of marriage,' writes Aquinas, 'carries with it a certain shame, because the movements of the genitals unlike those of the external members do not obey reason.'

Latent paganism

The unrelenting monotheism of the ancient Hebrews was difficult for most people to accept. They did not want the remote, 'jealous' God of Israel, Abraham and Jacob, what with his ethical rigidity, moral absolutism and summary justice. They wanted their own cuddly gods, flawed as they might have been. And what was that row about graven images? As far as Hellenic men were concerned, there was nothing wrong with the familiar representations of their deities. Christianity, whose finer points were bound to escape them, provided an easy alternative springing from its explicit anthropomorphism and implicit polytheism (again, both features of Pauline Christianity more than Christ's as conveyed in the Gospels). The palpable God-man who was like them in his human incarnation was more understandable, more comfortable. And if God was even physically like them, logically speaking they were like him, a welcome elevation in status for men whose physical lives were dire. The global glossalalian gloom of sectarian fundamentalism we observe today demonstrates the pagan propensity of the post-Christian Modman – and the potential for paganism built into Christianity. Carrying anthropomorphism back to BC levels, the happy-clappy multitudes are, of course, as pagan in deed as they are Christian in word.

Social and economic egalitarianism

'But many that are first shall be last; and the last shall be first' (Matthew 19:30). This was a heady promise for internal barbarians who had to understand it in the crudest sense. They now could claim ascendancy over the uninitiated by a simple declaration of faith, a coup as irresistible as it was effortless. And let us not forget the money! Abraham's righteousness may have been rewarded by great wealth, but the masses always suspected the rich were nothing but thieves ('property is theft,' said Proudhon). And, according to the Scripture, they turned out to be right: 'Then said Jesus unto his disciples, Verily I say unto you, that a rich man shall hardly enter into the kingdom of heaven. And again I say unto you, It is easier for a camel to go through the eye of a needle, than for a rich man to enter into the kingdom of God' (Matthew 19:23–4). So what should the rich do with their money? Why, give it away of course: 'go and sell that thou hast, and give it to the poor' (Matthew 19:21). That idea was bound to appeal to the poor. To give credit where credit is due, the apostles practised what they preached: 'And all that believed were together, and had all their things common; And sold their possessions and goods, and parted them to all men, as every man had need' (Acts 2:44–5). 'To each according to his needs' grew straight out of this passage, appropriately perverted.

The apostles were not wealthy; surely they realized that spreading their meagre possessions among the needy hardly amounted to responsible economic policy. By redistributing their wealth they were seeking self-purification. But the subversive potential of such acts when misinterpreted by people not normally driven by high urges is obvious. It certainly was so to Pliny the Younger who was sent to investigate the catacomb congregations. In his report he testified that they were not just communal but communistic, similar to the group described in the Qumranian scrolls. Since then we have had ample opportunity to observe what happens to communistic ideas whose full potential is realized.

Once again, we are talking here about a predictable mass response, not the understanding of a subtle Christian soul. Thus, for example, comments Aquinas: 'The perfection of the Christian life does not consist essentially in voluntary poverty, though that is a tool of perfection in life. There is not necessarily greater perfection where there is greater poverty; and indeed the highest perfection is sometimes wedded to great wealth.' Unfortunately, few of us bear resemblance to St Thomas; and the Romans were worried by the revolutionary potential of the new creed. What they saw in it amounted to yet another proto-Modman element:

A promise of immunity for destroying the old order

Here too, Christ himself may have kindled their fears: 'Think not that I am come to send peace on earth: I came not to send peace, but a sword' (Matthew 10:34). Specifically, the Temple would not stand for much longer: 'And Jesus said unto them, See ye not all these things? Verily I say unto you, There shall not be left here one stone upon another, that shall not be thrown down. ... For nation shall rise against nation, and kingdom against kingdom' (Matthew 24:2–7).

People who emphasize the historicity of Christ to the detriment of his divinity often portray him as a revolutionary, some kind of Che Guevara of Judaea. As long as we agree that he was many other things as well, perhaps there is as much evidence in the Gospels to support this view as to disprove it. Witness Christ's behaviour in the Temple. The money changers were lawfully going about their business when he began to lay about him. The citizens of Jerusalem did not like that arbitrary outburst, and the Romans were not overjoyed either. Then Jesus told his apostles to carry arms to the fateful night in the garden, even though he prevented Peter from doing much damage with his sword. And the manner of Christ's execution, which Rome reserved for subversives, suggests that his ministry was not seen at the time as entirely peaceful.

Chiliastic determinism

Christian eschatology appeals to the internal barbarian partly for the same reason Marxist determinism does: it not so much expiates sin as makes it irrelevant. This is reinforced by many things Christ said, such as: 'Verily I say unto you, All sins shall be forgiven unto the sons of men, and blasphemies wherewith soever they shall blaspheme' (Mark 3:28). When Augustine postulated that human life is preordained to pass through eight stages, of which the first seven are a millennium of worldly happiness and the eighth is eternal bliss, it was all the internal barbarian wanted to hear, and never mind the rest of *The City of God*. The Reformation revived and magnified the early Christian idea of predestination, which had been muffled by the later doctrine of free will. Cranmer, in particular, expurgated from his Book of Common Prayer all prayers for the dead because to the Protestants the final posting of the human soul was predetermined from the start, not being sensitive to any good works undertaken during one's lifetime. After a brief recanting detour, this belief took the archbishop straight into the Counter-Reformation pyre opposite Oxford's Balliol College.

Appeal easily reducible to catchy slogans

Again, Christianity shares this with socialism. 'Eternal happiness' and 'universal love' go on banners as naturally as 'liberty, equality, fraternity' or 'workers of the world, unite.' And what could competitors offer to combat this early exercise in PR? When the great Rabbi Hillel was asked if he could explain the essence of Judaism while standing on one leg, he answered that nothing could be simpler: 'Do unto others as you will have others do unto you. The rest is commentary – go home and study,' an unappealing prospect to the internal barbarian, to say the least.

The ease of initiation and conversion

Conversion to Judaism involves years of assiduous study and a keen ability to ponder abstract points. The Talmud states that in the phrase 'To love the Lord and to serve Him' (Deut. 11:13), '"to serve" means the study of Torah' (Sifre Deut. § 41:80a). When the relative merits of study and practice were debated at the Diospolis conference in Hadrian's time, the conclusion was: 'Study is more important because study leads to practice' (Kid. 40b). On the other hand, in some present-day fundamentalist sects it is possible to become a Christian as fast as one can take a quick dip and say, 'I believe in Jesus Christ'. And, by any stretch of the imagination, that is a small price to pay for millenarian happiness followed by eternal bliss, especially since throughout history internal barbarians have been incapable of studying anything without a material payoff.

Instant and effortless attainment of superiority over infidels
A feeling of superiority is as essential for the internal barbarian as it is undeserved. Both Lenin and Hitler played upon this vanity with virtuoso mastery, especially since it neatly led to egalitarianism: the tiny class differences among the national-socialist Germans, for example, were dwarfed by the gigantic superiority all Germans were supposed to have over everyone else. Likewise, the international-socialist proletarians towered over capitalists, university graduates and other non-persons. Neither had to do much to earn an exalted status, the good fortune they shared with the poor fishermen Peter and Andrew: 'And he saith unto them, follow me, and I will make you fishers of men' (Matthew 4:19). People like to feel significant, especially if this does not involve much of an effort on their part.

Proselytism
The Jews never turned converts away, but neither did they actively seek them. Not so the Christians: 'And as ye go, preach, saying The kingdom of heaven is at hand' (Matthew 10:7). And not so the socialists: one of the first acts of Lenin and his apostles was to create a radio propaganda service that began to beam their sermons all over the world. Regardless of whether or not they believe the sermons, internal barbarians feel flattered by any attention. This also explains why, in the unlimited democracy they themselves have spawned, they like to see politicians grovel for their vote every few years – and greater, and more expert, grovelling will always win more votes than better statecraft.

Christian proselytism literally understood made Westman expansive, driving the crusaders on to their adventures. They too had mastered the art of understanding the Scripture in a selective way, but they took out nothing that was not there in the first place. It is just that when one tries to build a life of Christian or any other virtue, one should realize that what is critical in practice is not only the rectitude of various postulates, but also the balance among them. By accentuating one at the expense of all others the believer presumes to understand God's ways, a transgression usually punished by turning the culprit into an unpleasant fanatic. Thus a Seventh-Day Adventist who runs the Sabbath up the totem pole, or a Pentecostal who insists on talking gibberish in imitation of the apostles' speaking in tongues, is as far removed from the spirit of Westman's religion as any pagan. The same goes for secular fanatics, which is why we should be wary of single-issue politicians, even when we happen to agree with the single issue.

If we now review the italicized headings in this chapter, perhaps we shall agree that Christianity appealed to the internal barbarian the same way socialism does: by suddenly expanding the limits of the allowable and providing an ecclesiastical blessing even for the darker, or at least more shallow, side of human nature. The blessing was conveyed in a coy way. It was not envy that the two doctrines ostensibly blessed but the communal spirit. Not expropriation but sharing. Not hatred of traditional values but a higher loyalty. Not destruction but creation. But the internal barbarian is good at reading between the lines, seeing through verbiage, grasping at the straw of undeserved elevation. He took out of Christianity what he needed and dumped the rest.

That he would do so was hard to predict, but not impossible; making allowances for human nature could have helped no end. Thus, even without the benefit of hindsight, it should have been possible for the sixteenth-century Reformers to think twice before throwing out the baby of Westman exclusivity together with the bath water of clerical corruption, graven images, indulgences and the rest. Apart from its exaggerated trust in human autonomy, most things about the Reformation add up intellectually, making sense within the realm of reason. But most human actions are carried out outside this realm, which is why reformations of any kind are a dangerous game to play. The likes of Luther or Calvin, or for that matter Cranmer and Tyndale, should have realized that the internal barbarian would be more manageable if encouraged to remain where he was spiritually. They should have sensed that the West was not strong enough to withstand such a huge explosion, that the shock waves would never become properly attenuated. Alas, they were driven men possessed by reformist zeal.

Or else they were not aware of the law since then exhaustively proven: any reform is bound to produce effects that are different from those intended by the reformers. The likelihood of such effects turning out not just different but opposite is directly proportional to the reformers' zeal. That is why, while the main impetus of the sixteenth century was ostensibly different from the eighteenth, the latter would not have happened without the former in any other than the chronological sense. The reformers introduced into Westman's religion both pre- and post-Westman values, thus devaluing the object of their veneration and, because of their zeal, achieving a result opposite to the one intended.

The question is, if from its very inception Christianity has been carrying the seeds of its own destruction, why did it last? Why was Christianity so successful for so long in keeping the internal barbarian from emerging as the all-conquering Modman? The answer is simple: no competition. It was not until the early seventeenth century that the internal barbarian could lay his hands upon a secular creed that made all the same promises, but without demanding any service in return, not even lip service to liturgical conundrums. It was no contest; the secular creed had to prevail; and so it did, with Christianity going into an ever-accelerating tailspin that, one fears, it may never be able to reverse.

COMPROMISE AS THE MIDWIFE OF WESTMAN

As we have seen, the Gospels are a minefield strewn with explosive charges waiting to go off. Care is needed to negotiate one's way through; there are few safe paths. Take a wrong step and the world will blow up into a blood-stained mess. If we again go over the italicized subheads in the previous section we shall see that the Gospels are more than just revolutionary – they can be subversive. That is not wicked by itself. Much depends on what is being subverted, and what transpires as a result.

In the case of Christianity, as it was on the outskirts of the Roman Empire in the first century AD, what was being subverted was, in broad strokes, everything. Family, religion, social order, traditional institutions, the structure of Roman society all came under attack. The Romans could not put up with this, hence the infamous lions they did not habitually let loose at members of other religions. That much is obvious. What is less so is that the Romans were not the only ones who dreaded Gospel Christianity. The post-Roman Christian world had a problem with it too. One discerns in the early Christians a nostalgic longing for the Hellenic world, not just because of its polytheism but mainly because of its social stability. The only way to contain that longing was to mollify it, cede to it the periphery of Christianity so as to preserve its core.

That was precisely what the Church has achieved over the centuries and in doing so it redeemed whatever human transgressions it has committed, and there have been many. In fact, one could perhaps go so far as to say that reaching and maintaining this cultural compromise was the main task of the Catholic Church. Its mission was to retain the core of Christianity while mitigating the subversiveness of the Gospels – if need be by withholding them from the masses. That is why, or at least partly why, the cult of the Virgin is so central not just to the dogma of Catholicism but also to its civilization. The Virgin of the Church is the ideal embodiment of family, the Mother not only of God but of motherhood itself. Those seeking full justification for this worship in the Gospels are likely to be frustrated. The adoration of the Virgin came not so much from the Gospels as from a need to counterbalance them, restoring the family to its central social role.

Cultural antecedents of this worship can be found more easily in ancient pantheistic cults. In Christianity, the Virgin performed the role of reconciliation. It is a mother's duty to break up fights between her children, forcing them to shake hands and make up. This was what St Mary had to do as well, gently bringing the best in Hellenism and the best in Christianity together, cajoling them to be friends. It is this compromise that lies at the roots of Westman civilization. However, such an omnivorous tendency runs against the grain of monotheistic rigidity, which is why at its height Catholic thought had to turn to Hellenic thinkers. Plato and especially Aristotle became indispensable in the thirteenth century; Catholicism could not do without them any longer. It can be argued that Aquinas may have gone too far down the path of compromise, that he injected into the bloodstream of Christianity not just a dose of humanistic rationalism but an overdose. But the important thing is that, for better or for worse, Westman culture was a product of Catholic Christianity, not of Christianity in general. In that sense, the thirteenth century was indeed as pivotal for Westman as the eighteenth was for Modman. Westman religion may or may not have survived without the resuscitating influx of neo-paganism. But Westman definitely would not have lived past infancy without it.

As he was a product of his culture, Westman depended for his survival not so much on muscular strength as on creative impulse. Culture was for Westman what the earth was for Antaeus, a resuscitating source of strength. Alas, cultural creativity is at odds with rigid monotheism. Judaism is the most clear-cut example of this, what with its strict injunction against graven images and, since the destruction of the Temple, the banishment of instrumental music from its liturgy. This last despite a fine and ongoing tradition of chant in Judaism, a tradition that goes back further than Gregorian chant and may have influenced it. But that is where Jewish liturgical music ends; and of course Jewish painters had to delay their appearance until the world went secular. All this naturally flows from Judaic dogma. But why did Judaism discourage the arts that later became Westman's property, while attaching so much importance to learning? By all accounts, Hebrew literature rivalled both in quality and volume the literature of Hellenic antiquity; so the burning of the Alexandria library deprived Westman of that part of his heritage as well. But why just literature?

The answer has to be that the relentless monotheism of the ancient Hebrews could accommodate learning, but it could not countenance non-verbal creativity. A man assuming the role of a creator seemed a hair's breadth away from usurping the role of the Creator – an unspeakable heresy to the bookmen of Judaea. Pre-Thomistic Christianity shared this attitude to a large extent. For example, Clement of Alexandria wrote that painting contravened not so much the Second Commandment as the Eighth: by displaying creativity, man was stealing God's prerogative. In other words, pre-Christian and early-Christian monotheism frowned upon not just pictorial or sculptural representations of God, but on artistic creativity as such. Thus, while the tradition of book learning has been passed from one generation of Jews to the next throughout history, to a point where it now must be part of the Jewish genetic make-up in a Lamarckian sort of way, no such relay baton has been passed on in the non-verbal arts. That explains why there were no significant Jewish painters active before the twentieth century, or why there have been so few Jewish composers and – with the exception of Mendelssohn and Mahler – none of the first order.

For Christianity to have produced a culture unrivalled before or since, Westman's Judaeo-Christian religion had to find a compromise between monotheism and neo-paganism. In fact, one may argue that Christianity itself was the beginning of such a compromise. And it would be even easier to make the point that Catholicism, when leavened with Plato and Aristotle, became such a compromise within Christianity. Had Judaeo-Christianity not become Judaeo-Hellenic Christianity, there would have been no Bach and Mozart. This is an interesting example of a process for which it is difficult to find any parallels: on the one hand, Judaeo-Christianity creates in its communicants a craving for cultural expression of their religious quest. On the other hand, it proscribes, implicitly or explicitly, any attempt to satisfy this urge. What looks like a paradox to us must have seemed an unbearable stress to our ancestors, a stress that could have destroyed them had it not been relieved. The proselytizing violence of the Crusades partly resulted from an attempt to find such relief. 'Partly' is the operative word here, for most crusaders probably never doubted the stated purpose of their endeavour. But intuitively they felt the compulsion to seek the truth in faraway lands. God only knows where it would all have ended without the humanizing effect of neo-paganism that guided Westman past puberty and led to the burgeoning of his culture.

This, however, is not the end of the paradox. For, crucial though neo-paganism was for Westman culture, it caused – or, at least, contributed to – the long-term erosion of Westman civilization. The success of a Westman civilization, unlike culture, is directly proportional to the content of monotheism in the nation's soul. The more of it in a Western country, the more civilized and the less cultured it will be. Thus Germany and Russia, the most direct European descendants of Western and Eastern Hellenism respectively, are in modern times the most cultured and the least civilized of Europe's nations. And in both countries, the Jews have represented the most civilized, but not necessarily the most cultured, group. Those Jews who were at the cultural apex in Germany and Russia gravitated towards Christianity. Heine and Mendelssohn are prime examples of this in Germany; Pasternak and Mandelstam, in Russia. ('Nowadays,' said Mandelstam, 'every cultured man is a Christian.') What Christianity does for the Jews in Western countries, Catholicism does for the Protestants in Britain. Newman, Chesterton, Waugh, Muggeridge, Spark and countless others converted to Catholicism, presaging a spate of such conversions later in the twentieth century. Apparently, the British artistic intelligentsia senses the inner conflict between art and Protestantism, even the watered-down version as practised by the Anglican High Church. The nature of the conflict lies in historical continuity, which culture demands and Protestantism downplays. Part of being cultured, in Westman's sense of the word, is to understand history and one's place in it. This is not the strongest point of Protestantism. As Cardinal Newman put it in such a sinewy fashion, 'To be deep in history is to cease to be a Protestant.' This goes to show yet again that, just as Christ willed in the Scripture, his house in the west was built on the rock of Peter, not Matthew, Mark, Luke or John. The branches of Christianity that preached a return to the Scripture ultimately failed to shield the West from its explosive potential. The charges went off, and they were triggered by Modman, the implacable enemy of Westman. If we look at today's two core Modman countries, Russia and the USA, we shall find support for this view. Neither has ever had much of a link with Catholicism. So neither country has ever been truly Western, in the sense in which the word is used in this book.

Dostoyevsky was very much aware of this, hence his hatred of the Catholics, only matched by his hatred of the Jews. He sensed that Russia was irreconcilable with the Catholic West, which is why he believed that destroying the West was the holy mission of Russian Orthodoxy. Dostoyevsky's views never deviated from the belief that the Russians are 'the sole "God-bearing" people on earth who are destined to renew and save the world in the name of a new God and who have been vouchsafed the keys of life and of the new world.' 'Russian thought,' according to him, 'is paving the way for the great spiritual regeneration of the whole world.' This was not a sentiment Dostoyevsky invented; it was one he sensed with his seer's instinct for the intricacies of the Russian soul. Ultimately, he knew that Russia could not just vegetate. It had to march either straight to perdition or else westwards, with the Gospels, 'the living word of Christ', on her banners. Replace the Gospels with *Das Kapital* or some other secular text, and one can detect the same instinct in assorted Russian politicians, from Lenin and Stalin to Zhirinovsky and Putin.

America, with its sectarian Protestant roots, provides more evidence. Protestantism played the same role for the Americans as Orthodoxy did for the Russians. It removed the shield separating the internal barbarian from the Gospels, giving him unlimited access. This pushed the button for an accelerated evolution, and the internal barbarian turned into Modman, complete with his messianic self-righteousness. Modmen saw the light shining from the Gospels, and they are still guided by reflections of this light even though they have lost touch with its source.

Today, as we travel the west, we find Modmen in command everywhere. But the scope of their victory seems to be in inverse proportion to the erstwhile influence of Catholicism. The more Catholic the country was in the past, the safer it now seems to be for Westman holdouts. Thus, Spain, Italy and France today appear more, shall we say, Western than the countries of northern Europe. The latter had their defences stripped away by Protestantism, and Modman has had a field day. In Catholic countries, Westman holdouts are still fighting a rearguard action, even though they are unlikely to win. They have suffered setbacks in those lands, but to some extent they have all proved to be reversible. France of Robespierre, Italy of Mussolini or Spain of the Republic all saw Modman on the march, but somehow Westman holdouts managed to entrench themselves and fight off extinction. That France achieved this with many different types of government, Spain with a Westman-style authoritarian government, and Italy with no discernible government at all suggests that the problem lies outside the reach of politics. Politics is only a feeble reflection of the main conflict of our time, not the conflict itself. If Westman were ever to come back, he would have to send a note of thanks to his church or concert hall. Not to any political institution.

MODMAN'S FIRST VICTORIES

It is impossible to pinpoint the exact time when the internal barbarian evolved into an all-powerful Modman. What is clear is that this evolution could have happened only when Westman society was suffering either a lapse of vigilance or general enfeeblement.

Accelerated erosion of religion that took place over roughly two-and-a-half centuries ending in the tragedy of 1789 weakened Westman's power no end. Since we have already seen that Westman culture, and consequently Westman himself, cannot survive in any other than an aristocratic society, the demise of religion dealt this society a deadly blow. A Westman aristocracy cannot exist in the absence of a monarchy. If the hierarchical pyramid is truncated at the top by the removal of a king, aristocrats cannot survive as such, without a Duc d'Orléans becoming a Philippe Egalité on his way to the scaffold. And monarchs, in order to survive as such when their subjects were demanding a share of power, had to draw legitimacy from divine right, something they had believed in but did not have to invoke with much vigour in the absence of such pressures, say in Charlemagne's time. This is the general thrust of the scaffold speech delivered by Charles I, the king whose understanding of the logic behind monarchy was matched only by Louis XIV's. However, the circumstances under which Charles I delivered his speech suggest that his sensitivity to the new nature of his subjects was of lesser acuity.

Divine right cannot be enforced if the priesthood cannot wield a power approaching that of the king, albeit in a different field. The priests will never wield such power if they receive it as royal largesse: what the king gives he can take away (Henry II made this point clear). And kings, like the rest of us, would rather not have competition if they can help it. In other words, tangible clerical power can derive only from an ecclesiastical authority that is out of royal – or governmental – reach. In the West, that means the Pope.

These last few paragraphs emphasize the protracted chain reaction of Westman's decline: Westman is joined at the heart with his culture and cannot survive without it; his culture cannot survive without an aristocratic order; aristocratic order cannot survive without a strong monarchy; a strong monarchy cannot survive without the doctrine of divine right; divine right cannot survive without a strong priesthood; priesthood cannot be strong enough if it does not derive its power from a source external to the king's realm. Therefore, the Reformation, severing as it did the links with such a source, was detrimental to Westman's health.

The name of this great schism is a misnomer. A reform is an attempt to improve an existing institution, not to destroy it and not even to create a parallel institution that will compete with the original one. When such outcomes do ensue, then perhaps a different name, such as 'revolution', would be more appropriate – regardless of the reformers' original intent. Ostensibly, the sixteenth-century Reformation was driven by a genuine need to, well, reform. But the zeal that went into the process made a benign long-term outcome impossible. The blows that rained on Westman as a result were not limited to breaking the above chain of interlocked links. They struck against the very fabric of Westman society. For example, the nature of geopolitics had to change for, until the Reformation, Europe had been in effect a loose federation. Nation-states in our meaning of the term did not exist, and different princes had more things uniting them than those setting them apart. Wars did happen – boys will be boys. But, even when protracted and bloody, they were more in the nature of local feuds than the all-out wars of extermination so dear to Modman's heart. If the princes got on with each other, there was peace. Otherwise there was an occasional bloodletting, ferocious though it may have been. One way or the other, the rifts were never too deep.

The Reformation changed all that. Suddenly, France and Holland or England and Spain acquired a divisive difference, one that could not easily be settled by nuptial arrangements or by bartering territory. From then on, European countries were no longer just Christian. They were either Catholic or Protestant, and their respective churches had to take political sides. Thus one instant effect of the Reformation was the politicizing of religion, a development that had to be harmful to that institution. This is not to say that the Church did not contribute to its own troubles. Even as the Scripture, selectively read, can dribble oil into the barbarian fire, so the history of the Church in general and the papacy in particular could easily be held against it. But, as we discussed earlier, there are mitigating circumstances. Even as the monarchs could not survive without the popes, the popes could not survive without the monarchs; so they had to reach a compromise. Yet even after a deal had been struck, the popes could hold their own, after a fashion.

An eighteenth-century man studying the history of the Avignon captivity or of the Borgias, particularly if the study had been undertaken specially to find something unsavoury, would have been richly rewarded. Modmen love to hold Westman's creations down to the absolute moral standard, for they know in advance that no human institution will ever pass muster. But in reality Westman institutions were like people, neither exclusively good nor all bad. When we say that a man is good we do not mean that he has no bad traits, only that they are outweighed by the good ones. In this sense the record of the Church over 2000 years qualifies it as a good institution, especially if one compares it with such Modman Leviathans as the political state. Whether this relativist praise is good enough for an institution formed to uphold the absolute standards of good against evil, is, however, debatable.

The strength of the Church may have been a source of solace to Westman, but to the emerging new breed it was a direct challenge. Driven by a collective imperative to take revenge on Westman, the internal barbarians first had to divide and conquer by severing the link between monarchy and priesthood, a need perceived intuitively by those who were plugged into the new *Zeitgeist*. This is why the anticlericalism that was a direct result, or perhaps even the cause, of the Reformation, was so much more effective than straight atheism could have been at that point. Goaded by some clever people, internal barbarians gleefully added an anticlerical twist to the prevailing spirit of the time. Choosing the tactics was the next task. The fiery rhetoric of Luther and Calvin was effective in Germanic countries, where the people were known even at that time for a rather sombre attitude to life. In France that, along with Spain, had added muscle to the Counter-Reformation, wit was a sharper weapon. This is why in the two-odd centuries before the head of Louis XVI rolled into a wicker basket, the personage of a corrupt, lustful, crooked monk, priest or nun was ever-present in southern European literature both before and after the Reformation, from Boccaccio and Rabelais to Diderot and Voltaire. When we read those writers' works we should remember that they are not just brilliant literature. They are Iago whispering into Othello's ear, and this regardless of the author's personal beliefs. Even when those were quite orthodox, as in the case of Boccaccio, the *Zeitgeist* made the writer put his pen to wicked use.

There is nothing like a few centuries of mockery to discredit an enemy. Anticlerical ditties sung in the streets of eighteenth-century Paris by hundreds of guttersnipes were sounding a death knell. The Church, particularly in France, became more and more marginalized, its authority undermined, its ability to fight back eventually diminished by the expulsion of the Jesuits in 1761 and the dissolution of their order in 1773. When that happened, Louis XVI had 20 years left to live. Across the ocean, the American Revolution was three years away.

If anticlericalism was the practice of barbarian onslaught, then deism was the theory. While anticlericalism relegates priests to a purely ceremonial status, deism demotes God himself to part-time employment. Until atheism becomes socially acceptable, deism provides a painless alternative. Dismiss God with a curt admission that all right, he did create the world; grant him no further role in life, and there is no need for ranting off soapboxes. Just get on with the business at hand and wait for atheism to take over. The wait will not be unduly long: agnosticism follows deism as surely as night follows day, and then atheism is just round the corner. Atheism is agnosticism plus politics; agnosticism is deism plus logic. Characteristically, men like Voltaire and Rousseau, rivalling Marx and Darwin as the patron saints of atheism, were not themselves atheists but deists. They did not feel overburdened by paying occasional lip service to God while demolishing his house.

But another house had to be built in its stead – a place the internal barbarian could call his own. That house was the political state. Once it was built, the internal barbarian was handed the freehold forever. His offspring became Modman, and it is by this name that we refer to him here.

MODERN SCIENCE AGAINST WESTERN GOD

When the link between monarchy and religion was severed, theocracy became impossible in the West, while the absence of a theocratic arm made absolute monarchy untenable. That deprived the state of an eschatological aspect, thus creating a vacuum – something nature abhors and people try to fill. Once God was shunted aside as the eschatological dynamic, man himself remained the only candidate for the vacancy so formed. This sudden ascent was not so difficult to effect since the dominant philosophical doctrines had already made God more or less redundant.

First Locke and Hobbes and then, in a different way, Hume pushed the idea of empiricism to the forefront of public discourse. Locke, in particular, became perhaps the most popular philosopher in the eighteenth century (largely because of Montesquieu's enthusiasm for his work, an emotion shared by most of the *philosophes* and Voltaire). The embryonic Modman was attached to Locke: divine inspiration was no longer recognized as an essential cognitive tool, which was welcome news to those devoid of such inspiration. Knowledge, according to Locke, was what emerged once the facts obtained by sensory perception had been processed by reason. The world was knowable only empirically, and man needed to look no further than himself as the ultimate repository of knowledge and perfection.

Linked to this view of humanity was its political extension: liberalism. Empiricism and liberalism are a combination made in secular heaven. Indeed, if people were now independent of God, it followed that they should also be independent of lesser forms of authority, within reason. Equality before God now had to be replaced by social and political levelling. This may have been merely a theoretical deduction by Locke, the longing of a Modman in the making. But hindsight tells us that Westman's world was to find the fruits of liberalism to be poisonous. In that sense, even though both philosophical empiricism and political liberalism were born in the West, they are anti-Westman ideas. Belonging, as they do, to the armoury of Modman's weapons, neither is compatible with Westman's soul. Put together, they destroyed it.

The *philosophes* gobbled Locke up; when his time came, Hume, a thinker who, unlike Locke, distrusted reason if not empirical experience, became the darling of Paris salons and Rousseau's good friend. No wonder: his French admirers were lifting man to the pedestal previously occupied by God, and inchoate utilitarianism was a perfect winch. Man no longer needed a deity for any practical purpose; he was becoming both autonomous and sovereign.

The larcenous shift of the religious superstructure onto the new atheist foundations also relied on science. Exactly the same trend is observable there: until the eighteenth century, most scientists were believers who used science to get closer to God by learning more about his creation. Once science was torn away from theology, scientists turned away from God. As they were certain that reason knew no bounds, now it had been released from its tethers by the *philosophes*, there was no obstacle in the way of applying scientific methods to the task that now seemed possible: proving that God did not exist. Many scientists were prepared to go farther along that route than had been imaginable hitherto. They were not quite satisfied with the reasoning of Hume who, dissatisfied with both the a priori and a posteriori proofs of God's existence, inferred that in the realm of reason the existence of God can be neither proved nor disproved. Moreover, it is neither provable nor disprovable in perpetuity. The illogical conclusion Hume drew from this correct inference must have been that *ergo* God does not exist: he was an atheist after all. But his was not the atheism of his French friends – it lacked the fervour springing not so much from disbelief in God as from belief in the opposite of God. Hume's distrust of reason in general extended to his own reason in particular, which is a sign of an honest thinker. This distrust also immunized him against Lockean statism in politics. And even though it did not lead him to faith, he still did not go so far as to put atheism down on paper and pass it as irrefutable fact. This was lily-livered as far as the politicized scientists were concerned. They wanted to go Hume plus one better.

The goal of proving that man created God and not the other way around was more political than scientific; and once science starts pursuing political ends it loses whatever sense of high purpose it ever had. Just as words become vulgar when they take on tasks for which they are unfit, so does the problem-solving intelligence of a scientist begin to look trivial when applied to areas that are anything but. For someone like Pascal, scientific knowledge added an important cognitive tool to an already formidable collection. For the newly emerging totalitarian scientist it became the only tool, pitifully inadequate when applied to tasks other than solving little riddles with the help of ever more sophisticated instruments.

THE TOTALITARIAN SCIENTIST

It would not hurt to stop here and contemplate a subspecies of Modman: the totalitarian scientist (*Physicus totalitarius*) who first joined the world's fauna at about the same time as the internal barbarian begat Modman. This subspecies is characterized by tunnel vision, delusions of grandeur and unabashed smugness born out of its ability to peek at bare half-truths through nature's keyhole.

The totalitarian scientist wants to extend his domain beyond the natural world and over the spirit, for without such extension his power would be less than total. But this does not work; the spirit fights for its freedom. Its stubbornness can only mean one thing to these people: if science cannot control the spirit by explaining it, the spirit does not exist. Given enough time, the empiricist belief in reason and the senses as the only sources of knowledge will lead to the belief that anything outside the reach of reason is not worth knowing, which in turn will produce a certainty that nothing beyond this realm exists. Admit the existence of an extra-material spirit and suddenly all those evolutions with or without missing links are lowered to the level of trivia contests. The totalitarian scientist is aware of this. Consequently, finding physical proof that God does not exist, and that man is some kind of ape entirely describable by its physicality, is as important to the totalitarian scientist as belief in

God is to a clergyman: without the power of its convictions neither type can survive. That is why Darwin, the patron saint of the breed, was so irrepressible in spreading his theory around.

Darwin's critical contribution to the theory of natural selection was that of a propagandist who, either personally or by proxy, persisted for as long as it took to make his pet idea politically acceptable. Darwin could not claim an exclusive right to the discovery of natural selection: already in Hellenic times Lucretius observed that it was by their superior cunning and strength that all existing species were different from those that had become extinct. Plutarch made a similar observation when he wrote about wolves devouring the slower horses and thus contributing to the survival of the faster ones. In the generations immediately preceding Darwin's, neither evolution nor natural selection was unknown to Lamarck, Cuvier or Darwin's own grandfather Erasmus. And Alfred Russel Wallace, Darwin's contemporary, described natural selection independently from him and in fact passed his ideas on to Darwin in 1858, thus triggering the publication of *The Origin of Species*. Wallace, however, did not develop his ideas further as he was unable to explain, by natural selection alone, the human brain. No such compunctions for Darwin, the prototype of the modern totalitarian scientist – he was out to push the boat of biology towards Locke and Hume, perhaps Marx as well. But compunctions were called for, especially where man was concerned.

A man and his bull terrier both have kidneys and a urinary tract, and so both are capable of passing urine onto the wall of a nearby building. The totalitarian scientist notes this similarity and leaves it at that, ignoring the salient difference: Fido can only irrigate the building; his owner can also design it. Against the background of this undeniable fact, the endless atavisms dug up as proof of man's descent from lower organisms serve exactly the opposite purpose. The trite similarities emphasize the sublime difference, much as darkness makes light seem brighter.

Any honest observation of life reveals an incontrovertible fact: man is unique in that he alone among all living beings possesses a soul, consciousness, mind, will – things of that nature. Adding archaeology to honest observation, one finds no evidence of any incremental development in this faculty, even though there may be some indications of a physical evolution. On the contrary, the earliest signs of man's habitation show him to be already as intelligent as most scientists, and quite a bit more artistic. Until we have conclusive evidence to the contrary, it is intellectually honest not to disbelieve too passionately that the ape became man not over millions of years but the moment God breathed a soul into its body. This event completely overshadows any previous or subsequent evolution of the body. For all we care, it might indeed have evolved the Darwinian way – uninteresting, if true.

An animal man may be, but he is not just an animal. His life is not limited to survival and propagation of his genes, a theory that the likes of Richard Dawkins, the popularizer of neo-Darwinism, are trying to turn into orthodoxy. Looking at man's deeds through the prism of hagiography makes it clear that an exertion of the spirit often compels him to sacrifice his physical being. Massada zealots and John Hus, St Stephen and Thomas Cranmer, St Catherine and Thomas Becket were all driven by their souls to do something no ape could ever do. And when monks and nuns choose salvation of their souls over gene propagation, it is in principle and not in degree that they differ from apes. This argument is as old as the hills, and totalitarian scientists have had plenty of time to refute it. They cannot do so, but it is curious to see how they get around this. '*Proof!*' they scream. '*Show us proof that man has a metaphysical side to him! Prove that man is created in God's image!*' Proof, it goes without saying, can mean only one thing to them: a compilation of empirical evidence that turns a hypothesis into a fact – until new evidence turns the 'fact' into an amusing memory.

The answer to their shrill demand is that Hume and Kant were right. There is, and there can be, no proof. But there are many indications, such as Bach's *The Art of Fugue*, Mozart's 39th Symphony, Rembrandt's portraits or Shakespeare's *Dark Lady* sonnets. Such things are not only superfluous to man's survival but, in a society run by Modmen, can be downright perilous to it. Therefore they came into being as a result of an extra-material inspiration, soaring above the threshold reachable by empirical proof. Anyway, the very insistence on holding faith down to the same standards of proof one expects in a lab betrays a wilful misunderstanding of the spiritual mechanisms involved.

The totalitarian scientist often tries to mask his true animus by pretending to be reasonable, acknowledging magnanimously that science cannot really explain everything. It is in this pseudo-accommodating spirit that he expects us to overlook all those Darwinian missing links, the likes of which would invalidate any theory that is less politically charged. The totalitarian scientist thus expects the same kind of leeway a believer grants his faith. But he is not entitled to it. Yet again he demonstrates a weak understanding of the difference between religion and science. If his endeavour lies in the sphere of reason and empirical proof, then no missing links are acceptable. When, as in this case, he cannot explain everything, he can explain nothing. For left outside of his scope is not just the most but the only important distinction between man and beast, and never mind the petty similarities. An aeroplane may resemble a tricycle in that both are made of metal, have three wheels and can transport people. Anyone offering this explanation to a visiting Martian without mentioning that aeroplanes fly, however, is not partly right or almost right. He is either mendacious or mad.

It is the confluence of reason and intuitive inspiration that is responsible for man's highest achievements. Activated by intuition, reason travels to the limit of its ability. It then stops, steps aside modestly, releases inspiration and watches it soar towards perfection – sulking, for it knows that the ultimate perfection is unattainable; but also rejoicing, for even the most remote of approximations can yield breathtaking beauty. It is outside reason's reach that true understanding lies. Schubert tells us more than Darwin about the origin of man.

As if to validate Chesterton's view that philosophy more or less ended with Aquinas, modern philosophers abet the totalitarian scientist by developing an even more blinkered view of life. Logical positivism, exemplified by A. J. Ayer, modernizes Hume as best it can by insisting that there exist only two valid forms of knowledge: empirical and analytical. If a proposition can be proved, or for that matter disproved, by neither, then it is off limits, not even worthy of serious discussion. When applied to scientific matters, this postulate rings true. When applied to what it was really designed to debunk, namely the existence of God, this postulate rings false as it denies the higher forms of knowledge. At the risk of being branded illogical negativists, we can try this neo-empiricism on the more palpable manifestations of the human spirit, only to find it wanting. Empirical and analytical aspects alone may explain some of Handel, but they will explain none of Bach.

Science is a different matter altogether. It may owe many of its discoveries (such as those by Newton and Mendeleyev) to an intuitive and instant perception of the whole, not a Hegelian transition of quantity to quality. But cognition based on facts is as indispensable to a scientist as 'creativity' is to an ad man. There is nothing pernicious about that, as long as we remember that the former relates to real knowledge the same way as the latter relates to real inspiration. When extended to other areas of life, this type of cognitive process reduces knowledge to a collection of sensory data supported by a bit of rationalization. That narrows, if not quite eradicates, the gap between man and beast. For dogs and other animals are also capable of collecting sensory data and processing them into a semblance of problem solving. Some of their data-gathering mechanisms are superior to ours, some are not. On balance, man's overall superiority in this area is demonstrable, but it is a difference of degree, not quality. The totalitarian scientist makes a mental note of this and smirks in a QED way. And since he always marches as one of a crowd in step with the *Zeitgeist*, he is capable of trampling over the feeble resistance coming from the few extant Westman holdouts. As they are stamped deeper and deeper into the ground, he stops noticing them altogether.

While Darwin himself was rather cautious in his comments on man, at least in *The Origin*, there is little doubt what his views on the subject were. At his time man was still considered the clearest indication of God's existence, and Darwin's work was self-admittedly devoted to proving the opposite – hardly the mindset of a scientist who worships at the altar of objectivity. Those who know the subject say that Darwin was, nonetheless, a great naturalist and they must be right. But *The Origin* and his subsequent work on the descent of man are not, at least not merely, scientific works. They are political propaganda conducted by means of science, which is as different from pure science as commercial jingles are from Schubert's *lieder*.

As a true propagandist, Darwin tended to assign undue significance to the data that supported his theory and ignore those that did not. His disregard of fossil evidence, for example, is characteristic. There was already enough evidence in Darwin's time to make him doubt the validity of natural selection as the only mechanism of evolution. He kept repeating Leibnitz's fallacy of nature knowing no leaps, of everything having developed gradually. His contemporaries (scientists, not theologians) doubted that idea. Our contemporaries reject it outright. We know now that the earth was created, and know roughly when: four-odd billion years ago, with biological life having been in existence for approximately a billion and a half years. Whether God or some mysterious 'big bang' created it is irrelevant.

Darwin's theory has lost its critical premise, namely that gradual evolution was supposed to have had unlimited time at its disposal. Natural selection, as we now know, has a limit: we cannot go further back than a billion and a half years. At first sight this seems to be a respectable length of time, but it becomes risibly inadequate when one imagines the amount of evolutionary change required to turn a single-cell organism into a human being, even one as flawed as Richard Dawkins.

Our knowledge of other planets, unavailable to Darwin, reinforces the pre-Darwinian, Westman belief in the exclusivity of the Earth, even as modern science, in spite of itself, continues to demonstrate the exclusivity of man. Desperately as Darwin's followers try to find life on other planets, they are failing to do so. Much to their chagrin, all those Venuses and Jupiters appear devoid not only of human but of any biological life, while our own planet continues to astound and delight man with its endless variety of flora and fauna, melancholy rivers and rowdy seas teeming with fish, craggy mountains, wild forests and gentle hills alive with birds and beasts.

Confounded by mounting scientific evidence, today's totalitarian scientists, the Dawkinses and Wolperts of this world, try to reconcile modern science and its advances in genetics, molecular biology and palaeontology with orthodox Darwinism. Like their patron saint, they simply must justify their hatred of Westman's God by hook or by crook. To that end they leave their smelly labs and enter the fragrant world of popular scientific journalism. That is a mistake. For, by lowering their arguments to the level of laymen, they can no longer cloud their afflatus with esoteric terminology. Mere mortals are allowed a peek, only to notice that the emperor's clothes are missing. When confronted with the evidence that humans share 99 per cent of their genes with apes or 92 per cent with fruit flies, we get the chance to shrug it off by stating the obvious: clearly the remaining 1 per cent or 8 per cent is much more important.

Westman holdouts must never be misled into accepting Modmen's slogans at face value. We should resist the temptation of being swayed by the sound of Modmen's words into believing that there is a hidden meaning behind them. There is no hidden meaning. There is, however, a hidden emotion: hatred of Westman. Armed with the thesis–antithesis bludgeon of Hegelian dialectics so beloved of Marx, Modmen simply have to destroy every fundamental tenet of Westman. And no tenet is more fundamental than belief in the exclusivity of man and the planet created as the stage on which his drama is played out. That is why Modmen misspend untold billions looking for evidence, however implausible, of man's place side by side with other animals.

'Religious belief is incompatible with science,' pronounces Lewis Wolpert, another influential neo-Darwinist, with his usual avuncular condescension. But in fact it is precisely Westman's religion-derived belief in the exclusivity of man that accounts for the unparalleled flourishing of science in the Western world. The root of Westman's ideas on the subject of man and nature lies in his founding document: the Bible. 'Be fruitful and multiply, and replenish the earth, and subdue it: and have dominion over the fish of the sea, and over the fowl of the air, and over every living thing that moveth upon the earth,' says Genesis (1:28). That one verse removes at a stroke all ethical or intellectual barriers in the way of studying nature. By contrast, the pantheistic monism of Hellenic, or indeed today's Oriental man constitutes just such a barrier. If a botanist feels compassion for a falling petal of cherry blossom, or an anatomist believes that a monkey is part of the same continuum of nature that he is, then the former may find it difficult to slice up a petal or the latter to lead an animal to a vivisectionist's table.

Modern science was made possible by the great theology of the twelfth and thirteenth centuries, even though St Francis's monism was close to latent paganism. It was, after all, not only great cathedrals but also great universities that were founded in the

Middle Ages. The myth of heroic scientists bravely plying their trade in the face of murderous theological opposition is just that, a myth. The Church did offer feeble resistance to certain lines of scientific enquiry, but on balance Westman's religion added more to scientific progress than it ever took away. That is why important scientists of the past, from Copernicus to Maxwell, from Newton to Mendel, were believers who saw their mission in following the guidance of Genesis 1:28. They, and indeed many of today's scientists (as many as half, by Wolpert's own mournful admission), saw how science and religion could complement each other. It is only for totalitarian scientists that they become incompatible. Science thus has followed many other of Westman's possessions into Modman's slavery. Instead of continuing its noble mission of helping man to know and subdue the earth, scientists have been corrupted into joining Modman's crusade against everything Western. Shifted into Modman's domain, their mission was hijacked and their minds perverted.

Science is not the only challenge to the exclusivity of man springing from the oneness of God spelled out in the Scripture. Today we observe a closely linked phenomenon: a lamentable rise of eastern creeds in the west. Far from continuing the respectful discourse between Maimonides and Averroes, this penetration is subversive, acting as yet another battering ram of modernity. By striking against Westman's anthropocentricity derived from the centrality of God in whose image man is made, European and American advocates of Zen, Taoism, Shintoism and so forth are doing a destructive job. These creeds may be spiritual nectar for Oriental men. For us they are poison.

From the 1960s onwards Buddhism, in particular, has had a wide influence in a West corrupted by Modman's agnosticism. Admittedly, that influence has been the strongest at the modest intellectual level personified by the likes of Richard Gere, but then such people rule Modman's world. For all its mysticism, Buddhism is, in a Westman sense, theodicy with a foreign accent:

a non-religious creed based on regarding our world with its every manifestation as corrupt simply because it accommodates disease, old age and death.

Westman regarded all those as both relatively unimportant and, in view of original sin, predictable. By seeking God, Westman sought to atone for sin and to overcome the material anchor of life. The scales fallen off his eyes, he would then see the beauty of God's creation, the inner logic of it that, as Einstein admits, dwarfs the logic of any man. Illuminated by spiritual vision, physical suffering can be accepted as a direct consequence of a moral failing; death only as destruction of the part of life man himself corrupted. The concept of God, whose kingdom is within man and who, as the Creator, is also without, gave Westman a direct link between the personal and the superpersonal, turning him into God's co-author. A Buddhist, on the other hand, is devoid of the superpersonal. Since he relies on his own spiritual resources only, suffering for him is senseless and therefore wrong, as is the world that allows it. The only logical way out is seeking nirvana, a personal mystical transport away from a corrupt world. This desire to withdraw from the world, rather than improve it, explains why the Orient has made a relatively minor contribution to science. By contrast, Westmen believed that, as part of achieving personal immortality, they should leave the world the better for having provided them with temporary accommodation. This belief follows from Genesis 1:28.

Personal immortality is impossible for a Buddhist, and though his idea of reincarnation is superficially similar to Westman's idea of eternity, it is its exact opposite. For, by merely hopping from one body to the next, a Buddhist's soul does not gain a higher form of life. It just acts as one card in a non-stop reshuffle, a process that is predestined and has nothing to do with one's own spiritual quest. Curiously, Buddhism can happily coexist in a Western context with positivism, utilitarianism, Marxism or any other pet modern belief. Westman's religion cannot, and, by derivation, neither can his culture, his civilization or indeed Westman himself. Modmen take to Buddhism and its Eastern offshoots with alacrity because they welcome a slight tinge of mysticism on their own purely materialistic creed. Buddhism thus gives Modmen a metaphysical dimension, however flimsy. Eastern monism makes Modmen more self-reliant for longer, which makes it dangerous to Westman holdouts. In that sense, an Eastern-style vegetarian is a greater threat to us than even a murderer. The latter can kill the body; the former may destroy the soul, and never mind his sunny, flower-child smile. It is shocking that these days even at some of Britain's best schools up to a third of the children are vegetarians, having been corrupted by their teachers into contemplating the morality of eating meat. At these same schools Christianity is allocated equal study time with the four other major religions of the world, an even-handedness that is guaranteed to turn students into insufferable little children. Following this trend, the Prince of Wales has pronounced himself to be 'not the defender of the faith, but the defender of faith.' Jack of all faiths, Supreme Governor of none.

It was Ortega y Gasset who first described the subspecies of Modman here referred to as 'totalitarian scientist'. 'By 1890,' he writes, 'we find a type of scientist without precedent in history.' 'Today's scientist is the very prototype of the mass-man.' '[He] knows his own minimal corner of the universe quite well. But he is radically ignorant of all the rest.' 'We shall have to call him a learned-ignoramus, which is a serious matter, for it means that he will act in all areas in which he is ignorant not like an ignorant man, but with all the airs of one who is learned in his own special line.' Ortega deplores not so much scientists as a society that accepts them in the role of intellectual leaders. But Modman's society has no other shining lights. Without religion, science has to provide, or at least reinforce, the justification for the kind of individual sovereignty declared by the *philosophes*.

THE UNENLIGHTENING ENLIGHTENMENT

'Nous ne voulons pas la contre-révolution, mais le contraire de la révolution.'

(J. de Maistre)

In acclaiming the secular sovereignty of the individual, the *philosophes* acted with sleight of hand, shoplifting Westman's ethos. In the West-man tradition, the self-importance of the individual derived from the all-importance of God. Prostrate humility before the latter was a pre-condition for the proud self-assertion of the former. The *philosophes* snipped off the wires of this connecting ganglion, letting God float away and simply shifting such concepts as freedom, individualism and universal love into the new secular domain. Suddenly the individual was encouraged to feel proud not of the fact that he was created in the image of God but of his own feeble self. This closed the loop of the vicious circle inside people's brains, and their heads swelled.

The internal barbarian growing into Modman liked what he heard. For centuries he had been taught that he had to spend his whole life atoning for original sin. Suddenly he was told all that was nonsense: he was good to begin with and, what was more, further perfectible. While before he had had to toil to become good, now he could devote the same energy to becoming happy, while others would take care of perfecting him. No effort was required on his part. Happiness thus ousted virtue as the aim of life. But earthly happiness can last only as long as life itself, whereas virtue used to be seen as a bridge to eternal salvation. However, uncertainty had already been cast into the heart of the internal barbarian invited to doubt everything by Descartes. Once there, doubt gnawed at the old certitudes until they were devoured.

So far so good; internal barbarians were ready to become deliriously happy by right. But, more specifically, what exactly was happiness? Rousseau and some *philosophes* were not stuck for an answer. They reminded the internal barbarians how in the unlamented past they had been taught they were all equal before

God. Now it had all changed: we are born equal not only in that narrow sense but in every respect. Alas, we do not grow up equal. At birth we all resemble the primitive man, *noble sauvage*, before he was corrupted by Western civilization. That chap, even though he was, well, a trifle savage, felt unabashedly happy every time he tossed his hirsute female onto the grass. Moreover, he was good, not having yet been exposed to the corrupting influence of the West. And he was equal to other noble savages in wealth and social status. Alas, that good individual was destroyed by those who had a vested interest in his subjugation: kings, priests, aristocrats. Presented that way, the conclusion had to be clear. Let us get rid of these exploiters and return man to his original happy-equal state socially and politically, while still allowing him to keep the trappings of more modern wealth.

Equality was thus portrayed as both a desirable and achievable objective, and Fichte was to write later that promoting universal equality was the only real function of the state. However, Rousseau and the *philosophes* did not push the idea of equality to its logical extreme; that had to wait until the nineteenth century, when it was fulfilled in theory, and until the twentieth, when it was attempted in practice. They still acknowledged that, because people differed from one another in certain characteristics, some could become slightly happier than others. But as long as these were the only inequalities left standing, all people would be more or less happy, and certainly happier than they would be otherwise, in the presence of even vestigial social privilege.

However, the *philosophes* themselves were Westmen culturally if not spiritually. All of them had received serious education. They must have realized that the culture they had acquired with so much effort would be in jeopardy should their theories be put into practice. In common with most cultured people at any time in history, they must have spent the odd joyous hour poking fun at the uncouth. What set them apart from most cultured people was their deep-rooted contempt for man in general and the common man in particular, which is not quite the same as a good-natured sense of cultural superiority. Because of this contempt they were so ready to peddle self-acknowledged fibs.

Liberty and equality meant about as much to those people as 'brand positioning' to a marketing man. The latter will communicate to the market those aspects of his brand that he knows from experience are likely to trigger the desired response, while talking about helping the consumer to make an informed choice. But what he is really after is sales, not providing a service to consumers. Likewise, the shibboleths (many of them shared with the Freemasons, which has given rise to many a conspiracy theory) spouted by the *philosophes* and the revolutionaries had little to do with their true intuitive objective: revenge. Each of these men had his own chip on his shoulder, but revenge is an accurate description of their common driving force. Naturally, in their psyche both God and believers figured prominently as objects of envy and targets for revenge.

How a man acquires so much bile as to let it dominate all other humours is not for us to say. One thing is clear: he has to be evil to allow that to happen to him, someone driven by a destructive force. The same force enables him to spot and exploit similar qualities in the mob, turning it into an obedient tool of his revenge. This is a common characteristic of the kind of people Dostoyevsky called demons, a characteristic that is both necessary and sufficient. If we pick at random any decent biography of people like Robespierre and Danton, Marx and Lenin, Stalin and Hitler, we shall see the same pattern. Men whose social and professional standing in early life had fallen short of their ambition, and whose background had not provided an automatic means of elevation, they were all driven by a desire to take revenge on the whole world, what with the sheer impossibility of pinpointing the specific culprits. Many of them, such as Robespierre, Hitler and Stalin, were at first dismissed as mediocrities by their political rivals. The dismal fate of those rivals yet again demonstrates human folly: gradations of intellect are specks of dust when compared with mountains of evil force. Even Marx managed to kill his opponents by driving them to suicide with character assassinations – what he would have done had he grabbed political power defies imagination.

The *philosophes* and revolutionaries could not have been wholly sincere in their rhetoric on the subject of equality. They had to believe they themselves would be exempt from whatever levelling the rest of society would have to suffer at their behest. Since they advocated elimination of traditional privilege, they had to have an alternative in mind, a way of controlling the mob about to be unleashed. That alternative could only have been the modern political state, run by present-day philosopher kings. In their minds' eye they must have seen themselves cast in that Platonic role. There is poetic justice in that few of the thinkers who made the revolution possible lived to see it: Helvetius died in 1771, d'Alembert in 1783, Rousseau in 1776, Voltaire in 1778, Diderot in 1784 and so forth. The justice would have been even more poetic had they lived to see the revolution but failed to survive its feral cruelty, the fate that befell Condorcet. Anyone with any sense of aesthetic balance would have loved to see the mob hack the likes of Rousseau to pieces at the same church in St Germain where this macabre deed was perpetrated on 316 priests in one day of 1792. Alas, that kind of justice had to wait another century-and-a-half, when few of the leading Bolsheviks got to die in their own beds.

Clever as they were, the *philosophes* did not possess prophetic powers. They were staking claims to an uncharted territory, and there was no hindsight available to them, as it is to us, that would have warned them to watch their step. The only revolutions of which they had any knowledge were the one in England, which had not devoured its young once it triumphed, and the one in America, which too had been benign. Since an orgy of internecine violence did not follow those victorious revolutions, it was a natural mistake to ascribe such herbivorism to all revolutions, rather than to the cultural and constitutional peculiarities of the English people on either side of the Atlantic. In every practical sense the *philosophes* were taking a stab in the dark. Once Westman's house became divided against itself, it could not stand; they had no doubt about that. But there was residual resistance to overcome: Westmen had not seen the writing on the wall as clearly as the *philosophes*. And, horror of horrors! they were not ready to go. They wanted to hold on for a while.

MODMAN DIVIDES INTO TWO

Westmen's residual resistance had two basic patterns to it, followed with minor deviations everywhere. For convenience's sake we shall be referring to them as the English and the French. The latter represented a principled, intransigent stand based on a sense of rectitude. French kings and aristocrats espoused the traditional view of their role in society, and would never see that role as an unbilled walk-on. That is why, for example, they opposed Turgot's free-market ideas that were similar to Adam Smith's. They believed, correctly, that, by providing an outlet for human energy, a free or even predominantly mercantile economy would not fail to produce a new class that could compete against their own. Turgot, who read the signs with the clarity of a prophet, warned that revolution was the only alternative to his reforms, and he was right. But French Westmen were unable to act out of character. They did not want compromise; their disdain for the internal barbarian was too deeply ingrained. This meant that the emerging Modmen turned against them armed not only with reason but also with passion. Modmen no longer just wanted them out. They wanted them dead.

The English pattern was more interesting, and it was extolled by those *philosophes* who did not have the stomach for massacre. In England Westmen had learned to resist in a cleverer way, and so they could have been ousted only by attrition, not by frontal assault. The English constitution, evolving over a millennium, was

116

balanced between the interests of every estate. It thus gave English Westmen a perfect tool for fashioning a compromise at a time when one of the estates, the common man, was no longer prepared to accept the traditional balance. Compromise, however, can be a perilous harbour towards which to sail. As Burke's exegesis of it showed so well, the English constitution embraced every liberal tenet, in the classical, Lockean sense of the word. What Burke did not mention was the kiss of death implicit in that embrace.

The liberals were wrong, and they have been proved to be wrong. For no true compromise is possible between Westman and the internal barbarian. Placating the latter into a semblance of self-confidence only creates the habitat for his unimpeded evolution into a victorious Modman. Social compromise is a useful stratagem for preventing social upheaval. It is an attempt to bribe the internal barbarian into abandoning his sanguinary instincts and agreeing to win in a non-violent way. But it cannot prevent his victory. Thus, though England has more or less managed to avoid the physical murder of Westmen within her borders, she could not prevent their gradual fading into the social background or, worse still and more widespread, converging with Modmen.

The rearguard action was fought well nonetheless, and its echoes can be picked up simply by walking the streets of central London lined with the townhouses of the Georgian nobility. Their plain, unadorned façades are in contrast to the opulence of similar dwellings in France. The statement made here is not so much aesthetic as social: the English subspecies of Westman suspected that envy was the animus of the internal barbarian, and it could be diffused only by hiding everything enviable away from his prying eyes. The French, on the other hand, haughtily flaunted what they had, which is why their Westmen ended up shorter by the head. English Westmen wanted the internal barbarians to believe that there was little difference between them, that they were all brothers. The danger in such a ruse is that what begins as pretence can end up as reality. And sure enough, as a result of this self-fulfilling claim English Westmen ended up barely distinguishable from their Modman conquerors.

The martyr king Charles I was perhaps the last English West-man who tried to use, indeed presage, the French pattern of resistance. Unfailingly, it produced the French type of response from the neonatal Modmen. However, they overreacted, attacking the compromise constitution from the other end as vehemently as Charles had assailed it from his. The Restoration got the com-promise back on track, making it possible for the internal barbarian to revert to attrition as the pattern of his evolution into a victorious and vengeful Modman. In this he became so successful that a statue of Oliver Cromwell now stands proudly outside the Houses of Parliament – the regicide saboteur of the constitution rubbing shoulders with the putative champion of it.

Because Modmen had to react to the two types of resistance in different ways, over time the breed split into two subspecies. We can refer to them as the nihilist and the philistine. The nihilist evolved in response to staunch French-style resistance. His chief *modus operandi* is violence on a scale never before perpetrated by any other human type. This violence is usually directed against groups of people, rather than individuals. The nihilist needs to wipe out any group, no matter how large, that will predictably contain a proportion, no matter how small, of Westmen. If the group numbers millions and contains just hundreds of Westmen, that does not matter. Numbers do not affect the principle, even as to a Westman a theft of £100 is morally as reprehensible as a theft of £1,000,000. For example, the Cluny Abbey in France was destroyed when it had just seven monks living there. To the new breed, that was seven too many.

The nihilist type could be found among the English and the French at the time of their revolutions, and subsequently any-where else where Westmen's resistance followed the French pattern, Russia in particular. The Modman philistine appeared in

118

response to the English type of resistance by subterfuge, the resistance that pretends not to be what it is. His main weapon is attrition, a slow imposition of philistine values on society, accompanied by gradual acquisition of political and economic power that he can then use to force Westmen into compliance. The United States is the birthplace of this subspecies, but not its sole habitation. The success of the philistine in America provided a springboard for his leap over the ocean, so now he is the dominant type in any country described as 'Western', a popular misnomer based solely on geography and not on any cultural content.

An important thing to observe is that neither the nihilist nor the philistine ever exists in an undiluted form. Just as Westmen carried both good and evil within them, with only their ratio varying from man to man, so do the philistine and nihilist coexist in the breast of a Modman. Given his natural inclination and outer circumstances, one of them can at times assume a greater importance, but not to the point of ousting the other. Thus even the most bloody-minded nihilist can still dream of material comfort, whereas the most complacent philistine will still harbour violent feelings towards Westmen. That is why Modman cannot coexist with Westman any more than a sentiment from a rap song can fit seamlessly into a Shakepeare sonnet. 'Shall I compare thee to a summer's day and then carve thee up, thou bitch,' does not quite ring possible.

As if conspiring to vindicate a law of Hegel's dialectics, the nihilist and the philistine are two opposites that appear to be in conflict but are in fact parts of the same whole. The differences between them are only those of degree. Fundamentally they are about as close as, say, a poodle and an Alsatian: different enough in appearance and behaviour, but still capable of producing common offspring. They are closer to each other than either is to Westman. And as their evolution advances, the differences between them fade away. For example, Americans and Russians like to remark how similar they are, even though both know there are many traits they do not share. But in principle they are right, for similarity between them runs deeper than the rather superficial distinction between, say, democracy and communism.

As a quick experiment, imagine a leather-jerkined Soviet commissar of the 1920s having a drink with a modern American. Now say to them that not all people should pass judgement on how they are to be governed simply because most do not know enough about the business of government. If you are so inclined, quote Burke on the desirability of people's interests being represented, but not necessarily their wishes. Even though the commissar would only pay lip service to the idea of the 'people' governing themselves, while for the American it would be an article of faith, both would react in a violent manner. The commissar would reach for his Mauser, and the American would suggest that you are full of faecal matter. For both subspecies of Modman feel equal hostility to anything that resembles Westman thought. The only difference is in the mode of expressing this hostility, and the philistine way has proved to be more successful than the nihilist one. The reasons for this are roughly similar to why a seducer tends to run up a higher amatory score than a rapist, no matter how diligently the latter applies himself to his gruesome pursuit.

The kinship between the two subspecies of Modman became more obvious in the twentieth century when the philistine seems to have wasted numerous opportunities to nip the nihilist in the bud. For example, when Hitler attacked Poland in September 1939, and after Britain and France had declared war on Germany, the allies could have easily finished the war there and then. On the Western front, the French army alone had a 3.2 : 1 superiority over the Wehrmacht in manpower, with 2850 tanks to Germany's none. Add to this the British Expeditionary Corps and it becomes clear why even the German generals knew at the time that any serious offensive against their western flank would quickly carry the day for the allies. Yet no such offensive came, as none, in any meaningful sense, followed the Bolshevik revolution in Russia. Contrary to a popular misapprehension, such negligence was not a result of the philistines' weakness, cowardice or stupidity. In fact, the liberal democracies of the West showed a great deal of courage when finally made to fight. The real reason was the philistines' deep-rooted sympathy for their nihilist relations, which is akin to a righteous brother still loving his wayward sibling. Once again, the differences of principle – as opposed to the verbiage they favour or the methods they choose – between, say, a communist and a liberal are small. Their negative animus is identical: desire to do away with Westman. Their positive aspirations are also the same: universal equality and prosperity. Where they differ is in the balance between the negative and the positive, but that difference can only manifest itself in tactics, not in intuitive rejection of everything the opposite number stands for. In the absence of such visceral rejection, one should not be surprised that the English did not heed Sidney Reilly's plea to rise in a 'holy crusade' against the 'midnight terror' of bolshevism or that the French did not squash Hitler after his occupation of the Rhineland and subsequent attack on Poland. In both conflicts a little effort would have stamped out the nihilist energumen once and for all, long before it gathered enough momentum to cause untold misery. But in such matters even a minimum of effort requires a maximum of commitment, which the philistine could not muster when confronted by his nihilist brother.

THE FIRST POLITICAL STATE

'We go to Europe to be Americanized.'
(R. W. Emerson)

The Westmen of the two would-be reference Modman countries, Russia and America, followed the French and English paths of resistance respectively. That is why Modmen in Russia had to

121

exterminate Westmen physically, while Modmen in America were prepared to be benevolent and allow vestigial Westmen to converge with them peacefully.

This the American Westmen eventually did, but not without the hiccup of a civil war in which America suffered heavier casualties than in all her previous and subsequent wars combined. Such inordinate bloodshed was to be expected: that was the only war in which the American Modman philistine fought a Westman opposition. For it was to the South that Westman holdouts had drifted. Perhaps they were attracted by an economy that revolved around agriculture. It is also likely that the French and Spanish, which is to say Catholic, influences in that area added a tinge of Westman civility for which settlers with Westman leanings tropistically reached, realizing that Modman would reign supreme in the mercantile North. In any case, a Westman oasis flourished in the South. The odds, however, remained stacked against it, and the breath of fresh air had to be drowned by the smoky stench of modernity.

Both sides displayed an all-out commitment to the Civil War, sensing that no conflict between Westman and Modman could ever end without a decisive victory for one side. Hence the unrestrained savagery displayed by the victorious Yankees in the closing months of the war; and hence the gallant effort of the Confederates who stood to the last man. The North realized that nothing short of a 'scorched earth' policy would do. The South knew that the North did not just desire the end of slavery – it craved the destruction of Westman's American habitat, the South. In the process, certain iconic personages behaved in a way that belied their subsequent reputation. Abraham Lincoln, for example, closed down 300 pro-Southern newspapers (and had their presses smashed), suppressed the writ of habeas corpus and, according to the Commissary General of Prisoners, had 13,535 Northern citizens arrested for political crimes from February 1862 to April 1865. Comparing his record with that of the hideous Mussolini, who only managed 1624 political convictions in 20 years and yet is universally and justly reviled, one begins to see modern hagiography in a different light.

Apart from the temporary aberration of the war, the convergence between the two subspecies proceeded apace until Westmen in America became extinct as a breed. On the other hand, the Russian Westmen put up a protracted struggle and therefore had to die in millions. One way or the other, the two countries became thoroughly modern and, in a perverse sort of way, similar. That is not so surprising since, even as Westmen thrived on diversity, Modmen subsist on uniformity. The two strands eventually got close enough together to be woven into the single cultural rope strangulating Westman.

Of the two, the United States is more straightforward. Its founding fathers, apart from such rare exceptions as Fisher Ames, came, *mutatis mutandis*, from the same line of cultural descent that led from Locke and Hobbes to Condorcet via Hume. Local colour came from the nature of American society formed as it was by immigrants from diverse cultural backgrounds who had all drifted to America for their own reasons. Most of the reasons, however, fell into two broad categories: religious and economic. Many of the early Americans were sectarian Protestant dissenters of a fundamentalist type, such as the English Puritans, Dutch Calvinists or German Mennonites, who had run foul of authorities in their native countries. Many went to the New World simply to escape poverty; they were attracted by the promise of a vast continent awaiting colonizers. The rhetoric of the American Revolution could not ignore either group, which is why the Locke and Helvetius ingredients of it had to be spiced up by dollops of deism and a generous handful of Turgot and Smith. Free enterprise was particularly important to the Americans, as aggressive economic activity was a common element all the disparate groups shared. But these rhetorical spices could not mask the decidedly Modman taste of the dish.

We do not need to be aware of the personal ties that linked the likes of Jefferson and Franklin with the *philosophes*; just reading the Declaration of Independence tells us all we need to know. This document is the first of its kind, the original statement of intent coming from a near triumphant Modman. Almost every word in it can yield a rich crop if analysed within the framework of this essay, especially in the first two paragraphs where the moral justification for independence is established.

The colonists insist on their right to 'assume among the Powers of the earth, the separate and equal station to which the Laws of Nature and of Nature's God entitle them.' They go on to say that they 'hold these truths to be self-evident, that all men are created equal, that they are endowed by their Creator with certain unalienable (*sic*) rights, that among these are Life, Liberty and the pursuit of Happiness.' People are entitled to organize their government on such principles that 'to them seem most likely to effect their Safety and Happiness.' This is all Modman's talk. No Westman could have written that, or indeed signed his name to any of it. He would have objected that:

a) Regardless of what Locke and Paine had to say on the subject, 'separate and equal station' for either individuals or countries cannot be derived from 'Laws of Nature'. There is no law of nature that says a colony is entitled to independence from the mainland. There exists, however, a tendency among Modman revolutionaries to pass their aspirations as rights. A 'separate and equal station', desirable though it may be to some, can only be achieved either by agreement or by force. No group has equality built into its reclaimable biological makeup. Portraying independence as a right that somehow supersedes the law was Modman demagoguery at its most soaring.

b) Pantheistic 'Nature's God' is clearly there to mollify believers of a more primitive type, those who react to the word 'God' by reflex and for whose benefit wise people (who were, of course, above such nonsense) had to put the word in. 'God' or at a pinch 'God's nature' would have been proper Westman terms, based on the assumption that God created nature and not vice versa. The author of the Declaration illustrates the pitfalls of a cavalier treatment of God. For Thomas Jefferson had a selective approach to Christian morality: some of it was acceptable to him, some was not. He clipped the acceptable passages out of the Bible and pasted them into a notebook, thus creating his own Scripture. One can argue that possibly all Protestants and certainly all deists go through the same exercise in their minds, if not literally. Atheism is the inevitable result, even if it is masked, as in America, by fulsome protestations of piety.

c) God is the only truth that can be regarded as 'self-evident' in that, by definition, it is either taken on faith or not at all. Any other truth, before it can be accepted as such, needs to be proved. A Westman is congenitally on guard against such phrases as 'self-evident', 'it is obvious that', 'it goes without saying that', 'needless to say'. He knows that they are either a sign of intellectual laziness or, worse, an attempt to dupe the gullible with falsehoods.

d) That 'all men are created equal' is, self-evidently, rather the opposite of truth. Again this is an attempt to pass wishful thinking for a fact. All men are created unequal physically, intellectually, morally, socially. Westman is a direct product of this inequality, and his very survival depends on it. What the phrase actually means is this: 'Would it not be nice if all men were created equal? We then would not have to go to the trouble of having to get rid of Westman.' Apart from displaying intimate familiarity with the works of Thomas Paine, the use of this phrase echoes the theories of the *noble sauvage* beautiful in his state of primitive grace, a *tabula rasa* on which Modman can scribble his message to the world.

e) It is questionable whether the term 'rights' has any value in serious discourse on political matters. Today we are served up any number of rights: to marriage, education, health, development of personality, leisure time, orgasms, warm and loving family or – barring that – warm and loving social services, employment, paternity leave and so forth. These 'rights' are manifestly bogus as they fail the test of not presupposing a concomitant obligation on somebody else's part. When a 'right' presupposes such an obligation, it is not a right but a matter of consensus. Thus, one's right to employment would mean something tangible only if there were someone out there who consents or is obligated by law to give one a job. One's right to a developed personality (guaranteed by the 1948 UN Declaration of Human Rights, which was signed by such authorities on human rights as Stalin's Russia) presupposes an obligation on somebody else's part to assist such development. One's right to a fulfilling sex life ... this can get too silly for words. Far from being natural, all these rights become tangible only if they are granted by others; and anything given can be taken away, so there go all those pseudo-rights alienated right out of the window.

f) The right to outward political 'liberty', as opposed to inward spiritual freedom, is also a pseudo-right, as it has to be derived from consensus. 'Liberty', along with all its cognates, is a word fraught with semantic danger: one man's liberty is another man's licence and yet another's anarchy. In any case, there again has to be a strong element of consensus there; the concept of liberty is too open to debate for it to be tautly definable. For example, is the absence of anti-homosexuality laws a factor of liberty or licence? If the answer is the former, then we ought to ponder the fact that the first modern country without such laws was Soviet Russia between 1917 and 1934, a place and period not otherwise known for a *laissez-faire* attitude to life.

g) The right to life mentioned in the Declaration is legitimate as its enforcement does not presuppose an obligation on anyone else's part. The question it raises, however, is not, 'Is it legitimate?', but, 'Is it terminologically useful?' For instance, the English Common Law, in force in the colonies at the time, provided adequate provisions for the protection of life, which would seem to have rendered any invocation of this right redundant. If the law was being abused or not enforced properly, then the practice of it needed to be addressed. This could hardly have been helped by dragging in a new theoretical concept that was always more likely to confuse than elucidate the issue. Moreover, as with all redundant terms, this one is not without some potential for casuistic abuse either. Is the death penalty a violation of the natural right to life? Is abortion? How is it that the proponents of the latter are almost always opponents of the former and vice versa, with this redundant right invoked in each case?

h) 'Happiness' was at the time a vogue term denoting a secular substitute for metaphysical virtue as the purpose of life. What-ever meaning one chooses to assign to it, and there are many possibilities, the word describes the exact opposite of Westman's essence. This is about the pursuit of truth, inner freedom and salvation, a pursuit more likely to result in suffering than happiness. But, even apart from such lofty objections, the word is nebulous at best, meaningless at worst. Recognizing this, some of the framers of the Declaration, most notably Alexander Hamilton, took the time to explain later, in the *Federalist* papers and elsewhere, that what they really meant was quite simply money – an admission of laudable honesty if dubious subtlety. The pursuit of money, assuming it does not involve arbitrary separation of other people from theirs, does pass the obligation test, but it runs head-on into the same objections raised earlier. This right is not spurious; it is redundant. Laws against theft, burglary, robbery, fraud and the rest derive from the Decalogue and do not need a modern term to bail them out. On the contrary, it was precisely the separation of such laws from their true source and their shift into the modern, secular area of 'rights' that made their enforcement so difficult in the west.

The right to property, one of the few real rights, is a case in point. Born out of the ethos of 'rights', the modern political state, while continuing to assert 'pursuit of happiness' as canonical law, has elevated judicial confiscation of people's property to a level unthinkable, say, in the Hellenic world. For example, Caracalla who, according to Gibbon, 'crushed every part of the empire under the weight of his iron sceptre' by increasing the inheritance tax from 5 to 10 per cent (thankfully, 'the ancient proportion was restored after his death') was a babe in the woods compared with a modern democratic parliament that will hit one for 40 per cent faster than one can say 'classless society'.

Of course, for the nascent American state, the pursuit of fiscal happiness was more important than for Europe, where at the time Westman indeed regarded ancient title to land as self-evident and therefore not needing reiteration. Pursuit of money was, after all, an important part of what brought most Americans together. It was thus more crucial than almost any other founding tenet of the new state. However, what made those states united was not just acquisitiveness but also an earnest commitment to the eradication of Old World survivals, grudges against which were part of the baggage many settlers had brought from Europe (this hostile intent was passed as the creation of a new type of man, the American). Here money was useful too, for it could function as the stick, not just the carrot. When all is said and done, the human qualities required for making money often are diametrically opposite to those that form Westman. The moment money became the universal yardstick with which human worth was measured, the death knell sounded for Westman. (In American English, 'how much are you worth?' has replaced 'how much money do you have?') From then onwards he could only stay afloat and lead a dignified existence by either turning into Modman or else living a double life.

Even these days, when the battle against Westman is long since won, Americans emphasize protection of property more than do even conservatives in Europe who still, for old times' sake, tend to regard it as only one of many conditions for a civilized society. However, Americans usually manage to seduce Europeans into accepting the transatlantic pecking order of virtues. Such acquiescence is a mistake. We already know that putting the accent in the wrong place is another pet trick of the victorious philistine subspecies of Modman.

The USA is unique in that it was conceived as a Modman state and created as such in a wasteland shorn of Westman's influence. With little indigenous Westman heritage to dispose of, pursuit of happiness proceeded apace, creating the 'happiest' society the West has ever known, and consequently the least Western. But the downside of pursuing happiness and not, say, virtue, justice, honour, dignity or the truth, goes beyond the yawning ennui America tends to induce in Westman throwbacks. For, in spite of all the lip service Americans pay to God in their Pledge of Allegiance, the USA is a Modman, which is to say relativist, state. Without the underlying supremacy of absolute moral strictures, society loses its moral fibre, which has many unpleasant ramifications. Law enforcement, for example, is difficult in the absence of an absolute criterion with which to distinguish between *malum prohibitum* and *malum in se*. Without this distinction law becomes amoral and runs the risk of becoming arbitrary. More important, when God's law is no longer recognized as an authority that is superior to man's regulations, the law loses its link with human nature, becoming instead an instrument of coercion. As a result, people treat it with fear but without respect, and fear alone is not a sufficient deterrent. That is why a high crime rate is an automatic levy modernity imposes, and the more modern the society, the higher the crime rate.

Business activity, central to the pursuit of happiness, also has to become amoral in a modern state. Not doing anything wrong disappears as an in-built starting point and is replaced by not getting caught. By itself that would be almost bearable if so many clever people did not spend their time, and waste ours, by thinking up cloying encomiums of what they call 'free enterprise'. However, freedom is a child of responsibility. When 'responsible' walks out, 'free' becomes an orphan. If certain of impunity, a Modman businessman would market potassium cyanide instead of potassium chloride, this to the chorus of 'conservative' economists singing hosannas to both the merchant and his victims for striking important blows for freedom of choice. One should never forget, even when extolling modern achievements, that the same company that gave us aspirin also gave us Zyklon B. In America and other Modman societies the inherent amorality of business, when conducted in a secular society, is dressed up by elevating business activity to a moral high ground it never used to occupy in Western countries. Someone like Milton Friedman or George Gilder will drive us to distraction, explaining that the cycle of free enterprise has more to do with charity than with acquisitiveness. In that sense they resemble their supposed antipode Marx who also had a knack for creating in his head a picture of economic life that had little to do with reality.

One wishes Messrs Friedman, Gilder and their friends studied the American economy as it is, rather than the idealized picture of it they see in their mind's eye. They would then realize that the New Deal corporatism that dominates the pursuit of happiness in America today has as little to do with free enterprise as the Korean People's Democratic Republic has to do with Korea, people, democracy or republicanism. And, rather than glorifying indiscriminately the founding institutions of America, they would perhaps see that this freedom-stifling corporatism is directly traceable back to the pursuit of happiness laid down in the Declaration of Independence.

When this narrative reaches the twentieth century, we shall spend more time on this. For the moment, suffice it to say that no true freedom, be that of enterprise or anything else, is possible without the ultimate discipline imposed by a suprahuman authority. When such absolute authority is replaced by politicized relativism, liberty becomes licence, equality becomes levelling, and fraternity turns into a faceless mass of humanity bossed around by bureaucrats. To this there are no known exceptions.

THE ROLLING JUGGERNAUT OF THE MODERN STATE

The USA became the first successful Modman state in history and, as such, veered from the traditional substance of Westman society. More copycat states followed, sharing similar desiderata of creating a new type of man.

The objective of society is to prepare the young for adulthood; the objective of the modern state is to keep them perpetually adolescent. Adults, with notable exceptions, are capable of being constructive. Children, with few exceptions, are destructive. Not to worry, says the state. Destructive adolescents are better at goose-stepping, and it takes a youthful testosterone count to bayonet a designated opponent of the state with gleeful finality. And when they return home, hollow-cheeked and empty-eyed, they will be so much easier to control, better prepared to accept the state's dictate on every aspect of their lives, from diets to sexual techniques. Thus the hectoring provider state replaces the loving provider family as the core of Modman's world; the only thing left for the family to do is to fade away. And it does.

The family is a building block of society but a direct competitor of the state, which always makes it the first target when the sniping starts. Today's political state in the West, while still not strong enough to abolish marriage and family, is strong enough to erode them by squeezing its huge bulk into the slot formerly occupied by the father. Thus, made redundant in his social role of provider, the father disappears, especially since divorce is easy to get. For the modern state to become big, today's family had to shrink to its average size of 2.7 alienated Modmen, eating overbaked modern meats full of antibiotics, and spouting half-baked modern 'ideas' full of egalitarian cant. The neonatal political state thus follows Rousseau's prescriptions to the letter: it overrides all conflicting loyalties as part of a concentrated assault upon Westman. And, like any baby, it has to be born covered in blood. That is why, just as Napoleon appeared on the crest of a revolutionary wave, so have even moderate political states been unable to avoid formative bloodshed. America is a case in point. It was immediately after the War of Independence that the Americans went about creating the first successful political state in history, the prototype of many a political state to come. This type of state, Modman's political expression, is different from the authoritarian state of the past.

The only objective of the traditional state was to go about its business, whatever it was. The people did not have many political liberties, but that curiously made them relatively free from political pressures. They were expected to toe the line and not to prevent the state from doing things necessary for its survival. At times of emergency they had to take an active part in state affairs and, if called upon, die in the act. But one thing they were not expected to do was to adjust their personalities to the needs of the state. In peacetime the central state was for them something that occupied the folk in the capital. It had little to do with their own lives. Once they had sorted the local squire out, greasing his palm with taxes, they were, well, free is as good a word as any. A characteristic of all authoritarian states is respect for traditional, familial institutions that always acted as a gasket separating the authoritarian ruler from his subjects. The ruler saw those institutions, rightly, as a foundation of his power. The people saw them, just as rightly, as the guarantors of their liberty. That is why monasteries, guilds, local self-government and, above all, families could all flourish under authoritarian rulers.

Not so with the modern political state, adumbrated by the

philosophes and first perfected by the Americans. Unlike the traditional authoritarian state, it did not evolve over centuries; it was created, in historical terms, overnight to illustrate political theories, each at least partly animated by Modmen's desire for revenge. The political state was an Enlightenment construct made real by violence, bribery and propaganda, and the intent went far beyond mere subjugation of the people. The underlying goal of any political state, be that a liberal democratic regime or its totalitarian variants, is not just to run people's lives but to change their nature. That is why the rulers of Modman states could tolerate no gasket separating them from the objects of their didacticism. Traditional institutions had to go because they diminished the power of the state to affect people's lives. Lest any doubts should remain of the true purpose of the embryonic political state, we must listen to the booming voice of one of its midwives, Jean-Jacques Rousseau:

> The state should be capable of transforming every individual into part of the greater whole from which he, in a manner, gets his life and being; of altering man's constitution for the purpose of strengthening it. [It should be able] to take from the man his own resources and give him instead new ones alien to him and incapable of being made use of without the help of others. The more completely these inherited resources are annihilated, the greater and more lasting are those which he acquires.

Modman taxonomists tend to display their characteristic obsession with form at the expense of substance by classifying Rousseau as a counter-Enlightenment figure. However, in everything of lasting, destructive effect, his thinking is indistinguishable from that of the *philosophes*. It is only in his Utopian aspirations for a bucolic state of nature that Rousseau diverges from the likes of Diderot, a detail not worth mentioning side by side with their towering similarity of underlying principle. Rousseau's *Du Contrat Social* succeeded in formulating the aspirations of the political state that extended from the physical to what used to be regarded as metaphysical.

The traditional authoritarian state had left the task of assisting in individual salvation to the Church. The political state usurped this function, but without inheriting the humility built into faith. Paternalism that loses the attendant humility stops being fatherly and becomes despotic. Some form of tyranny is thus not an unfortunate by-product of some political states, but an unavoidable offspring of the political state as such. The two most dutiful children of this parent, Russia and America, have fulfilled Rousseau's aspirations with equal success if by different methods. They truly deserve to be held up as Modman's model states, championing his nihilist and philistine subtypes respectively.

Whatever means a political state employs to reach its ends, and whatever slogans it puts forth, certain things remain immutable: to achieve the purpose stated by Rousseau, a modern political state has to be centralized and powerful. Neither can be effected without some form of coercion, and no political state has ever managed to avoid it at some stage, whatever pronouncements on universal love its founders made at the beginning. The French political state is a classic example of this. It started out with the *philosophes* pronouncing man both perfect and tautologically perfectible. It followed that good and further improvable people were qualified to govern themselves by the expedient of electing the worthiest among them to attend to the actual business of governing. It also followed that any other form of government was anathema, as it would block the paths that led from private goodness to public virtue. When these ideas were first put into practice, Frenchmen were handed liberty on a platter. But upon closer examination this piece of proverbial chinaware was instead found to contain a pile of severed heads.

First, the ruling class had to be democratically brought down a peg. Then the merchants had to be democratically dispossessed. Then the clergy had to have their property democratically confiscated. Then the army officers had to be democratically cashiered (violent hatred of the last two groups was one of Robespierre's less endearing characteristics). Then the farmers had to have their crops democratically requisitioned. And then they, along with many others whose sole crime was that Robespierre and his cronies did not like them very much, all met under the democratic guillotine. The latter went into high gear and ran up a score never before even approached by any authoritarian state not listing universal brotherhood among its desiderata. The only people set free in the process were the rabble: free to murder, rape and plunder. Soon, however, the newly elected tool of the people's power had to conscript the mob into the National Guard, so as to gain some control over it, while trying to counterbalance the old army that inclined towards scepticism about the advent of liberty, equality and fraternity. Almost overnight the country's armed forces swelled from 100,000 or so to almost ten times that number, and France fell under military control, which sooner or later was bound to produce a Napoleon. This demonstrates yet again Modmen's ability to pilfer Westmen's cultural heritage and apply elements of it to goals that are ostensibly traditional but in reality modern. Depending on the pilferers' talent, the larceny can fool more or fewer people, and Napoleon had talent to burn. That is why he so successfully channelled Westman's congenital expansiveness into Modman's expansionism. Even as Louis VII marched south at the head of a Crusade, Napoleon marched in every direction at the head of the *Grande Armée*. But while Louis had pursued Westman cultural ends, in however misguided a fashion, Napoleon was after modern political gain. He was a Modman answering the clarion call of a political state – with dire, but to him immaterial, consequences for millions of people.

Throughout the Middle Ages, and certainly in the preceding period that only those proud of twentieth-century Maidaneks and

Magadans can still be calling 'Dark Age', the nation state was non-existent, and people organized themselves into kindred groups closely patterned on the family: community, diocese, monastery, guild. The peaceful family reigned supreme and, until the Hundred Years' War, conflicts were few, usually localized and short. Then the authoritarian state appeared, and rulers began to put their militarizing foot down. But the foot usually stopped in mid-air. As long as traditional institutions were allowed to survive, the prince's power could not go very far.

No king ruling by divine right ever had the same power over his subjects as the modern political state, of either its totalitarian or liberal incarnation. Contrary to the prevailing academic view, the liberal and totalitarian states of modernity have more in common with each other than either has with the authoritarian Westman state. The authoritarian state sometimes stood above traditional institutions, but, unlike its modern antipodes, it seldom displaced them. Traditional institutions may have been paternalistic, but they were not cannibalistic. They encouraged man to create, while the faceless Leviathan that devoured tradition encourages him to destroy.

THE CHAMPION OF THE NIHILIST

On the surface, Russia's route to modernity was as different as different could be. Subsumed by despotism, Russia did not make a serious attempt to join the West until Peter I set out to 'chop a window onto Europe'. Much of this tardiness was involuntary: the country was too backward and unsettled to have embraced Western values even in a most superficial way. But a great deal of it was deliberate, as those Russians who had caught a glimpse of the West did not always like what they saw. Regarding Russia as 'the third Rome', the bearer of the Christian torch dropped by a flagging Byzantium, Russian rulers did not fail to diagnose some of the problems of the West in the immediate pre-Petrine period.

Besieged by those problems, the West represented to them a corrupting more than civilizing influence.

Peter's father, the second Romanov Tsar Alexei Mikhailovich expressed this proto-Eurosceptic attitude succinctly. When the English Muscovy Company, which had enjoyed a near monopoly on Russian trade since Elizabethan times, applied for an extension of its licence, it was floored by the short uppercut of the tsar's ukase: 'Inasmuch as the said Anglic Germans have slaughtered their own King Carolus to death, we hereby decree that none of the said Anglic Germans shall henceforth be admitted to Russia's lands.' The tsar's statement suggests that he grasped the main point about the contemporaneous West. It was becoming modern and therefore threatening to the well-being of absolute monarchs.

Peter was free from such prejudices. He was committed to leavening the savagery of Russia with the Western polish of an emerging elite. Part of this commitment was due to harsh necessity: Peter's survival depended on the obliteration of the traditional aristocracy that saw the Romanovs as dangerous upstarts. Part of it was neophyte zeal, a potentially more destructive component. Driven by it, Peter undertook a prolonged apprenticeship tour of Holland and England, where, among other essentials, he was to learn the hard way the difference between topiary and lavatories. However, he had to cut his education short and return home to suppress the mutiny of the Streltsy praetorian guard, the last serious threat to his reformist reign. As if to prove to the Russians that he had not gone soft on his Western travels, Peter hacked 80 of the Streltsy to pieces with his own hand. Having consolidated his power, Peter proceeded with the plan of turning Russia into a Western-style empire, a goal he had almost reached by the time of his death in 1725. More important in the context of this essay, he turned Russia into an excellent illustration of the key conflict between Modman and Westman.

Building on the reforms introduced by Patriarch Nikon in the previous reign, Peter modernized Russia's religion to a point where it shed some of its more Byzantine characteristics and began to resemble, however remotely, Westman's Christianity. He then attempted to create a Western-style cultural elite. In this he succeeded only partially, as an endeavour of that magnitude needed more time than Peter had at his disposal. As a shortcut he imported thousands of Europeans, some of whom, such as Lefort and Gordon, became his closest lieutenants. He also encouraged ethnically mixed marriages in the aristocracy, setting a good example himself by marrying Martha Skavronsky, a Livonian woman of easy virtue who was to become the Tsarina Catherine I. The stream of mixed marriages, previously condemned by the Orthodox Church, continued throughout the life of the Romanov dynasty, leaving its last reigning tsar, Nicholas II, with less than 1 per cent of Russian blood.

More important than ethnic cross-pollination was the speed at which Western culture was being absorbed into every pore of Russia's body. This was happening at a time when Westman was beginning to flag in his own natural habitat, and against the background of a population that was alien to the new trend not only culturally, but also ethnically and linguistically. For French and German had begun to play the same role in Russia as the French of the Norman conquerors played in Saxon England. Temporarily, Russian became a second-class language in its own land and had to wait almost a century before it began to acquire a serious literature.

Russia's religion was even more esoteric than the Catholic version of the Western confession. Moreover, with Russia's population largely illiterate in Peter's time, any Western culture was even more inaccessible than in the West. The arrival of the political state was still a couple of centuries away, the doctrine of divine right still reigned supreme, and the aristocracy enjoyed the kind of unchallenged privilege it had not tasted in the West for quite some time. Russia was thus going through roughly the same stages as the West had covered centuries before. While Western or, more precisely, quasi-Western man in Russia was still pre-pubescent, Westman in the contemporaneous West proper was already becoming senile. With typical youthful vigour, Russia forged ahead culturally, emulating Westman's path, but skipping many intermediate steps. Whenever things looked as if they would take too long to develop, the youngster would simply borrow them ready-made, making more or less good use of them.

The results of this accelerated growth were interesting. In due course they became tragic. The interplay with the West was particularly fraught with danger, for it began only when the West was getting less Western by the minute. But, even as Peter regarded the Swedish generals he eventually beat at the battle of Poltava as his teachers, so were his descendants ready to learn from Western culture, civilization and even politics. For the time being, that meant buying the West in its entirety as it was packaged then. Thus Catherine II was involved in a lively correspondence with Diderot and Voltaire. This most absolute monarch of her time routinely described herself as a republican and sought Diderot's advice on how to weave the ideals of the Enlightenment into the Russian political fabric. (This did not prevent her extending serfdom to the Ukraine.) Yet, for all her efforts to continue Peter's cause, Catherine did not succeed in making Russia Western. It was too late for that. Had the Westernization programme started not with Peter I but with Ivan the Terrible, who was Queen Elizabeth's contemporary and also her hapless suitor, Russia would have had many useful things to learn from the West at its peak, and the gap between her and, say, England would never have grown so wide. As it was, she struggled for a while to synchronize her step with the trundling of the senescent West and then forged ahead – with amazing results.

It is precisely her unquenchable thirst for things Western that makes Russia worthy of serious study. In spite of the clumsiness with which the Russians stuck Western saplings into their own soil, they succeeded in turning their country into a mirror image of the West. The mirror is both concave and convex, so it distorts the picture, but not beyond recognition. It is rather like a mimic doing an impersonation of a celebrity and conveying the character by accentuating the most salient traits. In borrowing things from the West the Russians mixed them with the bric-à-brac from their own ethnic store and animated them with the passion of the Slavic soul. Where the West had seething social unrest, Russia had manor houses burnt to cinders; where the West had the Bastille, Russia had molten pitch down the throat; where the West had Kautski, Russia had Lenin. And where the West was gradually taken over by the philistine subspecies of Modman, Russia was violently grabbed by the nihilist.

But the fact remains: if the West is Dorian Grey, Russia is the portrait. The nihilist is the image in the philistine's attic, and possibly vice versa. Even as Wilde's character was horrified by the grotesque mask into which his vices had turned the portrait, so should Westerners look at Russia not with scorn but with the sadness of someone whose soul has been turned inside out and its depravity revealed for the world to see. This is a good way to look upon Russia's nihilist history and the animus behind it.

Communist historians, both here and in Russia, have always felt duty-bound to squeeze this process into the framework of class struggle. However, their analysis does not hold water regardless of the historical period to which it is applied. The easiest way to disprove the class origin of Russian revolutions is to look at the men who perpetrated them. Since the Bolsheviks insisted on tracing their own genealogy back to the early nineteenth century, this is as good a place to start as any.

For those interested in Russian history, a group that should include any student of modernity, the uprising that took place on 14 December 1825 provides a useful blueprint. For the December uprising was carried out by aristocrats, members of the same class that produced the tsar and General Sukhozanet, the officer who issued the order to disperse the mutiny with grapeshot. In fact, many of the revolutionaries had come from much older families than even the Romanovs, never mind the Sukhozanets. That this uprising had nothing to do with class warfare is so obvious that one is amazed at the impudence needed to have put forth such a notion. But the Bolsheviks simply used a defunct doctrine to find a *post factum* rationale. The Decembrists were indeed the precursors of the Bolsheviks; however, what united them was not class but their shared hatred of Westman. They were Modmen, and this dwarfs any consideration of class or economics. By education and background the Decembrists appeared to be Western, many of them even spoke broken Russian. Their motives were similar to Robespierre's, but their French was better (just as Alexander I's was better than Napoleon's). Their links with France were particularly strong as many of them had served in the Russian occupation contingent in 1815. They had drunk deeply of the air of France without realizing it was poisoned. The Decembrists thought they had seen Christ walking on Western water but, unbeknown to them, what they had seen was Antichrist knee-deep in Westman's blood. The vision proved too much for the Decembrists, and they went mad.

These dashing aristocrats returned to Russia not only as vanquishing heroes, but as disciples who had seen the light. Gathering at night in restaurants or houses of dubious repute, they no longer just drank themselves to a stupor or discussed the more prominent attractions of gypsy maidens. Woven into their drunken toasts were those lovely French words *liberté, egalité, fraternité*, pronounced in their impeccable Gallic accents. Someone had forgotten to tell the wretches that *egalité* runs contrary to the other two aspirations. The very concept of equality, as used by the Decembrists, presupposes a forcible achievement of parity among large numbers of people. Freedom and brotherhood, on the other hand, are individual concepts. A social egalitarian cannot regard as a brother any member of a class superior to his own; whereas Westmen were taught to look upon any man, regardless of class, as a brother, a kinship achieved at a higher level than the transient matters of politics or economics.

It was a great tragedy that Russia began to borrow from the West at a time when the Western cultural coffers were beginning to be depleted. That is probably why the most impressive Russian successes were achieved in literature, the least indigenous art in the Westman scheme of things. While in music and painting, which were Westman's fundamental pursuits, Russia did not begin to speak in an original voice until late in the nineteenth century, her literature achieved both originality and greatness almost overnight. In size it was to become a small literature, entirely confinable, according to Nabokov's calculations, within 21,000 pages (approximately the size of Jules Verne's total output). But the quality of those pages was such that Russian literature instantly took its place side by side with other great literatures of the world, having the advantage of youthful exuberance over them.

A parallel we could draw with America is that the USA too has always found it difficult to make a significant contribution to any of the cultural pursuits of the West, literature again being the possible exception. And since traces of an aristocratic order only ever existed in America's Southern states, this region was responsible for producing most of the interesting American writers. However, American literature never has produced a Tolstoy or a Gogol. Partly, the reason for this is linguistic: having imported their language from the Old World, the Americans had to import its literature as well, and most of their nineteenth-century output suffers from epigonic provincialism. By the time they got around to developing their own idiosyncratic variant of English, the Western cultural springs that could have fed a great literature had gone dry. So the best American writers, such as Mark Twain, will for ever have to settle for the descriptor 'interesting', leaving 'great' to nations that have, in that respect, more fortunate histories.

Russia's situation was both fortunate and odd. It was fortunate in that Russia preserved a strict aristocratic order long after it had become a thing of the past in the West. Her cultured elite was even more estranged from the rest of the people, not even sharing its everyday language with hoi polloi. At the same time, its political power was absolute and its control of finances almost so. The economy was by and large agricultural and, apart from the two capitals, a great deal of Russia's life was conducted in the countryside. The ecclesiastical establishment, while not possessing much statutory power, exerted an influence on the people who did. One reason was the need to uphold the doctrine of divine right, which required a clergy able to exert a telling influence on the entire population. The other reason was practical. Because many members of the Russian royal family were not brought up in the Orthodox tradition, they had to convert, and many of them displayed the ardour of sincere neophytes (Catherine II and Tsarina Alexandra are good examples of this).

Religious figures often acquired an elevated status to which their positions would not necessarily have entitled them otherwise. One way or the other, the social preconditions for the appearance of Westman were there. The oddity of it all was that Russia was not Western. Her religion, while Christian, was not Western and so it did not benefit – or suffer, depending on one's point of view – from the Aristotelian influences that are so critical to Westman culture. Russia did not enjoy many of the liberties in the nineteenth century that, say, Englishmen would have taken for granted in the fourteenth. Even after the Petrine reforms her cultural intercourse with the West was minimal and tightly controlled. Her legal system in no way resembled any recognizable Western pattern. She never went through the formative cataclysms of the West: Renaissance, Reformation, Enlightenment. And yet the conditions she did possess – monarchs ruling a patrimonic state by divine right, a rigid aristocratic hierarchy, concentration of cultural, political and economic power in the same hands, a strong ecclesiastical element, preponderance of Western culture, proved to be sufficient even in the absence of all others. This suggests that those other conditions are irrelevant to the appearance of Westman as a dominant social type. On the other hand, we know now that eradication of the conditions that are indeed a *sine qua non* has proved lethal in the West. Thus Russia, cultural oddity as it is, was cast in the role of torch bearer for Westman culture at a time when real Westerners were busily turning into Modmen.

One feature the pre-revolutionary Russians borrowed from the contemporaneous West was a propensity for boundless criticism of tradition, as much the order of the day then as the culture of political correctness is in the West today. In both cases the perpetrators regard themselves as courageous opponents of the powers that be, refusing to acknowledge that they themselves are immeasurably more powerful. Dissenting, which is to say traditional, views become socially unacceptable and, in due course, intellectually suspect to a point where those who hold them begin to feel guilty for being unfashionably obdurate. Modmen are so obsessed with the destruction of the establishment that they often continue to fight it long after they themselves have become the establishment. Iconoclasm lives on long after the icons have been smashed.

PART 3
RECAPITULATION

HE WHO PAYS THE PIPER

As we move into the nineteenth century on the way to the fateful twentieth, Modman is fully formed as the dominant social type. Public opinion is firmly on his side and any digression from an undiluted modern agenda tends to be portrayed in the press and smart salons as either injustice or atavism.

By 1815, the time the nineteenth century really got going, Modmen had succeeded in compromising, if not yet uprooting, every basic tenet of Westman culture. While this achievement still fell short of their in-built objective, it had made the ultimate victory not only possible but inevitable, barring an accident of some kind. The situation resembled a chess game in which one of the players tries an unsuccessful experiment. He then finds himself under relentless pressure; his opponent has freedom of the board, controlling the key squares, applying a strangulation hold. The struggler will put up resistance, making his opponent sweat. But, in the absence of a blunder on the part of the opponent, there is only one winner.

Nietzsche, that notorious coroner to divinity, pronounced God dead in the 1880s and, as far as Modmen were concerned, he was describing a state of affairs that had existed for quite some time. Religion had lost its role as the bedrock of society, and culture derived from religion was no longer a characteristic of the dominant social type. Modman now saw himself as a central, almost divine figure towering above anachronistic culture. God as man had been replaced by Modman as God. He was, however, aware of one important difference between himself and God: having lived, if he was lucky, his three-score and ten, he was going to die. Mortality was thus a logical inconsistency from Modmen's standpoint, an insult to an otherwise faultless self-image. Science would solve this problem sooner or later, it had promised to do so, but Modmen were not so silly as to believe that deliverance would come in their own lifetime.

Physical life was all Modmen had, and so their only option was to cram as much as possible into it, making life even more physical, which is to say hedonistic. At the same time they were satisfied that, in doing so, they also were fulfilling their ultimate objective: destruction of Westman. Consigning God to his grave was Modmen's way of combining business with pleasure. Modmen today insist that the New Testament justifies their hedonism. Many misquote St Paul and hold up 'eat, drink and be merry, for tomorrow you die' as a divinely endorsed philosophy of life. Though one cannot expect intellectual rigour from Modmen, had they read Corinthians 1 (15:32), even they would have realized that their favourite passage means exactly the opposite of their wishful misunderstanding. For Paul was scathing about godless hedonism. He used the misquoted passage to show the depth of the abyss awaiting man in the absence of individual immortality. But what to Paul was unimaginable horror, to Modmen is a goal towards which to strive.

Their culture reflected their godlessness, even though it seemed even more introspective than Westman culture. With sleight of hand, Modman had stuck the ace of introspection up his sleeve, bringing it out only for larcenous purposes. Where Westman artists were introspective because only in that way could they understand their souls, approaching an understanding of God and thus fulfilling themselves, their Modman followers were introspective because their own self-expression had taken on huge proportions.

As ever, culture provides the most reliable insight. Since nothing illuminates culture as much as music, perhaps we should take a closer look at music in the nineteenth century. Starting with Beethoven who straddled two centuries and two epochs, music had changed to a point where it could now accommodate a new type of artist: the conscious innovator. Later, this type would move into other arts as well, painting and architecture particularly, but for the time being music was his home. What makes the term 'conscious innovator' pejorative is not the noun but the adjective. There is nothing wrong with innovation as such; on the contrary, the inner logic of art makes it ineluctable. Life cannot remain static; it has to develop. Music is the same. Just like baroque before it, classicism had had its day, with Haydn and Mozart having taken it as far as it could go. Perhaps Mozart took it even further than that, exhausting both himself and the style, which later prompted Glenn Gould's quip that Mozart died not too early but rather too late. Innovation had to come one way or the other, and it had to happen not because composers would suddenly decide that they ought to try something new, but because they simply could not write in the old style any longer. Having been stretched to the limit by Haydn and Mozart, classicism would have imploded trying to contain Beethoven and Schubert, Schumann and Brahms.

A transition from classicism was on the cards and it could only proceed towards something resembling romanticism as that was the general direction in which Westman was moving. Painting went through a similar stage at about the same time, the classicist stress on line being pushed aside by the romantic accent on colour exemplified by the likes of Goya and Delacroix. But the cards were being dealt from a stacked deck, for Westman was on a path to extinction, pushed that way by Modman. In that sense, romanticism was a factor of Westman's demise, a step on the staircase leading to perdition – this, paradoxically, irrespective of the masterpieces it produced.

Beethoven, a genius though he was, had Modman tendencies and drew not only human but even artistic inspiration from the 1789–1815 upheaval in France. This manifested itself either directly, in pieces like his 3rd Symphony and the 5th Piano Concerto, or indirectly in the bravura finales of many of his other works. In common with most Modmen, Beethoven believed that the future was knowable, plannable and rationally mouldable, which is why it had to be glorious. This misconception found its way into his music, demonstrating yet again that culture does not exist in isolation. The choral finale of the 9th Symphony, with people rejoicing over nothing, sounds particularly incongruous. Contrast Beethoven's finales with those of Shostakovich, a Westman holdout with first-hand experience of modern life. He ends many of his great pieces by almost cutting them off in mid-phrase, uncertain which way life would go, fearful it could only get worse. This creates an almost unbearable tension, and if the listener shares the same view of life he is left drained.

Being to some extent a Modman, the first one among composers of genius, Beethoven had a destructive aspect to his personality. That was mirrored by the ever-present corollary of self-destruction, with Beethoven showing the romantic way of dying to many a follower by slowly drinking himself to death. Though technically not suicide as such, this came as close as any great composer has ever come to killing himself (Tchaikovsky's suicide remains unproven). Music tends to discourage God-defying gestures in its practitioners, which is more than can be said for other arts. Suicide, slow or quick, is a slap in God's face, the only sin impossible to repent and the ultimate way to claim full sovereignty over one's own life. This is precisely why it is implicitly prescribed by romanticism and expressly proscribed by Western religion: Augustine, for example, regarded Judas's suicide as the greater sin than his betrayal. Throughout the nineteenth century and up to our time, Modman artists acted as if dying of old age would somehow render their lives illogical. From Byron and Lermontov, who sought death so persistently that they might as well have died by their own hand, to Kleist and Hemingway who did kill themselves, the list of artists who committed or attempted suicide is endless. Many of them also set a fine example for their exalted followers who imitated their idols' control of their own destiny. Called the 'Werther effect' in psychiatry, the very name of this copycat brutality is borrowed from one of the greatest romanticists of them all. This points at a uniquely modern nature of romantic suicide, different from, say, the suicide of Hellenic men like Zeno or Lucretius.

According to forensic psychiatrists, there exists a direct link between violence towards oneself and towards others. In Beethoven, the two urges were intertwined. Musically (and in common with any genius he had no meaningful life outside his art), this tendency sometimes manifested itself in a conscious attempt to break the old forms simply for the sake of breaking them. That dealt music a mortal, although delayed action, blow not because it resulted in Beethoven producing bad pieces, something a genius cannot do, but because his own great music paved the way for other conscious innovators of lesser talent. By instantly expanding the boundaries of the allowable, Beethoven pushed the first domino for a knock-on effect. Once again, this is not to say there is anything wrong with innovation as such; it is only conscious innovation that can prove destructive.

Hindsight enables us to see what kind of genie was set free by Beethoven and his followers. Art began to worship at the altar of subjective originality rather than objective truth. Yet until the nineteenth century it had been universally accepted that looking for truth was the real purpose of art. Because of that, traditional forms had a liberating rather than constricting effect. The artist could take the canonical foundation of his work as a given and concentrate instead on the higher goal. As long as truth did emerge, it did not matter to the artist whether he was the first to uncover it or the thousandth. Westman did not see life as a race, and he was free of the hubristic desire to be original at any cost. And even as it does not matter to a happily married couple that there exist many other happy couples, Westman was indifferent to originality as such. This humble respect for tradition did not lead to spiritual or artistic cloning, quite the opposite. An artist seeking a higher truth finds it as a vision inside his own soul, which is the only place to look for it. And, once found, the truth cannot help being individual, for people's visions always are. Just as two neighbours with identical backgrounds and outward lives still see different dreams in their sleep, so do real artists remain individual even, or rather especially, when they do not set out to be. Thus, for all the similarity of the forms they used, Bach cannot be confused with Telemann, one Scarlatti with the other or Haydn with Mozart.

A deliberate attempt to break the old moulds usually takes an artist to a level that is not higher than the one before, but lower. This applies to his social life as well. For example, Beethoven is commonly believed to have been the first composer to free himself from the shackles of aristocratic patronage. That is not quite true, but he was the first professing contempt for the very system of patronage. Granted, the humility of a Bach is alien to a Modman; his pride, the hubris of someone who is his own God, cannot accept the existence of a hierarchy in which he himself is not at the top. In common with Mozart, Beethoven did take steps towards freelance independence. But, in reality, he merely exchanged one form of patronage for another, proving yet again that great music cannot survive in a free-market way while remaining great music. Various electors, Counts Waldstein and Razumovsky, Princes Lichnowsky and Lobkowitz were all Beethoven's patrons at different times, even though most of them pretended to accept him as a social equal. This pretence continued at his death, when Beethoven became the only Viennese composer ever to receive a second-degree funeral, one up from Mozart (who, incidentally, got a perfectly respectable third-degree burial, which was a far cry from the pauper's grave of Modman's fantasy). Where Beethoven differed from his predecessors was in his desire to replace the He of Bach with his own I. Beethoven's I!!! screams from much of his music. Had he not been a genius, this musical egotism run riot would have been no worse than mildly irritating. As it was, it proved lethal.

Apart from reflecting Modman's self-deification suggested by Beethoven, the music scene underwent other deep changes in the nineteenth century. More and more the accent was shifting from the divinely inspired art of composition to the human art of virtuoso performance. In a way this shift reflected the gradual decline in direct patronage, which in turn mirrored the downward slide of the aristocratic way of life. With traditional patronage waning, artists had to seek alternative livelihoods, and box office receipts began to loom large. Modmen, philistine subspecies, were applying to art their chosen political technique, democracy, and their favourite economic tool, free enterprise. While we shall discuss both in greater detail later on, suffice it to say now that neither is applicable to the spheres of life for which it was not manifestly designed. The issue of good or bad in art cannot, or at least should not, be decided by a show of hands, each clutching a wad of banknotes. Yet this is precisely what happens when art is left to fend for itself on the economic battlefield.

By paying the piper Paul in preference to his fellow piper Peter, the public lets both know what kind of pipe playing it finds acceptable. Since neither musician can any longer survive without pleasing the public, he either has to devalue his art or abandon the habit of eating regularly. Devaluing is precisely what is involved, for serious art was not designed, and cannot be produced, for large numbers. If it is, it stops being serious art. A useful parallel can be drawn with fruit and vegetables over the last half-century. Victorious Modmen have decreed that most produce should be available to most people throughout the year, regardless of seasons. And so it is, except that to achieve that goal Modmen have had to sacrifice everything that used to make produce worth eating: taste, fragrance, texture, nutritive value. Such a fate has befallen art as well, and for the same reason, but Modmen do not mind. They have little taste anyway, so it is no hardship for them to munch what passes for food while listening with a half-ear to what passes for music. The pleasure of having rubbed Westman's nose in the dirt, on the other hand, is something they enjoy unreservedly.

Since numerical expansion leads to spiritual diminution, as early as in the late eighteenth century the public issued a mandate: never mind philosophical depth, let's see some fleet fingers. Musical performance quickly degenerated into improvised reproductions of birds' noises and other onomatopoeic rubbish. Of course, shows of virtuosity did not begin in the nineteenth century. As the famous keyboard jousts between Handel and Scarlatti or between Mozart and Clementi will attest to, aristocrats were not averse to encouraging nimble digital displays either. But for them such trivia served as spice, not the main course. Both the participants and the audience took it as read that the musicians involved were composers first and performers a distant second.

Not so the nineteenth-century public. For them musicians like Paganini and Liszt, while still composers as well, were the first pop stars, trained monkeys in the service of the paying public. And just like today's rappers, the pop stars of the past were expected to cultivate a diabolical image. Black cloaks with crimson linings, piercing gazes, shoulder-length hair – all these extra-musical attributes were helping to create the cult of musicians at the expense of music. In that sense, Liszt and Paganini were nineteenth-century equivalents of today's skinheads who perform in clouds of smoke symbolizing hell with a typically modern absence of subtlety. Just like today's lot they were playing into the hands of Modman barbarism. As if to prove that great music could not be created under such circumstances, both composers produced a mostly trite output, although Liszt's superior talent occasionally inspired him to create works that approached greatness, as opposed to relying on the technical innovations that are his main heritage. Unfortunately, as a composer, he was pre-occupied with sheer sound at the expense of intellectual depth and structural integrity. And, as a man, he was too busy building his personal cult, eliciting the nineteenth-century answer to today's pop hysteria. Instead of composing, or even performing, more of such powerful works as his Sonata or the E-Flat Concerto, Liszt kept regaling the paying public with dazzling, half-improvised variations on hit operas, such as Meyerbeer's *Robert le Diable*.

By injecting into performance the same creative energy that would otherwise have gone into composition, both Liszt and Paganini refined the technique of performing on their respective instruments, and their influence is still with us today. For example, playing vibrato on every note is a given for any post-Paganini violinist, be that Thibaud, Heifetz or Perlman. Unfortunately, they also bequeathed to us today the lamentable situation of the musician being more important than the music. The dazzling technique developed by the first travelling virtuosos eventually led to the appearance of a new profession: itinerant performing musician who did not compose the music he played. The first important pianists who fell into the new category, such as Rosenthal and Hofman, were taught by composer musicians (Liszt and Anton Rubinstein respectively). But they themselves stayed away from composition, apart from an occasional off-the-cuff vehicle for virtuosic display. Overnight, professional performers began to grow in stature, whereas composers were finding it more difficult to make a living as composers only or even primarily. Eventually, someone like Rachmaninov would be able to make in one concert tour more than he had ever earned from composing.

As with composition, in performance too a button was pushed for a delayed-action explosion. As Westman still had not become extinct, the second half of the nineteenth century and the first half of the twentieth did produce many musicians who were latently Western. As such, they dedicated their lives to understanding and then communicating to their public the deep meaning of the pieces they performed. So far untarnished by the creeping verbalization of modern art, musicians were still decades removed from the belief that the score provides everything there is in the music, and the performer's task is merely to play the notes accurately. For this belief to be enunciated and then acted upon, Modmen had to acquire the confidence to smash Westman culture to smithereens. When that eventually came about, towards the middle of the twentieth century, the signs were unmistakable: culture began to be infinitely attracted to literature, even as Westman culture had been infinitely attracted to music.

The mystery that lay at the foundation of Westman culture could not be expressed in words, which made cultivated people aware of the limitations of literature. Since Modmen refused to waste their quality time on mysteries, words and graphic symbols became their perfect media. Anything they had to say could easily be committed to paper. Music had to be downgraded to the status of entertainment – serious entertainment to be sure, but not something meriting any claim to enigmatic nature. That is partly why the score eventually began to be seen as coextensive with music, a literary document musicians ought to follow religiously and musicologists to analyse and pronounce on zealously.* The latter group gained in importance in parallel with the elevation of the score, for their domain now overlapped with music entirely. Articles and books on music eventually became so influential as to become dictates: musicians had to deliver what musicologists demanded. Both playing and writing thus became equipotent illustrations of the cultural *Zeitgeist*. For playing that illustrates the score without revealing the music behind it does not require any qualities beyond general musicality and digital dexterity. What it emphatically does

---

* 'The English,' quipped Chopin, 'love music, but they hate listening to it.' What for him was a *bon mot* for us is everyday life.

not need is an idiosyncratic individuality that alone can produce the ability to find and express the beauty hidden in a great work. In other words, it does not require talent. So talent had nowhere to go but out. The word, however, lives on. But these days it is applied to precisely the combination of musicality and dexterity that a century ago would have barely rated 'competence'. Words, after all, have to mean whatever Modmen want them to mean.

In the second half of the twentieth century this process produced a musical scene dominated by automatons who find in 'faithfulness to the score' a refuge from any need to become equal to the music they betray by their 'faithfulness'. Instead, they reaffirm Modman egalitarianism by being equal to one another, which is to say boringly identical. To take the piano as an example, the same music lover who could, listening to their recordings with his eyes shut, instantly tell Rachmaninov from Hofman or either of them from Fischer or Schnabel, today would be hard-pressed to tell apart all those Freddies and Borises. The culprit is the modern tendency towards levelling, not, as is commonly believed, some neo-classicist reaction to the excesses of the romantic era.

Given some ability, it is possible to learn the technique of playing classical music. The nobility of spirit required to understand Westman music, however, cannot be learned. One either has to be born with it or imbibe it from the ambient air. Unfortunately, the air exhaled by Modman is devoid of spiritual nobility. A youngster has to be a genius of Gouldian proportions to acquire a noble spirit in a culture that has made *Coronation Street* and *Jerry Springer* its crowning achievements. Alas, geniuses are few; so we shall forever have to settle for 'faithfulness to the score' as the surrogate of depth. Yet performers of old were aware that music is impossible to express fully on paper. If this were not so we would have recitations instead of recitals.

As audiences became mass-produced, so did performers. Conveyer belts in mushrooming conservatories were spewing out proficient robots, and those who could not quite hack it became musicologists. Towards the watershed divide in the twentieth century, the playing and writing nonentities had formed an implicit pact designed to keep real musicians out. Whenever one appeared (and the law of averages had not yet been repealed), they would unite against him, and before too long the poor overachiever would have 'eccentric' and 'irreverent' labels pasted all over him. Soon he would be driven off the concert platform either partially or totally. Someone like Gould had enough following to retreat into a successful recording career. Others have nowhere to retreat but to their own drawing rooms. Today there are more serious musicians among those who have no or little careers than among those whose names are plastered all over the papers.

Yet music still perseveres, with some decent pieces being written and a few real musicians appearing at a time when Westman holdouts do not seem to be there in sufficient numbers to keep it going. There must be something intrinsic in the genre to account for its unlikely longevity, something that explains why, for all the battering music has taken, it manages to survive after a fashion in the absence of the cultural and social conditions under which it appeared in the first place.

This something can be summed up in a single word: suffering. Westman is unique in history because suffering was a formative experience for him. If we accept that the pain Christ endured on the cross was also the birth pain of Westman, then suffering has a special place in the hearts of Westman holdouts. Western religion, whence came Western culture and Westman himself, attaches a deep meaning to suffering, something no other religion or culture has ever emphasized to the same extent. Suffering plays the same role in Western religion as peace and harmony play in Eastern faiths: it is central to Westman. Since music is the best way Westman has found to convey his religious feeling, it is also capable of expressing suffering better than other arts can. But the link goes further than that. While music is necessary to express the suffering of the Western soul, suffering in its turn is essential to music.

It is important not to interpret suffering simplistically as merely physical deprivation. Suffering is as essential for a Westman as comfort is for a Modman philistine, but Western suffering is more spiritual than physical. It is the anguish in the soul, not the pain in the body, at least not just that. Suffering is a corollary to freedom, the ability to make a free moral choice that is inseparable from Westman's ethos. Making a free choice is painful in itself and it can also lead to painful consequences. However, the only way to reduce the suffering implicit in freedom is to reduce freedom. Thus approximations of slavery, sometimes institutional but more often spiritual are the price we usually have to pay for less suffering. For Westman this price was unacceptably high. For Modman it is right; and that just may be the most significant difference between the two breeds.

Modman was born with no concept of freedom, which he tends to confuse with liberty. Westman, on the other hand, was defined by his soul and consequently by his inner freedom. Somewhere along the line this soul became moribund, and most Westmen were aware of it. Suffering was growing in acuity as Westman's inner self was dying – not only because his body was being broken on the rack of history. Music, therefore, had to record this process, which in turn fed music well enough to prevent it dying from starvation. Granted, suffering alone was not enough to keep music in luxuriant leaf. But it was enough to keep it going for longer than other arts. When modernity stuck the first dagger into Westman's back, the ensuing pain was recorded by Beethoven, himself more of a Modman than Westman, and the great composers who followed him. And, while Bach was equally adept at expressing the formative pain of Westman faith and rejoicing at its glory, romantic composers were at their best when expressing the suffering. Whenever they communicated the other constituent, one often detects more frivolity than joy. Suffering had become the only thing, not just the most important one.

That a great deal of suffering in the twentieth century had to do with a pandemic of violent death made things easier for musicians. As foxholes had long since become the only places with no atheists, death became the focus of religious feeling in Westman holdouts. That is why they are at their most poignant when inspired by mass mortality to answer the vague echo in the back of their own souls. In the twentieth century, when the first big war mortally wounded Westman and the second finished him off, music simply had to record the agony. This it did most typically through Shostakovich whose best works contain few happy notes. His emotional range reflects Westman's death throes by going from simply tragic to piercingly tragic to unbearably tragic. After that the Western soul had nowhere else to go. Having suffered its own tortures it now had to empathize with the pain of Kolyma and Buchenwald, Somme and Stalingrad, and the combination proved too much for it to bear.

Other cultural manifestations of Westman fared even worse. They were less equipped to resist the delayed-action explosion the button for which had been pushed in the nineteenth century by a massive shift towards conscious innovation. Painting, the other core Western art, demonstrates this amply. Towards the end of the nineteenth century, Impressionism appeared more or less simultaneously in both music and painting, but with one difference. In music it was introduced by the uncluttered artists Debussy and Ravel, whereas in painting, whose bolt had been shot in the seventeenth century, it was practised by less talented but more politicized figures. The former were latently Western, the latter modern, which is to say conscious, innovators. Apart from pursuing artistic ends, the Impressionist and post-Impressionist painters cultivated their style as a way of thumbing their noses at the Academy with what they saw as its stilted, archaic ideas. That Cézanne and Monet were more talented than their contemporary Academicians is neither here nor there: the latter, though men of modest abilities, were keeping alive a tradition that in due course could again have delivered sustained greatness. The Impressionists, however talented, shattered that tradition, thus making Damien Hirst unavoidable somewhere down the road.

At the same time they discovered the cult potential of iconoclasm, milking it for what it was worth. Just like musicians, these painters thrived when the accent shifted from art to artists, and their ability to develop into posthumous legends was in direct proportion to their capacity for aberrant behaviour, so highly prized by Modmen. Today, possibly nine out of ten people who are aware of van Gogh's propensity for self-mutilation or Modigliani's for alcoholism know next to nothing about the biographies of Rembrandt and Velázquez, never mind Zurbarán whose very name is unlikely to be known to them.

A scaled-down version of musical sycophancy hit painting as well, but with even more shattering effects. While some Impressionists were decent painters, their followers attempted to emulate their artistic iconoclasm without the benefit of concomitant mastery, such as it was. The resulting catastrophe reflects both the fact that painting started its downward slide from a lower height than music, and also the purely technical differences between the two genres.

First, while music had a ready-made fallback position in professional performing, painting had to remain a creative as opposed to an interpretative art. Also, music cannot be composed and musical instruments cannot be played professionally without technical proficiency, which has to be maintained by monastic practising. Such daily toil is a given, even for instrumentalists who would otherwise prefer just to 'express themselves', for without putting in time they would not get anywhere near a concert platform. With painting the situation is different: it is possible to produce graven images with little technical skill. Modmen, with their ideological commitment to ignorance, do not mind. For them, extra-artistic considerations are more significant because they are accessible to larger numbers than is the essence of art. Technique, especially of draughtsmanship, eventually came to be regarded as surplus to requirements. Since substance had fallen by the wayside to begin with, painting, now devoid of technical mastery as well, unerringly marched the way of pop music towards eliminating artistic content altogether, which peak was reached in the twentieth century. The reason why there still remained a few holdouts from the time when craftsmanship was *de rigueur* lies in painting's unique nature of sponsorship.

While music and literature were becoming increasingly dependent on mass support, painting was still financed by one-to-one transactions. Westman holdouts among lovers of music and literature are outvoted and outshouted with ease, and their tastes are sacrificed at the altar of pluralism. Painting is different. Even if Westman holdouts are in an infinitesimal minority among patrons of art, they can still influence events by providing demand in need of supply. So demand for real art was merely marginalized but never extinguished. However, painting has not been spared attrition just because it is the only art financed in roughly the same way as ever. In fact, it has fallen prey to the same pressure as all other arts, but in its case the pressure is exerted in a different way. First, because of the collapse of education, we can no longer take it for granted that people with enough money to patronize art will have the taste to know which art to patronize – quite the opposite. Second, as today's Walpoles usually have little taste for art but do possess a keen nose for investment, they have to rely on the 'expert' authority of the popular art press. That institution, however, is controlled by the Modman mob entirely, as it is financed by it directly. In practice, decisions on which art to patronize are forged in the same smithies of taste as decisions on which music should be performed and by whom. The choice between good and bad is made not by artists and people of refined sensibilities but by the modern gurus of 'art appreciation'. The corrupting effects of this arrangement are felt not only by today's artists but also by the old masters who are these days reassessed in accordance with modern criteria. Witness the inflated prices van Gogh continues to fetch, especially compared with painters of the more distant past. One can only lament the unfortunate oversight on the part of de Hooch or Morales who somehow neglected to ensure record-breaking marketability by removing portions of their anatomy. Also, Caravaggio has been posthumously pronounced a first-rate genius, and no wonder. So far as Modman is concerned, Caravaggio fills the bill perfectly. As a man he enjoyed the uninhibited lifestyle (including the odd bit of murder) so beloved of Modmen. And as an artist he combined an indifferent spiritual content with formal innovation, again an ideal marriage for Modmen.

IS THE WORLD SAFE FROM DEMOCRACY?

'The most may err as grossly as the few.'

(J. Dryden)

Cultural victories scored by Modman in the nineteenth century had obvious parallels with politics, economics and with their intellectual rationalization, which passes for Modman political philosophy. Modmen were already dominant but they were still unaware of how dominant. They were saving the worst of their smugness for the next century. For the time being they were flexing their muscle and probing gently to see how far they could push.

Their right to happiness had already been asserted and, in America, institutionalized. But America, what with its absence of indigenous Western tradition, was a soft touch. Disdainful of unsporting victories, Modmen were becoming confident enough to take on the strongest bastion of Westman: Europe. The time was ripe for conquest, for the Napoleonic wars had left Europe exhausted and European Westmen without much resolve to fight. Aristocratic regimes were losing ground, even if they had so far managed to weather some of the nastier storms.

The restoration of the Bourbons in France did not fool even their staunchest supporters into an illusion of security. Monarchy there was seen more as a stopgap arrangement than a return to pre-revolutionary times. Assorted German principalities, their inherent weakness having been shown up by Napoleon with contemptuous ease and their number reduced dramatically, were coming under the sway of Prussia, while the latter was hastily developing the groundwork of a modern political state. It was in the nineteenth century that Prussia, culturally the least Westman of the German states, demonstrated how far ahead of her time she was. Waving the carrot of economic benefits and social security under the noses of the smaller principalities, she dragged one after another into a customs union first, single currency second, single superstate third. Where the carrot did not work, as in the case of Schleswig Holstein, the stick saw the light of day. Also coming with the advent of Prussia was feverish industrialization and with it the inevitable dominance of Modman. One way or the other, Westman was not faring well in Germany. Monarchy in Russia managed to hang on by the skin of its teeth following the uprising of 1825 and was doing well on the surface. But the rot had set in to a sufficient extent for Marx to have singled Russia out as the likeliest candidate for a communist takeover.

That left England as the champion of Westman. The English, however, were having none of this: the role they chose instead was that of pathfinder for the philistine subspecies of Modman. Even as the agnostic empiricism of Locke and Hume had provided the philosophical basis for Modman's first tentative steps, the utilitarianism of Bentham and Mill now propelled him to the shining bauble of the Industrial Revolution. In a way, Bentham followed Hume as logically as Marx followed Bentham, what with morality gradually disappearing from Modman's philosophical equations. Of the major philosophical schools, utilitarianism was the first amoral one. Bentham and Mill eschewed Hume's ill-advised yet honest attempts to find a basis for absolute morality outside faith. In doing so they abandoned absolute morality. Instead of Westman's polarity of virtue and sin, they postulated

162

Modman's polarity of happiness and pain as the starting point of moral choice. Happiness was good and therefore virtuous. Pain was bad and therefore sinful. Also, the two concepts easily lent themselves to a switch from the positive to the negative and back. Thus, absence of pain could at a pinch pass for happiness, while a deficit in the latter could easily be seen as being painful. It followed that moral choice had to lose its independent value and become subsumed in the relativity of the new polarity. There was no a priori morality any longer. The morality of a choice had to be judged a posteriori in relation to its outcome in achieving happiness or causing pain. If a choice led to the former it was moral; if it produced the latter it was not. A few decades later Hemingway expressed this concept of morality with a typical forthrightness: if something feels good it is moral. Following this dictum, one has to believe that Mr and Mrs West, the mass murderers and torturers of youngsters, were paragons of morality because their shenanigans undoubtedly made them feel good.

Happiness cannot function as the universal criterion of rectitude because it is relative. Your neighbour may feel happy about playing pop records at maximum volume, but his happiness is your misery. According to the utilitarian logic, there was only one way to settle such a conflict: a show of hands. Thus, to judge the morality or indeed utility of an action we were supposed to count the number of people the action made happy or otherwise. If the balance was positive the action was utilitarian and therefore moral. If the balance was negative the action was neither. It was as simple as that. Moreover, this was exactly the kind of simplicity Modmen loved. The complexities of Judaeo-Christian ethics were now in the public domain, but their accessibility was of no use to Modmen. Like the internal barbarians of yesteryear, they had no time for complicated things; their time could be spent more profitably on achieving happiness. Bentham and Mill made sense to Modmen. 'The greatest good of the greatest number' was a licence to destroy every cultural possession of Westman, which had been produced for few people by fewer still. Secure in the knowledge that they had numbers on their side, Modmen were ready to start tightening the screws so as to create what de Tocqueville was to describe as 'the tyranny of the majority.'

In his late works Beethoven abandoned the revolutionary optimism of his earlier periods. Likewise, towards the end of his life Mill developed doubts about utility as the universal yardstick, and he too began to talk about the tyranny of the majority as its likely consequence. There were no such doubts for Bentham. He was logical to the end, allowing his utilitarianism to lead him to the denial of everything that had flown out of tradition, from trial by jury to parliament. That is the logical way for rationalism to go: who needs Burkean prejudice and prescription when one's own reason can solve every problem life throws up?

Once absolute standards of good and evil stopped being a social dynamic, the numbers game began to be played in the arena of morals and aesthetics, areas not hitherto available for mass pageantry. Politics and economics naturally had to follow suit. Bentham died in the year the Reform Act crowned the first stage in the political ascent of the philistine subspecies of Modman in Britain. Since the greatest happiness of the greatest number was now seen as both utilitarian and moral, it followed logically that the greatest number should have a direct impact on their political happiness. This meant that the franchise had to expand and that the extent of its expansion was no longer dictated by prudence but rather by the utilitarian expedient of how much Modmen could get away with at any given time.

The English constitution had suspended the sticks and carrots of social influence in fine balance: all estates were represented in the division of power. The people had their interests, if not necessarily their wishes, adequately represented in the House of Commons. The people thus had a defence mechanism they could activate at the slightest threat of tyranny from above. Unfortunately, the liberal principles that lay at the foundation of this constitutional arrangement also had an offensive potential. Modmen, the new group now wielding social and political power, were not about defence: an important part of their reason for being was assault upon Westman. Now that they had made their début on the historical stage they were ready to use parliamentary representation as an aggressive weapon. All they had to do was ensure that their greater numbers would tell and, to achieve that, the franchise had to be pushed towards universality.

These days, people who jealously guard modern democracy against invective miss an important point, which is that they are in fact defending not real democracy but its perversion. Britain, along with other Western countries, has had two democracies, not one. The first belonged to Westman, the second to Modman. The first was genuine, the second, the one still with us today, bogus. The democratic aspect of the English constitution reflected Westman justice and a sense of social balance. Both sprang from the creative nature of Westman who, for all the blunders and crimes he had committed, was out to create a world that would agree with his understanding of God. Modman, on the other hand, is by nature a cultural vandal. He was brought into this world to do away with Westman, a mission of which he is either consciously or viscerally aware. To that end he hijacked the concept of democracy and turned it against Westman. Expanding the franchise *ad nauseam* was the surest way to undo a constitution based on the assumption that voting was a privilege to be earned.

According to Burke, there were in his contemporaneous Britain about 400,000 people qualified to vote. Discounting population growth and Shirley Williams's educational mayhem of the 1960s as two factors cancelling each other out, one could venture a guess that in his view today's number would be roughly similar. Aware that the British electorate today is in fact some 100 times greater than Burke's figure, one fears that perhaps the requirement for proper qualifications has been dropped along the way. This fear is justified, along with the attendant suspicion that democracy is now used for some nefarious purpose and not as an instrument of self-rule.

'One man one vote' is an unconstitutional concept leading automatically to the political dictatorship of the crowd and the inevitable demise of Westman. But, as a slogan, it performed the same useful service for the philistine subspecies of Modman as '*liberté, egalité, fraternité*', '*vsia vlast sovietam*' (all power to the Soviets) and '*ein Volk, ein Reich, ein Führer*' performed for his nihilist brothers. The success of the democratic slogan is largely owed to those good Western people who, unaware that they are victims of an awful trick, cannot find it in their hearts to say anything bad about democracy. When a Modman mocks a Westman holdout by such jibes as 'if you are in favour of ['elitist education', 'curbs on public spending', 'private medical care' or some such], you are against democracy', it takes suicidal courage to say, 'I am only against your kind of democracy. I wouldn't mind returning to the constitutional democratic arrangement the likes of you have perverted.' Few of us are brave enough to fight a losing battle. In the absence of such courage, Modman is unstoppable.

It stands to reason that Bentham was a great champion of the one man one vote system, so it was fitting that he had to die in the year in which the English constitution suffered the crushing blow of the Reform Act. As the blow fell, his followers were making fire-eating speeches on the morality of an expanded franchise. In fact, 1832 was the year when parliament stopped being an instrument designed to protect Westman against arbitrary rule and became instead an instrument of Modman putting his tyrannical foot down. Once the principle, if not yet the practice, of universal franchise became accepted as a moral tenet, Westman no longer had a chance.

Modmen either ignored or pretended to ignore the substance of a parliamentary arrangement in which the function of democracy is to act as a counterbalance to the unelected power of the king and aristocracy. Any accent on substance is of course Western.

Modmen are obsessed with form, and substance has been ceding its positions inch by cowardly inch. Democracy is part of the same obsession, what with Modman's form being consistently used as a weapon against Westman's substance.

An antidote to this political sabotage would be a clear under-standing that no political formation should be an aim in itself. What is important is not method of government but the kind of society it creates. Democracy or any other political technique should be weighed in the balance of our ideals, desires and expec-tations – and judged accordingly. Yet Modman's philistine sub-species denies our right to judge democracy, just as the victorious nihilist banned the right to question Lenin or Hitler. Modmen run it up the pole and salute the democracy of virtually unlimited suffrage with unquestioning devotion, the way Westmen used to worship God. In doing so, Modmen know they are worshipping themselves.

Once again, this devotion reflects the ascendancy of form over substance. Modmen know that the essence of their society would not stand up to scrutiny, so they cling desperately to the outer shell instead. One interesting example of this compulsive formalism is the reaction of both Britain and the USA to the 1999 coup in Pakistan. Both countries felt called upon to pronounce a verdict on that development, Britain because a Commonwealth country was involved, America because, having appointed herself Leader of the Free World, she has to make sanctimonious comments on everything. The politicians of the two countries started out by acknowledging that (a) the overturned government was corrupt, tyrannical and unpopular, (b) the military coup brought in a government that was none of the above and (c) it was just possible that the abrupt change of government may have averted a nuclear war between India and Pakistan. To a sane Westman these reasons would have sufficed if not to welcome the new regime with open arms then at least to give it the benefit of the doubt. But to Modmen any sane arguments that question their tyrannical formalism are taboo, so American and British leaders had to rebuke the new regime for being undemocratic irrespective of anything else. 'We cannot,' said one of them, 'accept that some coups can be better than others.' Why, pray tell, not? One would think that such discernment should be a necessary job qualification for people entrusted with the conduct of foreign policy. Would it not have been wonderful if a coup against, say, the democratically elected Hitler had succeeded in 1938? Fortunately for politicians, people who ask such questions are kept a safe distance away from power.

The situation is getting worse by the minute. Even a mere half century ago Western politicians still tried to refrain from blatantly silly pronouncements. As a hypothetical example, had the 1944 generals' plot against Hitler succeeded, one finds it difficult to imagine the Western leaders of the day reacting as our own contemporaries reacted to the coup in Pakistan. One cannot picture Churchill signing his name to a communiqué that said something like:

> We must moderate our joy over the recent events in Germany. Admittedly, it is difficult to deny that Herr Hitler was an implacable enemy of this country and her allies. Moreover, we are none of us unaware of the crimes his regime has perpetrated and the misery it has caused. The incoming government has already declared cessation of hostilities against the Allies, and obviously we, along with our peoples, welcome peace. At the same time, we must not lose sight of the fact that, unlike the military junta that has ousted it, Herr Hitler's government was democratically elected. Therefore, we cannot welcome the generals' plot unequivocally. In fact, we denounce it for the denial of the democratic principles HMG is here to uphold.

Let us extricate ourselves from this thrall of democratic form for a moment and ask a subversive question: so what kind of society do we wish to result from political process? Westman holdouts might argue about this, but most will probably settle on four essential attributes: justice, liberty, security and stability. At the same time, intellectual honesty compels one to admit that, if queried, most of the same hypothetical people are likely to express the conviction that democracy of universal suffrage is the best, some will say the only, realistic route to these desirable ends. In Anglo-Saxon countries today this belief drinks from a cultural rather than political, brook and cuts across the entire red-to-white political mainstream. And of course Anglo-Saxon possessions are cherished by Modmen the world over, along with McDonald's, Coke, pop music and verbs made out of nouns.

That is why 'democracy' is proudly emblazoned in the constitutions of such contrasting nations as Denmark and the Korean People's Democratic Republic. Both Lars and Lee feel that democratic is the thing to be. They have forgotten to go through the requisite weighing exercise mentioned earlier, a forgivable oversight in Lee who does not really mean 'democratic' and a lamentable one in Lars who ought to know better. Refusing to succumb to this amnesia, one returns to the scale of desired attributes only to find Modman democracy wanting.

Before we do anything else, it is important to strip unlimited democracy of its non-partisan mask. Unlike the limited democracies of Hellenic antiquity and Westman polity, universal suffrage is a radical idea that came to the fore after Modmen pronounced man to be good to begin with and, what is more, infinitely perfectible. It followed ineluctably that good and further improvable people, all of them, are equally qualified to choose their leaders and govern themselves. It also followed that any other form of government was unthinkable. As mentioned earlier, once Modmen elevated universal suffrage to secular sainthood, active opposition to it became impossible in the West. Even timidly expressing reservations about this kind of democracy was becoming increasingly more difficult. However, Lord Acton was to remark that the main conflict during the French Revolution was 'a great struggle between democracy and liberty,' thus implying that the two words Modmen insist on uttering in the same breath might be mutually exclusive. Acton sensed that arbitrary power, whether vested in prince or people, is always tyranny.

The eighteenth century, with its demolition of religion, deprived governments of an eschatological aspect. But other redemptive creeds were bound to appear so as to fill the vacuum. In the nineteenth century democracy elevated Modman to a god-like status and gave him a DIY technique for expiating secular sin. The *philosophes*, abetted by British empiricists, had even managed to weave scientific threads into the democratic promise, presenting democracy as a social answer to the scientific revolution of the seventeenth century – a trick that was to stand both socialists and communists in good stead. Socialism and communism, Modman's other redemptive creeds, are unlimited democracy's first cousins once removed; they activated the same response mechanisms marching in parallel with democracy and just a step behind. Like universal suffrage, both are weapons in Modman's armoury. Socialism is democracy with logic; communism is socialism with nerve. All such beliefs spring from a characteristic liberal ignorance of and contempt for human nature – a condition disguised by incessant encomiums on the goodness of man.

Democracy of universal suffrage, as the very etymology of the word suggests, is almost as pregnant with mendacity as is communism. 'Democracy' implies the promise of self-government and the premise that such an organizational arrangement will *ipso facto* preclude tyranny, which is simply not so, as the democratically elected Messrs Hitler, Perón, Mugabe, Putin and Macîas Nguema (who gratefully murdered a third of the population of Equatorial Guinea that had voted him in) could have testified. It also implies that sovereign power rests with the people. Yet Modman 'democracies', along with their ultimate supranational extensions, today never tire of demonstrating how far this is from the truth. Witness the travesty involving the democratically held referenda in Denmark, Austria and Ireland a few years ago. In the first instance the Danes rejected the Maastricht Treaty; in the second Austria voted in Herr Haider who may or may not be unsavoury; in the third the people of Ireland voted not to ratify the Treaty of Nice on the enlargement of the EU. In all three instances the European Union, that great champion of pooled democracy, put its foot down and the boot in. People's choice is all fine and well provided it is the choice Modmen favour at the moment. Otherwise people will have to choose again – and keep choosing until they get it right.

Neither is unlimited democracy a particularly time-honoured creed. The word 'democracy' in both Greece and Rome had no one man one vote implications and Plato used it in the meaning of 'mob rule'. The American founding fathers never used it at all and neither did Lincoln. But towards the end of the nineteenth century the word gained a little currency as the more intelligent Modmen found it a useful smoke screen, while the more gullible among them actually believed the implicit promise. But in reality the promise of democracy is larcenous when democracy is unchecked by the power of other estates. By atomizing the vote into millions of particles, democracy renders each individual vote meaningless. What has any weight at all is an aggregate of votes, a faceless impersonal bloc. Consequently, political success in democracies depends not on any concern for the good of the people but on the ability to put such blocs together. This has little to do with statesmanship. Coming to the fore instead are such qualities as disloyalty, a knack for demagoguery, photogenic appearance, absence of constraining principles, ability to tell lies with convincing ease, cold disregard for *bono publico*, selfishness and an unquenchable quest for power at any cost – all typically, though not exclusively, Modman traits.

When these qualities succeed the newly elected leaders fear they will be found out, so they strive to put some serious acreage between themselves and the people who have elected them. They seek to remove every remaining bit of power from the local bodies that stay close to the voters and to transfer it to the centralized Leviathan, claiming all the time that the people are governing themselves. Thus, expanded franchise inevitably leads to greater centralization and, for that reason, it is wrong to complain, as today's conservatives often do, that growing centralization undermines democracy. It is like saying that pregnancy undermines sex.

While perpetrating centralization run riot, the ostensibly democratic but in fact Modman-tyrannical state acquires more power over the individual than any monarch who ruled by divine right ever saw in his dreams. French subjects, for example, were shielded from Louis XIV by several layers of local government and the Sun King wielded more power over his loftiest courtiers than over the lowliest peasants. The King was aware of this and his famous pronouncement on the nature of the state fell more into the realm of wishful thinking than reportage. By contrast, a freely voting French citizen or British subject of today has every aspect of his life controlled, or at least monitored, by a central government in whose actions he has little say. He meekly hands over half his income knowing that the only result of this transfer will be an increase in the state's power to extort even more. Clutching the few remaining notes he hopes that Leviathan, no longer athirst, will let him keep them for his family. He opens his papers to find yet again that the 'democratic' state has dealt him a blow, be that of destroying his children's education, raising his taxes, devastating the army that protects him, closing his local hospital or letting murderers go free. In short, if one defines liberty as a condition that best enables the individual to exercise his freedom of choice, then democracy of universal suffrage is remiss on that score.

And neither is understated liberty the price Modmen pay for security. Unlimited democracy, whose penchant for aggressive statism is predetermined both historically and psychologically, has demonstrated time and again its chronic inability to avoid murderous wars – or at least to win them quickly once they become unavoidable. This was proved in the twentieth century, the first in which Modmen ruled supreme from beginning to end. Westman democracy, already reeling in the run-up to that fateful century, died as it unfolded. With its congenital mendacity, Modman democracy tried to pass defeat for victory, even as Robespierre and Danton had tried to convince the French that martial law was liberty. Modmen refuse to admit that the 'victory' in the first big war of the century empowered two satanic creeds, while the second delivered half the world to one of them.

Ever since unlimited democracy achieved the public-relations status of the only possible alternative to tyranny, hundreds of millions have died violent deaths (a number that includes victims of crime that democracies are unable to combat). Universal suffrage implies universal military service, a fact that is at least as responsible as technological advances for the amount of blood spilled in modern wars. If medieval kings had to beg their vassals to spare a few men for the army, today's democracies can simply conscript the entire population if they so wish and prosecute anyone who refuses to join up. Still, conscription would be just if defence of the realm were the issue at stake. But Modman democracy is not about defence of the realm, which after all is one of the few legitimate functions of government. It is about manipulating votes here and now. No Modman politician is capable of thinking beyond the next election he realistically expects to win; few Modman voters are capable of thinking beyond the quiet comfort of today.

Giving people the vote was easy; teaching them to cast it in an enlightened and responsible fashion has proved impossible in conditions of universal suffrage. As a result, Modmen of the philistine variety have got to a point where they see nothing as worth dying for. This means that the next time their nihilist brothers fancy a bit of fratricide, the philistines are unlikely to find the backbone to fight – unless they feel that fighting is the only way to preserve their comfort. Any other concession, including independence, would be proffered with alacrity, unless of course the philistines could pay other nihilists to do their fighting for them. Rome had this kind of arrangement with the vandals and we all know what happened in the end. So much for security.

And unlimited democracy does not provide stability, quite the opposite. One can argue that the democratic body politic carries the gene of instability, even as it is forever plagued by the demons of *ad infinitum* centralization. Here too, this most factional of political systems suffers from the heredity of its liberal mother and radical father. That is why democracy infinitely gravitates towards social democracy (a euphemism for socialism that in itself is a euphemism for the dictatorship of Modman), leaving little room for conservatism, which is a popular but imprecise word for Westman politics. Looking at the three major European democracies of today, Britain, France and Germany, it would be hard to argue that democracy is a factor of political stability. In a mere century Britain has gone from being a constitutional empire to being a non-constitutional crypto-republican province of the European Union, France from being an international power to being first a part of Germany and then its junior partner, and Germany – well, we all know about her. Having started the twentieth century by keeping some vestiges of Westernnness, the glorious trio ended it as a set of snuff movies starring Westman as the principal attraction.

Modmen, helped along by utilitarianism, have created a situation wherein it is no longer possible to look at a society and ask not 'is it democratic?' but 'is it just?' Modmen do not ask this question because their founding impulse propels them not towards justice but towards creating conditions for humiliating Westman. Justice has no meaning in the absence of the concepts of absolute virtue and sin, and these concepts were the first casualties of the rape of religion adumbrated by the *philosophes* and welcomed by the utilitarians. Secular justice is by definition both relativist and casuistic. It is the former because exactly what constitutes justice becomes a matter of opinion. It is the latter because laws designed by fallible men seem these days to contain the entire concept of justice. So they cannot be expressed in simple language conveying eternal truths. Instead, Modmen have to wrap their regulations into layers of arcane jargon, reducing justice to protracted attempts at making heads or tails of self-perpetuating cant. What transpires as a result is a mocking perversion of justice.

Now, a mere two centuries after the victory of secularism, Modmen do not cringe when served up 'social justice', for example. In fact, 'social justice' is nothing but levelling, which is about as opposite to justice as one can get. Economic levelling is not economic justice; social levelling is not social justice; political levelling is not political justice. They are, however, as natural to Modman democracy as envy is to man.

GETTING DOWN TO BUSINESS

'Honour sinks when commerce long prevails.'
(O. Goldsmith)

Like any other modern revolution, the Industrial Revolution of the nineteenth century exacted a heavy toll on Westman, the sociocultural type that until then had been struggling to retain its weakening hold on power.

To borrow Lenin's term – and one should always learn from experts – the beginning of the century was marked by the presence of a 'revolutionary situation' wherein the upper classes could not and the lower would not live in the old way. In other words, Westman was losing his nerve while the impassioned Modman was spoiling for a fight. His philistine subspecies found the economy to be a perfect battlefield for carrying the fight to the enemy. Not that the social potential of financial success had ever been lost on people before. Throughout history, wealthy merchants had bought their way to social success, which used to be defined as leaving one's humble beginnings behind and joining the ranks of what here we call Westmen.

The class of gentlemen was formed by the part of the aristocracy that was not off limits to newcomers and by the socially mobile and talented members of other classes. For many who were just below the gentlemen's class it provided an aspiration. Those even further down the social scale may not have desired any cultural prizes, but they did want to make money. When they succeeded, they had to jump on the cultural bandwagon willy-nilly. Thus, upward social mobility always included a similarly vectored cultural component. For the reverse to become the case, Modman first had to vanquish.

The internal barbarian always realized that money could have a civilizing effect on him possibly, on his children definitely. In Western society, the internal barbarian was likely to regard such a development as desirable. Even if Westman culture had no value for him as such, in a society whose terms were set by Westmen culture could act as a social hoist. Therefore a would-be Westman could swallow his pride and merely seethe inside at the snide putdowns in which the less intelligent Westmen indulged. He knew his money was as good as theirs, or even better for being younger and more vigorous. Sooner or later he would join their ranks either directly or vicariously through his progeny. If he had to spend millions on their charities towards that end, then so be it.

Westman's ethos, when it was still dominant, was impelling internal barbarians to better themselves by adding cultural self-elevation to either martial valour or business acumen. It also steered them towards abandoning their usual selfishness and acting in a manner consistent with Westman ethics. Great charities, hospitals, universities, museums and opera houses were endowed by internal barbarians seeking to become Westmen. They had picked themselves up by the bootstraps and placed themselves firmly amidst a culture they had hitherto seen as hostile. That required a massive effort, but then so does any achievement worth having. Not many internal barbarians were willing to make such an effort, but the few who were joined Westmen and were greeted if not exactly with open arms then at least with equanimity. Here we are more interested in those who instead joined the ranks of victorious Modmen when an opportunity presented itself.

This opportunity goes in history by the name of the Industrial Revolution. As it gathered speed, fewer and fewer Modmen felt like bettering themselves in Westman ways. Modman middle classes were appearing, and they were able to satisfy both their philistine and nihilist cravings without having first to adopt Westman cultural values. Eventually, Westman ways stopped being seen as a factor of social betterment. When that happened, self-made fortunes stopped being a factor of Westman prosperity. Instead, like democracy, they became ammunition for the guns levelled at Westman.

Modman democracy has many things in common with Modman economic activity. Both are driven by impassioned men able to manipulate great numbers of people devoid of such passions. Both are held to be off limits for criticism by Westman holdouts, especially by those who were politically active when free enterprise was a popular target in intellectual slinging matches. Say anything at all against free enterprise, and suddenly the good people who used to man the anti-collectivist trenches start looking at one the way lions used to look at pious Christians. A natural response, as in the case of democracy, would be to remind them that to Westmen substance ought to be more valuable than form. What is important is not how an economy runs itself but what it achieves, and at what social and cultural cost.

As with many aspects of life, including democracy, Modmen have contrived to retain some formal features of free enterprise while falsifying its substance. As with democracy, it is not the substance that is worth criticizing but the modern perversion of it. Like democracy that tends to self-destruct as it expands, free enterprise has a potential for becoming less free as it gets bigger. And, in common with democracy, free enterprise is not God who possesses an intrinsic and absolute moral value. It should therefore be open to a worldly exegesis. To be sure, before Westman became a museum exhibit, free enterprise had had a positive moral content, mostly by virtue of not being its opposite negative. As most have now learnt, an economy wholly planned by the political state is a slave economy that has to include labour camps as an unavoidable component. Moreover, this kind of economy is bound to fail – a theoretical postulate proved in every country where command economy has been tried in earnest. But the fact that command economy is invariably bad does not make free enterprise invariably good. Just because the opposite of it is monstrous, free enterprise does not automatically become some-thing it is not – a charity. Yet, if one listens to conservative economists from von Mises and Hayek to Friedman and Gilder, one realizes that is exactly what they are saying. This is, crudely, how their argument goes (paraphrasing is quicker than a direct quote from George Gilder's *Wealth and Poverty* would be):

> The starting point of free enterprise is a charitable act, not unlike giving a Christmas present. The entrepreneur has to guess what the recipients will want and invest his money to get it for them. But it will remain a guess, for no investor can be sure that the supply he is creating will find a demand. To be sure, he expects something in return for his outlay, but then so does the bearer of Christmas gifts. The latter goes out every year and spends what in Britain is a silly amount of money on mostly useless trinkets, expecting to receive his fair share of useless trinkets in return. But the return is uncertain as he can never be sure that his generosity will be reciprocated in kind. He may offer a bottle of sweet sherry (retail price £5.97 at an outlet near you) and receive a miserly pack of flower-patterned paper napkins (retail value £2.56 at a corner 'shoppe'). His investment has thus produced a net loss of £3.41 and can be described as a 60 per cent charitable act. Moreover, the recipient of his alms may pour that stuff

down the sink, telling himself that no one who drinks such a beverage can ever be his friend again. So the hapless charity worker cum investor will not even be able to recoup his outlay next year.

Similarly, an entrepreneur who, say, plans to open yet another Indian restaurant has to spend thousands of his own money plus frequently tens of thousands of someone else's on what essentially is a gift, for he has no way of knowing that the market is not already saturated with Indian restaurants to a point where the locals will stay away in droves. And just as the bearer of Christmas gifts secretly hopes to receive a more valuable gift in return, so does the entrepreneur hope to be rewarded for his generosity in the future, but fears he may not be. His enterprise thus represents a selfless act that places him in the ranks of secular saints.

This line of thought doubtless makes sense to Modmen, especially those who have read Ayn Rand. They are, after all, more interested in form than in substance, and in utility than in morals. In fact, utility for them has a moral dimension and, because they know free enterprise has utilitarian value, they seek morality in what essentially is a morally neutral, which is to say amoral, activity. They are seeking in vain. For, as a Westman would know, the motive behind an act is more important than the consequences. Judging the value of an act solely by its result means taking the moral aspect out completely, which is tantamount to regressing to what Nietzsche called 'pre-moral times'.

Utilitarianism constitutes such a regression. It perverts Westman morality according to which the origin of an act makes its result morally irrelevant. A maniac who fires indiscriminately at a crowd is a murderer even if, unbeknown to him, the only people he hits are child molesters. By the same token, a man who jumps from a bridge into the river to save a drowning woman is a hero even if he accidentally lands on the woman, breaking her neck. Thus an entrepreneur whose motive is self-interest is, at best, committing a morally neutral act. 'At best' are the operative words here, for entrepreneurs are seldom reluctant to push the laws governing their activities to breaking point. Superficially, a successful businessman finds himself in a situation similar to that of the erstwhile Westman. He too is at the numerically disadvantaged end of a socially pregnant dichotomy, fighting rearguard action against the advancing masses. But since the rewards he is after are purely material, his *modus operandi* is different. Westmen genuinely cared about those less fortunate and, when they remembered, tried to improve their lot as best they could, hoping they would be rewarded in eternity. The Modman entrepreneur is driven by a selfish need to feather his nest as much as he can and, since his life still has to end at around three score years and ten, as quickly as possible. That goes a long way towards explaining the lamentable decline in charitable donations throughout the Western world.

To be sure, even as the Westman ethos pushed his ancestor, the internal barbarian, into civilized behaviour, the Modman entrepreneur is pushed by the utility he deifies into what may look like charity to the uninitiated – hence his attempts to attenuate profit-busting industrial unrest by social-security schemes, reasonable wages, pension plans and what have you. But Modman's utilitarian ethos is different from Westman's ethos, for it is devoid of moral content and so does not produce irreversible personality changes for the better. Thus, the same entrepreneur who had the foresight to turn his workers into his market by paying them $5 a day (a seemingly charitable act at the time) could use his gains to support both satanic creeds of twentieth-century modernity.

While Henry Ford was not the only major businessman who helped either Hitler or Stalin or both, his is a more interesting case than most. In his public persona Ford was and still is regarded by American conservatives as one of them. This political tag presupposes the championing of traditional values and individual liberty in the face of collectivist oppression. And sure enough, in his public pronouncements Henry Ford did come across as holier than James Madison – if one overlooked the rabid anti-Semitism immortalized in his robust pamphlet *The International Jew*. But even if one adopted a 'boys will be boys' attitude to the anti-Semitism of such leading business figures as Ford and J. P. Morgan, one still should not be too hasty in letting them get away with a claim to conservatism. A slight delay should be caused not by what they said but by what they did – always the more reliable sign, especially with men of action.

Ford had been financing Hitler's movement since before the *putsch*, which was first reported by the *New York Times* in December 1922. In recognition of this support Hitler had a wall of his private office decorated with a portrait of Ford. In 1928 Ford merged his German holdings with I. G. Farben, a chemical cartel that also financed Hitler from the start and whose impressive product range later included the custom-made Zyklon B gas for the needs of Germany's growth industry. Ford's holdings in Europe prospered during the war, thanks in part to extensive use of free labour generously supplied by Auschwitz. In 1938 Henry Ford was awarded the Grand Cross of the German Eagle, the highest Nazi decoration for foreigners, which, incidentally, Francisco Franco had turned down. But Ford's greatest reward was the opportunity to profit from the war on both sides of the conflict. His plants in Germany and France assisted the Nazi war effort as much as his Detroit facilities helped the Allies. The war was to Ford an opportunity, not a threat. There is even evidence that the US Air Force spared American holdings in Germany, including Ford's factories. The RAF Bomber Command operating against targets in France was either not party to that arrangement or else Sir Arthur Harris got carried away, but in March 1942 the RAF hit the Ford plant at Poissy. Justice was done, however, when the Vichy government paid Ford 38 million francs in compensation, with profuse apologies for having been lax in their anti-aircraft defences.

Lest one may accuse Ford of playing favourites, in 1929 he signed an assistance agreement with another champion of free enterprise, Stalin's Russia. This agreement culminated in 1931 when Ford's Gorky plant was completed. While known to every Russian as the maker of GAZ lorries, it is also known for its true military output to those who are aware of the real function of such factories in Soviet Russia. Also in 1929 the Americans built the Stalingrad 'tractor' factory, then the largest manufacturer of tanks in Europe. The entire facility was built as modules in the United States, transported across the Atlantic and re-erected in Stalingrad by American and German technicians. Later, again with American help, the Stalingrad plant was cloned in Cheliabinsk and Kharkov.

It is generally believed that businessmen like Ford or Morgan, who financed both the Bolsheviks and the Nazis, were atypical. In fact, the opposite is true. That is why it is pointless to ask why oh why questions along the lines of why did Henry Ford and his son Edsel, both political conservatives and American patriots, build factories in Russia that produced the armoured cars and personnel carriers used in Korea and Vietnam to help kill 100,000 Americans? Or why did American businesses in general, most of which are run by 'conservatives', build up the Soviet Union's military machine, which then cost the American taxpayer billions of dollars to counteract and which still may not have said its last word? Such questions are pointless because Modman business is not only amoral but also apolitical. Regardless of what beliefs businessmen profess in their spare time, during office hours they will act according to the inner logic of their profession. This can be demonstrated empirically by talking to businessmen or financiers. The more educated of them will joyously chat on any subject under the sun, from politics to baroque orchestras to existential philosophy. But the second the conversation veers towards money, levity gives way to gravity. The businessman's jaw tightens, his eyes begin to reflect steely resolve and his sense of humour disappears. One senses that this subject is real life while everything else is a game. In today's America, where most people are businessmen even if their business is philology or some such, one will observe this phenomenon when talking not just to merchants but also to painters or economists.

The latter have acquired tremendous prestige, which is incomprehensible, for economics is a dubious science. Science goes beyond common sense; economics does not, or at least should not. People in general are useless at grasping the difference between Glenn Gould and Evgeni Kissin, but they are fairly good at making money – provided they are left alone and allowed to get on with it. Economic casuistry only comes into play when people are not allowed to get on with it, when the political state steps in and chops Adam Smith's 'hidden hand' off at the wrist. The state has no common sense of its own and its usual contribution to the economy is to override other people's for political reasons. By taking common sense out of distribution of business gains and, often, out of such essential controls as prices and wages, the state destroys the natural cycle. This creates muddy waters in which economists can then fish, using their computer models as rods. Instead of merely describing the way people make a living, economics becomes an arena for a political free-for-all, providing a nice comfortable battleground. It is part of modern reductionism wherein a complex phenomenon is boiled down to a few sloganable shibboleths. Delving deep into the real conflict of modernity leads to uncomfortable thoughts, impossible for an establishment insider to get away with or indeed to conceive. It is easier to reduce it all to a polarity of free enterprise versus command economy and chant, along with Orwell's animals, 'free good, command bad!' or vice versa. The debating parties can thus stay within the comfort zone of Modmen. This also makes labelling easy, and Modmen love labels because they obviate the need for real thinking. Thus Margaret Thatcher, a Whiggish radical who did not have a conservative bone in her body and who in all her years at the helm did little to promote the cultural cause of Westman, proudly wore the tag of a conservative. This was made possible by her championing of free enterprise. Somehow those who hail 'Maggie' as the conservative standard bearer ignore the unconservative things for which she is responsible: the Single European Act, the leasehold law, failure to arrest the collapse of education first as education secretary (when she closed down more grammar schools than any 'left-winger' ever did) and then as prime minister, a steady growth of public spending and real taxation with the concomitant increase in the state's power.

Supporters of free enterprise *über alles* would be well advised to take a broader look at society. This would enable them to see that although competitive free enterprise may be a necessary condition for civilized society, it is certainly not a sufficient one. For one thing, unlike conservative economists, men at the cutting edge of free enterprise do not believe in competition. Quite the opposite, they would like to nip it in the bud by bankrupting every business but their own. A free entrepreneur *par excellence* can exist today only in a start-up mode, or else at the level of a corner sandwich shop. Once his business has become successful, his thoughts gravitate towards putting an end to competitive activity. He wants to put competition out of business. At that end of economic thought he is greeted with a fraternal embrace by his brother the democratic bureaucrat who, for his part, used to believe in pluralism while he was clawing his way up the party ladder. Now he has reached the top, pluralism means only one thing to him: a threat to his position. The modern brothers instantly recognize their kinship and have no difficulty in striking a corporatist partnership.

Free enterprise in the West today occupies about the same slot as it did in Lenin's Russia during the New Economic Policy (NEP). Faced with economic collapse and mounting famines, Lenin allowed most of the service industries as well as some small-scale manufacturing ones to go private. But what he described as the 'commanding heights of the economy', which is to say banks, heavy industry, foreign trade, large-scale manufacturing, exploration and control of the natural resources, remained firmly in the hands of the Bolsheviks. Replace 'Bolsheviks' with 'the bureaucratic corporatist elite' and today's situation in the West is not a million miles away. For all the Sherman Acts and Monopolies Commissions in the world, big business has to gravitate towards monopoly – one of the few things Marx got right. That is, he was right in his observation but not in his explanation. The capitalist wants to achieve a monopoly so as to oppress not so much his economic inferiors as his cultural superiors. A Modman businessman has a psychological need to achieve total control of his market in the same way and for the same reasons as a Modman politician wishes to achieve total control of his flock. Class has no role to play here – one of the many things Marx got wrong. Modman prays at the altar of uniformity and melts down any class differences until they are reduced to quaint idiosyncrasies: modernity tends to gravitate towards an amorphous middle. In today's Britain, for example, the differences between 'the proles' and 'the toffs' seldom go deeper than the number of buttons on their jackets.

What drives the modern 'free' businessman towards monopoly is the same utilitarian impulse that paradoxically drives many aristocrats towards socialism: they know that putting the clamps on the socially dynamic strata of the population will prevent any serious competition appearing. Here the entrepreneur's longings converge with those of his employees who tend to act as a collectivist bloc. Their motivation is old-fashioned envy coupled with the deep-seated belief that it is possible for some to rise only at the expense of others falling. By the same token, the ruling bureaucracy has a vested interest in keeping businesses as large, and consequently as few, as possible for this will make control easier and more total. In short, the only people who do believe in free enterprise are big businessmen waiting to happen, those who are still climbing towards the summit and do not want their rope cut. Once they have got to the top they will realize the error of their ways and start acting accordingly.

Another dynamic at work here is a tendency towards the global-
ization of business closely mirroring a similar trend in Modman
politics. Like Modman life in general, business tends to lose its
national roots. In the absence of protectionist tariffs, known to be
counter-productive at least since the time of David Ricardo, an
aspiration to monopoly drives a big business towards foreign
expansion *ad infinitum*, which is another form of protectionism
but one that does not provoke retaliation in kind. This megalomania, along with a tendency to dissipate ownership by financing
expansion through stock market flotation, leads to a situation
where 'free enterprise' becomes neither. The 'capitalist', Marx's
bogeyman, is eliminated in philistine Modman societies as
efficiently as he used to be shot in nihilist ones. Most international
corporations are neither run nor controlled by capitalists, if we
define the breed as the owners of capital (or of 'the means of
production'). That type, rather than having been created by the
Industrial Revolution, was killed by it, albeit by delayed action.
Today's captains of industry do not necessarily own the capital of
which they dispose, and they do not live or die by their success or
failure. The risks they venture are usually taken with other
people's money and they stand to gain untold fortunes by achieving success, while personally risking next to nothing in case of
failure. If they fail they take the king's ransom of redundancy and
either move on to the next bonanza or, should they so choose,
retire to a paradise of philistine comfort.

Qualities required for a rise through modern corporations are
different from those needed in the early stages of the Industrial
Revolution. They are, however, close to those required for careers
in government bureaucracies. This is partly due to the growing
disparity between the ever-expanding outlook of the management
and the ever-narrowing outlook of the specialists who make the
products. In the old days, someone who designed bridges could
advance to the next rung in his company by demonstrating ability.
Once he got there, he continued to design bridges, but with added

responsibilities. People at the top rung would thus be of the same stock as those several steps below, although their duties would be different. This is not so for modern corporations. Growing specialization creates a different situation: the people in production represent a different breed from those in the boardroom. The latter are hardly ever drawn from the former. Most leaders of giant modern corporations come from legal, sales or marketing rather than manufacturing backgrounds. Curiously, when Marx wrote *Das Kapital*, the gulf between workers and management could still be bridged by hard work and ingenuity. The industrial conditions imagined by Marx were in fact a self-fulfilling prophecy: it is only when some of his ideas were acted upon that an unbridgeable chasm appeared between the corporatist management and the narrowly specialized labour force.

Even as the governments of philistine modernity grow more corporatist so tautologically do actual corporations. A new elite is thus formed and it is a homogeneous group whose members are indistinguishable from one another regardless of whether their original background was business or politics. Witness the ease with which they switch from the corporate to the government arena and back, especially if they come from the international end of either (George W. Bush's cabinet provided a few examples). The spiritual father of the breed was Walter Rathenau, managing director of AEG in Germany in the 1920s. One of the leading theoreticians and practitioners of corporate socialism, he prophesied that, 'The new economy will ... be ... a private economy [which] will require state cooperation for organic consolidation to overcome inner friction and increase production and endurance.' Here was the original politician cum businessman, and there was poetic justice when he was murdered in 1922, 11 years before his dream became a reality in Germany, and by the same people who made it so.

As their budgets begin to rival Belgium's GNP, international corporations forge even closer links with financial institutions: the latter form part of the corporatist government world not just by inclination but by statute, having to forge a unity with the quasi-independent setups that control the money supply. Organizations like the Federal Reserve, European Bank, the Bank of England, Deutsche Bank and Banque de France are more independent of their national governments than they are of one another. Like Modman businessmen and politicians, they do not feel they owe loyalty to their people, much less to any moral principles. Their loyalty is pledged to the international elite that increasingly supersedes national interests.

It is instructive to follow the history of the Federal Reserve, for example. From inception, its executives have operated to achieve ends that only ever overlapped with American interests by coincidence. One sees people who were to become key figures in the Federal Reserve financing Lenin both before and after his takeover, assisting in Trotsky's passage from New York to Russia, helping Hitler out of a tight spot or two, and helping the Nazis design their New Order and Roosevelt his New Deal. Incidentally, the participation of some of the same individuals in formulating those programmes may partly explain their striking similarity. Three figures are particularly interesting. One is Gerard Swope of General Electric (a company closely involved at the time in assisting both the Bolsheviks and Nazis) who more or less formulated Roosevelt's New Deal policy while sitting on the board of AEG, the German subsidiary of GE and one of the principal backers of Hitler. Another is Paul Warburg of the Federal Reserve Bank of New York who was on the board of the American I. G. Farben, while his brother Max sat on the German board of the same company. And then there was Walter Teagle, also of the Federal Reserve Bank of New York, chairman of Standard Oil of New Jersey, the company whose German subsidiary Deutsche-Amerikanische Gesellschaft had intimate links with the Nazis. This known Nazi sympathizer was one of the principal authors of FDR's New Deal package and also acted as economic consultant to the authors of Hitler's New Order. When Herbert Hoover referred to the New Deal as a 'fascist measure', he may have meant not just the nature of this policy but also its architects.

All this should not come as a surprise. Supranational corporations and other international organizations, unburdened by moral concerns, adore statism. To them, a big omnipotent state represents not tyranny but economies of scale. It is for this reason, for example, that Western philistine states try so hard to put small farmers out of business. Those chaps are too independent for their own good. The bureaucrats who run huge agribusinesses are more likely to toe the line, even if they do make us all eat tasteless, chemical-laden stuff. The bigger the state's substructure, the more the state likes it.

THE FALSE PROPHET

'Marx's teaching is omnipotent because it is true.'

(V. I. Lenin)

The philistine subspecies of Modman gathered power throughout the Industrial Revolution by attacking Western society's cultural and social fabric. A population explosion made the job easier. Europe's population tripled in the century demarcated by Waterloo at one end and Verdun at the other. The numbers game was stacked against Westman, as the demographic shift was placing him in an ever-dwindling minority. However, the shift was not just demographic but also geographic. The demands of a growing industry were drawing more and more people out of the countryside, Westman's natural habitat, and into the burgeoning cities, whose sprawling anonymity made Modmen feel at ease. Political power, thanks to expanding suffrage, was also shifting away from Westman.

The nihilist subspecies was beginning to do as well during the Industrial Revolution as its philistine relation. Both were helped along by Marx, the first deliberately, the second inadvertently.

While rejecting the revolutionary content of Marxism, philistine Modmen were ready to welcome some of its assumptions: the primacy of matter and the all-conquering significance of the economy vindicated the basis of modernity. Marx's portrayal of social life as a product of struggle among hostile classes also struck a chord with the philistines who were Modmen after all. Their deep-seated resentments had found an updated intellectual base. They had been shown a clear path to social advancement that did not require a dedicated effort to join Western culture. A class structure based on people's relation to the 'means of production' made it easy: just make money and up the class ladder you climb. The philistine was acquiring a springboard to social elevation by simply being good at making a living. That is why, even though the fallacy of Marxist economics has been amply demonstrated, in countries run by philistine Modmen many of the Marxist assumptions still persevere. Most Englishmen in particular accept the class view of society as a given. This leads them up more garden paths than one finds in the Hampton Court maze. The lost souls become confused when someone like the multi-millionaire Alan Sugar describes himself as 'working class' or when someone like John Major (a Conservative prime minister!) talks about the delights of classless society. Conversely, those with titles but without two pennies to rub together do not sit comfortably at the top of a pyramid resting on the 'means of production'.

Had philistine Modmen read Marx instead of relying on politicized mouthpieces they would have known that the central doctrines of Marxism were false even at the time of writing. Marx wrote for political not intellectual ends, so he showed the way for many a Modman politician by suppressing data that contradicted his theories. For example, the first edition of *Das Kapital* gives most statistics up to 1865 or 1866, except those for the changes in wages that stop in 1850. The second edition brings all other statistics up to date, but the movement of wages again stops in 1850. Any serious study will demonstrate that Marx based his theories on industrial conditions that either were already obsolete at the time or had never existed in the first place. That is no wonder, for Marx never saw the inside of a factory, farm or manufactory. However, the point about Marx's selective treatment of facts is only worth making because of all the numerous claims to scientific truth made by, and for, him. Whatever else he was, Marx was not a scientist. He was not after truth, and all his writings were designed for one purpose: to stab a venomous sting into Westman's heart. In this he was so successful that both subspecies of Modman still live off his legacy to some extent.

Whatever service Marx provided for the philistine was unintended. It was the nihilist who stood to gain most from Marx's theories. For Marx gave the nihilist something he had been sorely missing: an eschatology to fit his instincts. Extermination of Westman could now be put on an intellectual footing. While the kingdom in heaven had been debunked beyond a comeback, the kingdom on earth was at last described in detail. Marx went one better than the likes of More, Campanella, Fourier and Owen by creating a utopia that did not look utopian. His ideal society appeared to be there for the taking, however long that took to achieve. It was a utopia nonetheless, but one put together with more thoroughness than any of his predecessors had been able to muster.

Since for 70-odd years the most formidable propaganda machine in history was dedicated to spreading Marxism, many feel they know what Marx is all about without having to resort to the primary source. That is a pity, for if more people had actually read the *Communist Manifesto* one hopes there would be fewer innocents who echo Modman propaganda by saying that Marx's ideals were wonderful but regrettably unachievable; or else that Marx's theory was perverted by Soviet practice. In fact, Marx's ideals are unachievable precisely because they are so monstrous that even the Bolsheviks never quite managed to realize them fully, and not for any lack of trying.

For example, the *Manifesto* (along with other writings by both Marx and Engels) prescribes the nationalization of all private property without exception. Even Stalin's Russia in the 1930s fell short of that ideal. In fact, a good chunk of the Soviet economy was then in private hands (small agricultural holdings, repair shops, construction and other co-ops and some medical care). And people were allowed to own cottages, flats, clothes on their backs, radio sets, pigeon coops, tools – really, compared with Marx, Stalin begins to look like a humanitarian. Marx also insisted that family should be done away with, with women becoming communal property. Again, for all their efforts, Lenin and Stalin never quite managed to achieve this ideal either, much to the regret of those Russians who could see an amorous payoff in such an arrangement. Then, according to the *Manifesto*, children were to be taken away from their parents, pooled together and raised by the state as its wards. That too remained a dream for the Bolsheviks who tried to make it a reality by forcing both parents to work, and leaving no place for their children to go but the state-owned crèches, kindergartens and young pioneers' camps. But that was as far as it went: kindergartens and young pioneers' camps were not compulsory, and those fortunate women who could get by without full-time employment were still free to read Pushkin to their children.

Modern slave labour, such an endearing feature of both Soviet Russia and Nazi Germany, also derives from Marx – and again Lenin, Stalin and Hitler displayed a great deal of weak-kneed liberalism in bringing his ideas to fruition. Marx, after all, wrote about the total militarization of labour to be achieved by organizing it into 'labour armies', presumably led by Marx as *generalissimo* and Engels as chief of the general staff. Stalin came closer to this than Hitler, but again fell short. No more than 10 per cent of Soviet citizens were ever in enforced labour at the same time. The rest still could more or less choose their professions and for some it was even possible to choose their place of employment.

The only aspect of Bolshevism and Nazism that came close to fulfilling the Marxist dream was what Engels described as 'specially guarded places' to contain the likes of aristocrats, the intelligentsia and the clergy. Such places have since acquired a different name, but in essence they are exactly what Marx and Engels envisaged. Here Lenin and Stalin did come close to fulfilling the Marxist prescription, but they were again found wanting in spreading concentration camps to a mere half of the world. So where the Bolsheviks and Nazis perverted Marxism, they generally did so in the direction of softening it.

Marxism answers Modmen's visceral need to find a justification for their hatred of Westman. That is why Modmen have a compelling need to believe at least some of it. If knowledge is the recognition of something already felt intuitively, then Modmen learned from Marx much of what they needed to know. A warm feeling of gratitude will never leave Modmen's hearts, no matter how many academics decide that their careers can now be advanced by abandoning Marxism, no matter how many Marxist governments now use 'ex' as their first name. Rumours of the demise of Marxism are exaggerated. True, for the time being the world's first Marxist state has erased the bearded face from its banners. But Marxism has been so widespread not because its home was in Russia but because it is in Modman's breast. It will persevere for as long as Modman does.

UNHEEDED LESSONS OF HISTORY

Armed with Marxist eschatology, the nihilist Modmen were ready to pounce. In Russia, the country that would eventually become the first prize fallen to nihilism, this particular piece of 'superstructure' was not, however, imported until the late nineteenth century. Nevertheless, homegrown dynamics were working towards the same goal.

It is hindsight that makes Russia a worthy object of study. A nineteenth-century writer would have been more justified in regarding France as the weakest link in the Western chain. The violence of 1848 and 1870 outdid any such events in contemporaneous Russia, and the débâcle of the Franco–Prussian war would have looked more damaging to France than the defeat in the Crimean War seemed to be to Russia. But hindsight is a more reliable tool than prophecy. From the height of decades, we can look down upon the mistaken proponent of the French theory. We know what happened, so why not borrow a Modman trick and suggest it was bound to happen?

Turgenev coined the term 'nihilist' in his novel *Fathers and Sons* (1862). The term apart, Russia was not the place where the nihilist first made an appearance, but it was an ideal arena for his lasting triumph. The year 1862 was remarkable in Russian history and not only because *Fathers and Sons* was published. It was the first full year that had passed since Alexander II, the 'liberator' tsar, had put an end to serfdom. This had followed years of heated campaigning in the press, fiery rhetoric on the part of what today would be called opinion leaders and the general rumbling of 'public opinion'. The last term deserves quotation marks for in reality there is no such thing as public opinion. What passes for it is merely a consensus in the leading media of the day. For example, 'public opinion' in any major European country today is circumscribed by a score of press journalists, half a dozen TV talk-show hosts, ten or so academics, perhaps five to ten PR types and a handful of government spokesmen. Let us round off that number at 50 altogether. That is a bit thin for a country of 60–80 million and certainly insufficient for a lofty claim to being 'public' opinion. Underneath that protruding tip there lies an amorphous mass of silent public-bar opinion, but silent it is and always has been. If 'public' opinion reflected the public-bar opinion, it could legitimately assert its status as *vox populi*, but the two bear little relation to one another. 'Public' opinion is well aware of this, but being endowed with plenty of contempt for the masses it does not care one way or the other. As long as public-bar opinion continues to be drowned by rivers of lager, 'public opinion' can brandish *ad populum* arguments all over the place. These may be totally spurious, but who is to know?

If that is the situation in Europe today with its quasi-free and semi-educated populace, what was going on in nineteenth-century Russia was much worse. A disfranchised, illiterate majority was in no position either to write for the papers or indeed to read them. All those chattering jousts for the right to pose as 'public opinion' were held between a few dozen liberal writers and half as many conservative ones. As is usually the case, the conservatives could not ignore truth completely and so they eventually were out-shouted. Their 'liberal' opponents were Modmen, mostly of the nihilist variety, so truth was the least of their concerns. They wanted to get rid of Westman by hook or by crook. This ought to be kept in mind as an important backdrop to the abolition of serfdom in Russia. On merit, that was a step in the right direction. But after the advent of Modman such things are never decided on their merits; the subtext tends to dominate the text. In this case, the subtext was the destruction of Westman's economic base in Russia, a powerful blow for Modman. A parallel with the abolition of slavery in the United States is crying out to be drawn. In a vacuum, with every atom of the Modman versus Westman conflict purged, that too would have been an unequivocally positive development. As it was, it pushed American Westmen to the brink of extinction.

Modmen were athirst and it was impossible to slake their cravings by surrendering to whatever slogans they chose to brand-ish at the time. The slogans, then as now, were mostly liberal. But it was self-delusion to believe that satisfying liberal demands would mitigate the underlying impulse. Even as a blackmailer always comes up with new demands after the first payoff, so do Modmen refuse to rest on the laurels of liberal victories. That is why it was logical that Alexander II was blown up by a terrorist bomb in 1881. It was the blood of Westman that the new order craved, not *zemstva* (local government bodies), constitutional monarchy or an end to serfdom.

In Russia it was not the philistine but the nihilist who had to become the standard bearer for Modman. The reasons for that were manifold. First, the aristocratic core in Russia remained fairly strong and determined while slowly dwindling away. Second, the liberation of serfs had brought to prominence a large body of people with emotional grievances against the post-Petrine, quasi-Western establishment. Third, a real industrial revolution was still decades away, so the ranks of philistines were not swelling to a point where their numerical superiority would reach a critical mass. And fourth, Russia was insufficiently removed in time from the savage ways in which political disagreements had been settled in the past. After all, the father and uncle of Alexander II died under mysterious circumstances, his grandfather was strangled, his great-grandmother ascended to the throne by having her husband murdered, the day of his father's coronation was spoiled by a republican uprising. And a mere century before, dismemberment, mutilation, quartering, impaling and other such niceties had been the common currency of political debate in the empire.

While the aristocratic core in Russia was determined to resist the onslaught of Modman, it was not inflexible in the methods it chose for such resistance. Since Western liberal influences were strong, Russian aristocrats attempted to follow Western models, often uncritically. Unfortunately, foreign implants do not invariably succeed in a soil all too ready to reject them. The reforms of Alexander II were one example of failure, punctuated by a full stop of an explosion. Other examples came from the trial of the nihilist Netchayev gang and the case of Vera Zasulich. The Netchayevites were tried for the murder of their former comrade Ivanov whose loyalty they had begun to doubt. This was the inaugural case for the newly instituted trial by jury. Though the defendants were found guilty of murder, only four were sentenced to penal-colony imprisonment. A message was thus sent to society that honest hatred of the establishment went a long way towards exonerating even murderers. The message was taken and an open season on tsarist officials began. Vera Zasulich (named by a contemporaneous French magazine as 'the most famous woman in Europe') was tried for an attempt to murder F. F. Trepov, chief of St Petersburg police. The jury of Miss Zasulich's peers found her innocent on the grounds of her political, rather than simply criminal, motive. This miscarriage of justice demonstrated the uselessness of jury trials in Russia; and from then on crimes with political implications were tried by military tribunals. Those proved only marginally less lenient, at least until nihilist terror reached pandemic proportions in the early twentieth century. Russian judges came to their senses then and, in return for the murders of 1600 officials between 1905 and 1907, passed about 5000 death sentences. But by then it was too late.

The failure of the Russian courts to save the country from nihilist outrages could have taught a useful lesson to posterity even in the West: institutions are only as good as the people who man them. Trial by jury, for example, cannot survive as an instrument of justice in the absence of a broadly based group of people who understand what justice is. That condition was not met in Russia in Zasulich's time, and it is not being met in the West today. Thus an argument that a murderer had an impoverished childhood has been known to produce mitigated sentences or even acquittals in Western courts; race has been seen as an extenuating circumstance and political motives have been accepted as being nobler than simple savagery. As courts in the West demonstrate their inability to deal sternly with criminals, the jury system looks more and more antiquated. Jurors have to be drawn from the available pool of humanity, which, alas, has been poisoned by decades of Modman cant. As a result, courts are beginning to act as rubber stamps of egalitarianism rather than agents of justice. Society predictably responds with a climbing crime rate that requires statistical larceny to pass for anything other than a social catastrophe: for example, in 1954 there were 400 muggings in all of Britain; 2001 produced 400 in Lambeth, a South London borough, in one month. Considering that the jury system is now barely operable in Britain and the United States, historically the bastions of Western legality, one should not be unduly surprised that the system failed in Russia.

Miss Zasulich was thus free to co-found in 1883 the first Marxist group in Russia, the Liberation of Labour, but then Marxism was not the most prolific expression of Modman's will in Russia. More widespread, and at the time seemingly more dangerous, were such organizations as People's Reprisal and People's Will, conspiratorial terrorists gangs. (*The Possessed* is based on the murder of the student Ivanov by People's Reprisal, and Netchayev appears in Dostoyevsky's novel as Pyotr Verkhovensky.) However, we should never lose sight of the direction in which all such groups, Marxist or otherwise, were pulling: the obliteration of Westman. Subtle differences in their doctrines have always been of paramount importance to sympathetic historians, both in and out of Russia. But an unsympathetic analyst would find it hard to distinguish between, say, Tkachyov and Plekhanov, Netchayev and Martov or Lenin and Trotsky. They were all possessed by the same energumen, and any differences in their methods were only tactical. Lenin, for example, was temperamentally closer to the Blanquist Tkachyov than to the Marxist Plekhanov. But he realized that Marxist jargon offered promising possibilities that did not exist in unadorned terrorism. Not that he rejected terrorism altogether, but his viscera had set a different task: not the odd bomb but the wholesale slaughter of millions.

Lessons of history are hard to learn without historians teaching them. Unfortunately, Russia, potentially the most valuable lesson of modernity, is not spoiled by a surfeit of Tacituses and Gibbons. In the twentieth century the country itself did not, for obvious reasons, continue the fine tradition of historical scholarship begun by Karamsin and developed by Solovyov, Klyuchevsky and Milyukov. Why Western historians were remiss in this field is harder to explain. But it is not impossible.

The events of 1917 had the same divisive effect in the West as did the upheaval of 1789. A cataclysm of that magnitude seems to have precluded objectivity: one had to be violently con or ecstatically pro. Much as we may sympathize with the former emotion or despise the latter, either makes penetrating analysis difficult. The most we have been able to expect from historians is unfalsified, or at least not consciously falsified, historiography, an important yet inadequate offering. After all, few of us are capable of making sense of the events that directly led to the slaughter of tens of millions and the enslavement of half the world. These require an explanation, not just a compendium of data. But fusing a multitude of facts into a single concept is not an easy task even for professionals. For people at large it is impossible. In the absence of real understanding, the lessons of Russia remain unlearned. That is why her folly is likely to be repeated.

GLOSSOCRACY: MODMAN DEVELOPS HIS OWN WEAPON

The twentieth century found Modman mature and ready to strike. Like an heir to the throne who has been nurtured for decades and now is impatient to claim his prize, Modman would not wait any longer.

He wanted ascendancy *de jure*, not just *de facto*; and he wanted it now. No longer possessing the moral scales required to weigh the human cost of this ambition in the balance, he was ready to go all the way. No price was too high. The resulting orgy of bloodshed is well documented, if not always well understood. We shall keep returning to it, but my purpose is not to produce a sequential history of modernity; it is to describe Modman as a sociocultural type. And neither the infancy nor senility of a group – or a person – is an ideal time to study its character; it is the years in between that afford the greatest insight. The twentieth century was the beginning of such a period for Modman; this century will probably be the end of it.

In wiping out Westman's heritage, Modmen ran the risk of losing a sense of destination and eventually they realized this. As Modman's founding urge, the destruction of Westman, came close to fulfilment, slight doubts became discernible. In a way, the proximity of the goal was proving both anticlimactic and disappointing; the journey seemed more desirable than the arrival. That is why Modmen added looting to murder. Killing Westman was no longer enough; stealing his possessions was becoming equally necessary. This is what constitutes the great larcenous shift of modernity wherein Westman's cultural property was broken off its religious underpinnings, dragged into the house of the new owner and adapted to his use. Thus Westman's expansiveness was transformed into Modman's expansionism. Westman's introspection became Modman's obsession with human psychology, understood in a materialistic way. Westman's striving to develop forms adequate to expressing the substance of culture turned into Modman's preoccupation with form as such. And Westman's nurturing of reason as a cognitive tool, one of many, reappeared as Modman's belief in reason as a be-all and end-all.

With its accent on formal perfection, the post-Christian world perversely resembles the world of pre-Christian classicism. But the resemblance is superficial: cultural winds can never return to their circles. As Modmen discovered, you cannot break eggs without breaking eggs. Their world lacked the serenity needed for an unhurried pursuit of formal harmony; this had been trampled in their frantic pursuit of happiness. Modmen's brutalism is as antagonistic to Hellenic as it is to Westman values, so they had to look for their own ways of ensuring lasting success. As we now know, this was achieved by a partial convergence of the nihilist and philistine strains.

But first Modmen had to consolidate their gains, making them as nearly irreversible as they could manage. Violence, no matter how boundless, could not act as the sole instrument of such consolidation, a conclusion that became inevitable in the face of evidence. Though one may argue that a century in which, on average, millions died violent deaths every year elevated violence to a qualitatively new level, it is nonetheless clear that killing has backfired on Modmen not just physically but also spiritually. Eventually, they proved unable to maintain their muscle tone at a level required to practise unlimited mayhem. Like those Nazi murderers who had to switch to gas because they no longer could stand the ravines full of blood (a development documented in H. Höhne's history of the SS *The Order of the Death's Head*), Modmen have lost their nerve. Like an ex-athlete whose body goes to pot when his sinews can no longer take the strain of daily training, Modmen have grown flabby. Playing war games on computer screens – albeit with real bombs tearing up real flesh – is still within their capacity. Pushing millions over the top into machine-gun fire is not: this would run foul of the philistine subspecies that has grown too strong to allow that to happen. One therefore admires so much more the prescience with which Modmen devised an alternative mechanism to power. For lack of an established term to describe it, we have to coin a new one: glossocracy, the government of the word, by the word and for the word.

For Westmen language was useful but not critical. A Bach fugue could communicate their essence more effectively than even a Shakespeare sonnet or Racine play, but this does not mean that Westmen were contemptuous of words – had they been there would have been no Shakespeare or Racine. They simply were aware of the limitations of words, an awareness that paradoxically had a constructive influence on language. On the other hand, Modmen's insistence on the self-sufficiency of language has had exactly the opposite effect.

The ascendancy of language reflected the ascendancy of reason. It is only through words that reason can make its presence known;

extra-verbal tools go to the bottom of the box. Even writers whose subject is inadequacy of language have to rely, illogically, on language to get their point across. Be that as it may, even as reason is severely limited, so is language. The pen can be mightier than the sword, but to become so empowered it has to cease being just a means of putting graphic symbols of meaning down on paper. Even as music had to stop being merely sounds to become the ultimate expression of Westman soul, so did words have to stop being just words in Modmen's hands. In the process they were to lose the poignancy with which Westmen had endowed them. But Modmen did not rue that loss: beauty had no place in their world. Neither aesthetics nor ethics was even a consideration; utility carried the day.

That is why language has suffered the same fate at the hands of Modmen as so many other Westmen possessions. It was stolen, shifted into Modmen's domain and used for their purposes. Westman's word was reduced to a microcosm of Westman's world and followed the latter's fate by having its substance destroyed and its form perverted. By depriving words of their true meaning, Modmen managed to turn them into lasting instruments of their power, something to stand them in good stead long after the edge of the seemingly more violent weapons has been dulled. Hence the nature of glossocracy.

In God's eyes, erecting 'a tower, whose top may reach unto heaven' with the subsequent disintegration of language was severe punishment: 'Go to, let us go down, and there confound their language, that they may not understand one another's speech' (Genesis 11:7). It would never have occurred to the writers of the Old Testament that a time would come when inflicting a Babel on the world would be done not by God as a way of unleashing his wrath, but by some men as a way of controlling others.

The unity of form and substance, with the latter having the upper hand, was as characteristic of Westman's language as it was of all his other possessions. Exactly how language works and how it relates to thought is both outside the scope of this book and beyond the comprehension of its author. But this absence of under-standing is common enough, for creating a precise model of lan-guage would be half a step removed from creating a model of the human mind. This task has not yet been achieved and is, one hopes, unachievable. Yet certain observations are possible to make.

Words represent a unity of semantics and semiotics. The semantic aspect is easy to understand at the point of production, though it becomes murkier at the point of consumption. Words have a meaning, but the meaning is never exactly the same to the utterer and recipient. If a nun were to discuss love with the publisher of *Penthouse*, chances are they would waste much time trying to understand what the word meant to each of them. But even without such hypothetical examples, it is clear that commu-nications based on semantics alone can never be an unequivocal success. The more common the cultural backgrounds of the speaker and the listener, the more their semantic understanding will overlap. But there always will be a piece sticking out.

That was what F. Tyutchev meant when he declared that 'a thought uttered is a lie'. Though the poet could use words with a precision that is outside the reach of most people, even he realized that language is inadequate to the task of carrying a thought to its destination intact. Something is bound to be lost along the way. The whole truth never reaches the listener; only a fragment does. And a partial truth is a partial lie. However, verbal communi-cations are never based on semantics alone. The semiotic and contextual aspects are always there, and they can either plug the semantic gaps or widen them. Words send signals that may have little or nothing to do with their meaning. Some signals are emotional. For example, in its normal context the word 'hooray' sends a powerful emotional signal and a weak semantic one; with, say, 'consubstantiation' it is the other way around. But we can imagine contexts in which the situation could be reversed. Thus we can talk about the 'hooray patriotism of 1914', producing little emotional effect upon our listener. Or if we offer 'consubstantiation' when trying to explain to a Christian what we mean by 'mythology', the effect could be very emotional. The impact that words have on the listener largely depends on both textual and contextual factors, and the link between the two can vary depending on how the words are used and what emotional, intellectual and historic baggage they carry. But if we were to abandon semantics altogether by denying the existence of any semantic aspect that is more or less immutable, words would stop being a means of communication and become an instrument of power – or nothing. They would be nothing if the speaker could not impose upon the listener the intended meaning of the word. They would be an instrument of power if he could. Lewis Carroll realized this perfectly, which is why he made Humpty Dumpty conduct this dialogue with Alice:

> 'When I use a word,' Humpty Dumpty said in rather a scornful tone, 'it means just what I choose it to mean – neither more nor less.' 'The question is,' said Alice, 'whether you can make words mean different things.' 'The question is,' said Humpty Dumpty, 'which is to be master – that's all.'

A word can communicate a notion only if there is a presumed parity, however approximate, between the speaker's and the listener's understanding of the word. For that to happen, all its users must accept the academically acceptable definition of the word. Under such circumstances, the communication remains essentially free, and the speaker does not have to bend the listener to his own will to make himself understood. Whatever misunderstanding did arise would be attributable to the personal colouring of the word, let us say 1 per cent of emotion etching 99 per cent of meaning. Not so when words are used in any other than their real meaning. To make himself understood, and his words acted upon, the speaker then has to be an institutional superior of the listener, a 'master'. He has to impose his understanding of the word at the expense of the listener's understanding. This can be done by downright coercion based on an implicit threat. Or it can be done by mind-numbing repetition where the listener gives up his own understanding in sheer exasperation and agrees to accept the speaker's meaning. In this case a certain amount of coercion may still be necessary, if only to make the listener stay quiet long enough for the endless repetitions to work. In either event, words will be used not to express a thought, or even to conceal it, but for the extra-lingual purpose of establishing or maintaining power.

Glossocracy is a power mechanism based on this linguistic background. Starting from the hollow-ringing promise of liberty, equality and fraternity, Modmen displayed a cavalier attitude to semantics. As hindsight tells us, liberty meant martial law, equality meant wholesale murder and expropriation of the upper classes, and fraternity meant secular egalitarianism under the aegis of Modmen. No matter. The more meaningless the word, the more powerful it is as a weapon. By the time the twentieth century rolled along, Modmen had perfected the art of desemanticizing words so as to turn them into weapons of crowd control. When used by the nihilist subspecies of Modman, this technique is called propaganda. When used by the philistine subspecies, it is called advertising. And when used by the hybrid of the two, it may be called political correctness.

It is interesting to see how both the nihilist and philistine glossocrats put the word 'free' to work. To the nihilist 'free' means the exact opposite of the dictionary definition. Lenin, for example, defined freedom as 'acknowledged necessity'. In that instance glossocracy worked because it was helped along by a physical threat. These days it can do well even without such a crutch to lean on, for Modman philistines distort the word 'free' in a more subtle way. Just as their government allegedly depends on the consent of the governed, so does their glossocracy rely on the consent of the populace to ignore the real meaning of words. Thus any advertising man learns that 'free' rivals 'new' for being the most effective message in marketing communications. What makes it so potent is precisely the consent of the public to disregard the real meaning of the word, thus accepting it as a tool of glossocracy.

For if they stopped to think about it, the 'punters' would realize that an offer to 'buy nine widgets, get one free' is larcenous in any but the strictly legal sense. The potential buyer is being offered nothing for free. He is being offered a modest 10 per cent discount designed to induce him to buy ten items for which his need could be lukewarm. In all probability he would not buy ten widgets without such an inducement; he might buy a couple or none at all. But he consents to spend a greater sum than he would otherwise as part of a broader consensus on which philistine glossocracy is based: he has been so conditioned to respond to desemanticized words that he now feels happy to do so.

If we extend the word 'free' into the philistine politics of Modman, we discover that it works just as well there, in, for example, such mendacious terms as 'free medical care'. 'Free', to a semantic rigorist, used to mean something for which one did not have to pay. To a Modman glossocrat it means something different. If pressed, he would admit that of course somebody has to pay for all those CAT scans and ECGs. Such things are expensive, and the more inefficiently provided the dearer they get. If patients do not pay for them directly, the payment comes from the government, which can only make money the old-fashioned way: from taxes. 'Free' thus means that the transfer of money from patient to hospital is mediated by the state acting as a general contractor with megalomania. But governments are less efficient than private enterprise. We must thus assume that mastectomies are more expensive when one pays for them through the government, whether one needs them or not, than they would be if one paid for them directly and only when one needed them. But when today's Europeans pay for state medicine, they do not just pay for mastectomies and scans. An ever-growing proportion of their money pays for the ever-growing state bureaucracy required to administer 'free' medical care, something for which they would pay less if medical care were not 'free'. But the Europeans do not mind paying taxes or at least claim they do not – in the same way in which Soviet people did not mind donating huge amounts to government bonds that never paid up. In both cases, it is glossocratic slavery that is responsible. Since steady growth of nationalized medicine is tantamount to the state extorting increasingly larger sums from the people, 'free' medical care places an ever-growing proportion of the nation's finances and labour force under state control, thus increasing the power of the state over the individual. In other words, 'free', translated from the Modman, means 'serving the state, not the citizen, and therefore being more expensive than it otherwise would be, not to mention less efficient'. Doctors complicate matters even further. In a survey of a few years ago, 90 per cent of the 'medical professionals' in the UK stated that people suffering from 'smoking-related diseases' ought to pay for treatment directly, on top of getting it free by paying taxes. Why? Because these diseases are behavioural, caused by the patients' obtuse bloody-mindedness. A Westman holdout reluctant to succumb to glossocratic tyranny asks, how about AIDS? It just goes to show how little he understands the meaning of 'free'.

Incidentally, that medical care can be used as an instrument of tyranny has been demonstrated by every political state in history, not least by Nazi Germany. In fact, reading about Hitler's medicine one cannot help noticing parallels with today. As firm believers in state medicine, the Nazis showed how it could be used for crowd control. Like today's bureaucrats, they emphasized preventive medicine, with nutrition featuring prominently in their health propaganda. Every German had a duty, according to the Nazis, to look after himself so as to prolong the part of his life when he could continue to serve the state. Likewise, in today's state medicine the need to relieve financial pressures on the state's purse can be neatly converted into a blanket dictate on citizens' lives. Conditioned to accept the dictates of the Modman state, Europeans do not cringe upon hearing from yet another health official yet another admonition on their dietary habits. 'And exactly what makes this your business?' is a question seldom asked. But if it were asked, the truthful answer would not be far removed from the Nazi rationale: the good of the state.

The Nazis waged an anti-smoking campaign that would be the envy of today's EU. It was the Nazis who first established the link between smoking and lung cancer and, as a result, lung-cancer statistics in Germany continued to be better than in other Western countries for a couple of decades after the war. As many other forms of research, this proceeded from the starting point of an axiomatic assumption, in this case that smoking had to be bad because the Führer was good and he did not approve of lighting up. Chemical additives and preservatives were roundly castigated by the Nazis; wholemeal bread was depicted as morally superior to breads made from blanched white flour. Like today's bureaucrats, the Nazis promoted vegetarianism (practised by Hitler, Hess and many others) and attacked medical experiments on animals (unlike us, they had no shortage of enthusiastic human volunteers). As the Nazis were godless, animals were to them not principally different from humans and were in fact superior to some. Hitler loved his Alsatian Blondie more than any woman in his life; in today's Britain veterinary medicine is organized better than the care of humans.

Of course, doctors in Nazi Germany were involved not just in preventive medicine but, most of them eagerly, in such less benign pastimes as eugenics and enforced euthanasia. It is comforting to observe how medicine in today's West is inching in the same direction. Euthanasia, in particular, is custom-made for Modmen, what with their devotion to the state. One cannot open the papers these days without reading a thinly veiled lament about the burden placed on the fragile shoulders of state medicine by an ageing population. And euthanasia is steadily moving towards the forefront of potential remedies. This is a paradox, for the governments' tireless propaganda of healthier 'life styles', coupled with advances in pharmaceuticals and hygiene, is designed to help people live longer. In reality, it is designed to increase the power of the state, but when medicine is used for that purpose one cannot be had without the other: longevity will grow. This creates yet another vicious circle of modernity: the state uses medicine to advance its own good by tightening its control on citizens' lives; but as a corollary to this, the state hurts itself by creating a multitude of old free-loaders who do nothing but sap the state's resources. To today's governments, euthanasia is the only logical way out, and never mind the effete arguments against it based on the outdated notion of the sanctity of human life.

As with many other of Modman's perversions, Holland led the way by legalizing euthanasia explicitly and encouraging doctors to expand its use implicitly to a point where Dutch doctors now execute more than 1000 patients a year and, as a recent survey showed, many old people in Holland are scared to go to hospitals because they think doctors will kill them. Other modern countries, including Britain, are only a step behind, eyeing Holland's progress with envy. In the USA, the fundamentalist lobby can still deliver votes (or not, as the case may be), so the American champion of euthanasia, the deranged Dr 'Death' Kevorkian, was eventually sent to prison, but not before he was allowed to kill God knows how many people. Such setbacks are, however, unlikely to stop 'progress' in general and the progress of euthanasia in particular. The political state has to be served first, and if such service involves a wholesale cull of the crumblies, then so be it. This is another example of the moral cul-de-sac awaiting humanists. They start out as secular preachers and end up as self-righteous executioners.

The British and other Europeans are unhappy about waiting lists at hospitals caused by a chronic shortage of hospital beds, but they miss the point. State medical care does not need hospital beds to perform its principal function: control over people's lives. For example, one British hospital recently created a new post of director of diversity at a cost of £100,000 a year – while cutting its number of beds for lack of funds. In fact, fewer hospitals have been built in Britain during the first half-century of its nationalized medicine than in the 1930s, hardly the most prosperous decade in British history. Servants of the state have to look out willy-nilly for Number One, defined not as themselves or their patients but their master. And, as Modmen of the nihilist variety have demonstrated, to be truly successful state control has to extend to people's private lives, not just public activities. Glossocracy can achieve this end by itself – for example, by brainwashing people into believing that there exists a valid moral distinction between driving after two glasses of wine or three. But glossocracy is slow, proceeding at the unhurried pace of natural forces. Why not help it along by issuing a direct threat: if you smoke and get emphysema, you can croak without any medical help, see if we care? No reason at all; every little bit helps. At least, medical care remains free.

A quick look at education confirms this semantic conundrum with the word 'free'. Before education in Britain became 'free' and 'comprehensive' in the 1960s, it had been good and cheap. Since it acquired those glossocratic modifiers, it has become expensive and bad. Advertising copywriters deepen the confusion even further by admitting tacitly that 'free' means nothing at all. That is why they routinely leave it unemployed in front of 'gift' that is perfectly capable of doing all the work by itself. Down into the semantic bin goes the lying parasite 'free', where it lands on top of the previously discarded political terminology of the philistine subspecies of Modman.

THE NON-LANGUAGE OF POLITICS

Few words in Modmen's political vocabulary are ever used in their true meaning. This vocabulary is there not to communicate ideas but to act as an instrument of glossocratic coercion. That this is achieved with the consent of the governed should not be used for *ipso facto* exoneration: as Hitler, Stalin, the tabloid press and the advertising industry have demonstrated, such consent, or indeed hysterical adulation, can be forged easily enough by deploying weapons of mass propaganda with consummate skill.

An examination of any routinely used political terms will confirm that they are not used in their true meaning. As a random example, we can look at the words 'Conservative' and 'Liberal', as they are spoken in Britain today. (Every Western country has similar examples, such as 'Republican' and 'Democratic' in the USA.) When these words were first used, Westmen still had vestigial power, and the Tories, also known as Conservatives, were, not to cut too fine a point, the party of aristocracy. They believed in a social order based on traditional hierarchy, although not without flexibility. Their attitude to the lower classes was paternalistic, akin to that of a father who feels that even his unsuccessful child deserves love. Since the lower classes were mostly employed in agriculture and nascent industry, Tory paternalism extended to those fields, taking the shape of what today we call protectionism.

The Whigs, also known as Liberals, while also respectful of tradition, believed in *laissez-faire* economics at home and free trade abroad. They were opposed to protectionism, and their success in having the Corn Laws repealed spelled Britain's economic success. Liberal ideas put into practice created in the Waterloo-to-Ypres century the greatest economic growth Britain has ever enjoyed, though at some cost to Westman institutions. At the same time Tory rearguard action was modestly successful in attenuating the shock waves of this growth and keeping the now threadbare social fabric from being torn to tatters too quickly. Then, in barged the twentieth century heralded by the roar of howitzers. Out went Westman aristocracy, gassed in Flanders, taxed in Whitehall. And all we see at the end of it is glossocratic Babel.

The Conservative Party is now explicitly committed to a 'classless society'. Enough has been said about this; suffice it to say now that we can no longer regard the Tories as the party of aristocracy or the aristocracy as the ruling class. 'Classless society' is the glossocratic for a systematic replacement of Westman class structure with that of Modman, which is even more hierarchical than its predecessor but less benign. After all, its hierarchy is not based on centuries of breeding and upbringing, and honour does not figure high in its list of virtues.

What does the word 'Conservatism' mean these days? Take aristocratic social order out of it and paternalism is more or less all we have left. In Modmen's terms, this means a gigantic 'welfare state', to the 'basic features' of which the true-blue Tory Peregrine Worsthorne wanted us all to pledge 'loyalty' as far back as 1958. That may be what 'Conservatism' means to the party faithful, but to the few remaining Westman conservatives it means something different. They have to acknowledge that the word is semantically inoperable as is, and add to it a typographic dimension by describing themselves as conservative with a lower-case 'c', thus renouncing knee-jerk loyalty to Modman's upper-case Conservative Party. Most definitions of that small 'c' probably include some aspects of what in Britain is inaccurately called Thatcherism: limited government, personal freedom, *laissez-faire* economics at home and free trade abroad; in other words, all those things that circumscribe the traditional domain of liberalism.

Is this what that word means today? Not at all, is the reply to the perplexed Martian student of English. In America, liberalism means, *mutatis mutandis*, socialism: replacement of individual responsibility with collective security, with as much government control and as little personal liberty as is achievable this side of concentration camps. In Britain, it means the platform of the Liberal Democratic Party, which stands for roughly the same plus the negation of Britain's independence. In this aspiration the upper-case Liberals go even further than the upper-case Conservatives, who used to swear by God, King and country but now tend to support multiculturalism, classlessness and European federalism. For the nineteenth-century liberal, the 10 per cent of the nation's income the government was then spending was too high. For today's liberal, the 40-odd per cent it spends now is too low. Thus if one wants to use 'liberal' in its proper sense, and it is after all a cognate of 'liberty', then one must either modify it with 'classic' or replace it with 'libertarian', thus dumping the word straight into the aforementioned garbage heap of lexicology.

At this inauspicious site it is piled on top of other cognates of liberty, for example 'liberation', as in 'national liberation'. When applied to places like Burundi, 'national liberation' means a transitional stage between colonialism and cannibalism. When applied to the 'former Soviet Union', it means a shift from *de jure* to merely *de facto* Russian control. When applied to Asia, it means Mao, Ho and Kim. Thus modernized, 'liberation' and its cousin 'liberal' go the way of 'conservative', which incidentally means Burkean Whig in America and, these days, Leninist Bolshevik in Russia.

Of course, today's Liberals are not descendants of the nineteenth-century Whigs. They are a splinter group of Old Labour, which in turn traces its roots back to the Luddites, Chartists and other trouble-makers of yesteryear. More important, it is umbilically linked with certain unfashionable continental doctrines, a link Labour does not mind emphasizing by adopting foreign tunes like the 'Internationale' and 'Bandera Rossa' as its party songs and the foreign red flag as its party banner. New Labour, so called because the unmodified term is a historically compromised election-loser and therefore a decommissioned glossocratic weapon, hangs onto the symbols but feigns to renounce the substance, claiming it represents the middle classes rather than the unions, also known as labour. In other words, Labour is not labour. It stakes a claim to the plot owned in the past by the Liberals, who used to be Whigs but are not any longer.

If such basic terms have lost their meaning to become glossocratic tools we should not be unduly surprised at the confusion with more amorphous concepts such as 'right wing' and 'left wing'. For instance, strident adherents of Old Labour do not mind describing Lady Thatcher 'as extreme right wing'. This designation is also applied retrospectively to the likes of Hitler. One infers that the political spectrum, as Modmen see it, starts at the extreme right exemplified by Thatcher and Hitler and ends up at the extreme left represented by the sort of chaps who in 1995 released Sarin gas into the Tokyo underground. For what did the 'extreme right' Thatcher stand? Why, *laissez-faire* economics at home, free trade abroad, limited government, individual responsibility and meritocracy. In short, she was an out-and-out Whig, even though she confusingly led the Tories. If A equals B, and B equals C, then A equals C. Applying this proven logic to the task in hand, we have to assume that Hitler, Lady Thatcher's fellow 'right-wing extremist', was a Whig too. But then we find out his beliefs ran more towards socialist ideals: big government, nationalized or at least subjugated economy, wage and price controls, strict tariffs, cradle-to-grave welfare, vegetarianism and the kind of genocidal peccadilloes that until (or after) him were practised on that scale only by socialists, who are undeniably left wing. Then we remember that Hitler's party was called the National Socialist Workers and ask the inevitable question: so who then is the right-wing extremist? And what does the term mean? Perhaps other countries can give us a clue. In America 'extreme right wing' usually describes Ku Klux Klan types. Importing the term here, we wrap Lady Thatcher in a bed sheet with slits in the hood, only to find the picture unrealistic, though white was definitely her colour. In Russia, right wing means communist and left wing means a Whig-Socialist mongrel. Thus no help is forthcoming from abroad; yet again Britain has to rely on her own resources to straighten out her mess.

Alan Clark, the late Conservative politician cum pundit, attempted to help by offering in a *Daily Telegraph* article of a few years ago that 'Thatcherism is in, and of, the past', and 'the Friedmanite orthodoxies ... were never entirely accepted.' 'Almost lost to sight,' he continued, 'remain the three principal functions of the state: to ensure that its citizens are secure, that they are gainfully employed, and that they are enlightened.' Of the three functions according to Alan, the first is another word for social conscience, the glossocratic for socialism; the second is another word for wholesale nationalization (the only way for a state to 'ensure' total employment), the glossocratic for socialism; the third is another word for 'free' education, wherein the government makes us pay through the nose for the illiterate Modman nonsense pumped into our children's minds. That, too, is the glossocratic for socialism. The three functions of the state can thus be reduced to one: being socialist. Therefore Clark's Conservative Party must become, if it is not already, as socialist as New Labour but not quite so socialist as Old Labour, and then one day it may win another election in the name of conservatism – but not of liberalism, which is what Friedmanism really is, and it is 'in, and of, the past'.

Clark was right, though not in the way he had intended. Socialism is indeed the ultimate political expression of Modman. Both of its models, nihilist and philistine, have struck a chord in his heart. The nihilist version, so ably represented by the Nazis (national socialists) and Bolsheviks (international socialists), has now been largely discredited, but we should not be misled into believing that there is no way back. It is just that at this time we are witnessing an accelerated convergence of the two types, with the nihilist version being incorporated into the philistine (glossocratic socialism, sometimes referred to oxymoronically as 'democratic') and vice versa. Who will eventually gain the upper hand in this meeting of minds is difficult to predict. But the nihilist is always with us because he is within us. Given favourable circumstances, he will strike again. The underlying impulse of all types of socialism is to subsume the individual, particularly the Westman holdout, into the morass of a giant corporatist state. It is the most effective way of disfranchising Westmen, making them duck for cover.

The glossocratic mechanism of power was custom-made for socialism, whose semantic mendacity starts from its very name and proceeds to its proclaimed goals. These are yet another example of the larcenous shift perpetrated by Modmen. In this case, the sharing and caring aspects of Christianity were stolen from the rightful owner who used them for individual salvation. They were then married forcibly to the collectivist, corporatist state and used for its self-vindication. But Westman holdouts should be able to see through the fog of glossocratic verbiage and realize that the modern state has only one natural goal: expansion aimed at pushing Westman to the margins and then into oblivion. Thus 'protecting the less fortunate' really means expropriating the more fortunate, 'investing in healthcare and education' really means expanding state bureaucracies and increasing taxes, 'investing in industry' means crypto-nationalization, and so forth. If most people in the world rejected glossocratic semantics and insisted on words used in their proper meaning only, glossocracy would come tumbling down like the walls of Jericho. But people have lost the capacity to distinguish between the semantic true and false, and this is precisely what makes glossocracy possible in the West. In fact, 'consent of the governed', another shibboleth Modman pilfered from Westman, must today be expanded to include 'to accept words as meaningless semiotic messages designed not to convey meaning but to make glossocracy absolute'.

A lie is possible only when words are expected to be used semantically, not when both parties to a verbal exchange agree to disregard semantics altogether. That is why only a shallow analyst of the modern political scene would conclude that politicians tell lies. They do not, at least not in any real sense. They simply go through a glossocratic ritual. Thus Stalin did not lie when, at the height of the bloodiest mass carnage and worst famines in history, he declared that 'Life has become better, Comrades; life has become merrier.' Neither does an advertisement lie in the strict sense of the word when it claims that a mass-produced beer 'refreshes the parts other beers do not reach'. In both instances it is not a man telling a lie; it is a glossocrat putting his foot down.

WHILE STOCKS LAST

It is only in this context that a sane man can understand Modman's political thought. Skipping all intermediate steps, it goes straight to its ultimate goal: acquisition of power unleavened by any other than glossocratic concern for *bono publico*. Likewise, a modern advertising copywriter reverses the traditional logical process by always starting with the conclusion ('Brand X offers what the much-touted Brands Y and Z can't possibly offer'), and only then sometimes touching on the intermediate steps. Once the conclusion has been understood, the Modman political glossocrat fills in the blanks by putting together a list of desemanticized verbal stimuli best suited to achieving the goal. This is an exact equivalent of commercial brand building.

The word 'brand', with its 'personality' matched to the 'market profile', is a glossocratic invention. Brand characteristics have little, often nothing, to do with product characteristics. If they in any way overlap, it is by serendipity. Any similarity between the two is no longer needed: the public has been conditioned to think brands, not products. A pub crawler selects a brand of lager not because he really believes that by doing so he appears more intelligent to his friends, but because he is satisfied that the marketers of the brand have activated the correct mechanisms of glossocratic response. What those mechanisms are differs from brand to brand, but only superficially. By and large, they can all be grouped according to which of the seven deadly sins they not only expiate but indeed glamorize. Modman's appeal is not only not modern in any true sense, it is downright atavistic.

Lust, for example, has been shown to be particularly effective for marketers of personal-hygiene products, underwear, cosmetics and cars. This appeal has become a self-fulfilling prophecy, which is a *sine qua non* for closing the glossocratic loop. Thus a belief that some brands of motorcar have a strong 'pulling' power has been communicated to the male of the philistine subspecies directly and to the female vicariously. Modmen expect, and their women accept, that the thrust generated by a powerful engine will reflect or perhaps even enhance the sexual potency of the man who drives a car thus equipped. That a Westman holdout may wince at this kind of transference is neither here nor there. What matters is not semantics but semiotics; not substance but form; not reality but make-believe. Similarly, the modern political process has practically nothing to do with reality, which is reflected in the unreality of the words that convey the meaning, or rather the symbolic meaning, of political concepts. If the parties' names mean nothing in any of the leading parliamentary democracies, then it is little wonder that the modern political process almost entirely bypasses reason, in whose name it was devised in the first place. Modman politics is neither democratic nor autocratic; it is glossocratic.

Modman politicians follow the same logic as Modman marketers, which is why they share the same techniques. Marketers have benefited from the polling tricks first conjured up by politicians, while the latter are relying ever more on focus-group research that has stood marketers in such good stead. Focus groups are put together for the purpose of identifying the semiotic actuators of the basic, not to say base, response mechanisms. Let us say research reveals that the public is more responsive to an appeal to lust than greed in the marketing of a Japanese car that resembles a sports car in appearance but not in performance. The resulting TV commercials will then show, say, a leggy creature, all billowing hair and rock-steady bust, running towards the car in which a muscular chap awaits. That is, if the intended target audience is male. If it is female, then a tall, dark and handsome chap will be shown first in close-up, contorting his unshaven features into a semiotic message of an impending erection, and then in a medium-wide shot, rolling his pectorals as he John-Waynes towards the car and its pouting female driver. Had the focus group suggested that avarice would be a more promising deadly sin to target, then exactly the same product would acquire different brand characteristics. It could, for example, come across depicting the driver as an astute youngster who has saved a fistful of cash by buying this car. The payoff for his thrift could again be sexual (a girl realizing that he would be a better father of her unborn children than the square-jawed creature who had wandered in from the adjacent lot) or it could be professional (his boss realizing that a young man who looks after his own money so well can be trusted to look after someone else's). In any case, the car's real characteristics will not come into it.

A marketer who wants to include some latent appeal to reason will be helped in his effort by an elaborate code of practice that frowns on outright falsehood but makes up for it by countenancing more subtle deception. To that end, our Modman 'brand builder' will be encouraged to use any number of tricks, of which the most illustrious are the unique selling proposition (USP for short) and its derivative, pre-emptive benefit. The concept of the USP springs from the correct evaluation of the Modman audience as an aggregate of persons who are incapable of responding to more than one message at a time. Thus the marketer of a brand uses his own judgement, fortified by every manner of market research, to 'position' the brand in a unique way. If this bears some semblance to reality, so much the better; if not, that is just fine too. Let us suppose that two brands of soda are identical in every respect except that one has a twist-off cap and the other has not. The twist-off cap becomes the brand's USP, and every piece of communication for this soda will feature comparisons between a silly lad who has to look in vain for a bottle opener and his clever rival who neatly opens his bottle in one graceful motion. The payoff will most probably be sexual, with the latter chap claiming the affections of a girl who looks down with contempt on the attempts of the other suitor to open a bottle with his teeth. Such communications will not tell a lie by stating that one brand of soda has a twist-off cap when it has not. But they will deceive by blowing this minute detail out of all proportion and by omitting the fact that in every other respect the two sodas are identical.

If even such a minuscule USP cannot be found, which is increasingly becoming the case in the conditions of uniformity so beloved of Modmen, then the pre-emptive benefit makes an appearance, which is a characteristic shared by all or most brands but claimed by only one. The marketers of this brand thus pre-empt the benefit of the whole product category by claiming it to be the unique characteristic of their own brand. Many years ago, for example, the marketers of a mass-produced American beer proclaimed that all their bottles were 'washed in live steam', implying pristine sterility. Unaware that all beer bottles are sterilized the same way, the public swallowed the campaign hook, line and sinker. But they would not have cared even had they known. Any sane individual would assume anyway that a commercially distributed liquid comes in a clean bottle, however this is achieved. What matters to a Modman consumer is the mating ritual of the glossocratic game, not facts.

The Modman consumer of political messages responds in exactly the same way. If we look at the slogans of any political campaign, we shall discern 'USPs' and 'pre-emptive benefits' galore: meaningless shibboleths, not real concepts. What makes the situation in politics even more pernicious than in commerce is that there are few legal restrictions on what a politician can promise. Unlike a marketer, a politician is not prevented by law from telling a lie, such as issuing a promise he has no way, or indeed no intention, of keeping. He may suffer for an unkept promise in the next election, but in all likelihood will not. The electorate is, after all, like a market: short on memory, long on the desire to see the glossocratic game played by the rules. And veracity is not one of them. Thus, when a politician promises to look after the least fortunate, only the most backward voters expect him actually to do so. The bulk of both politicians and voters are middle-class Modmen who could not care less about the poor. But voters who gravitate towards the left pole will not plug themselves into the glossocratic loop until they hear the right words, the eenie-meenie-miny-mo of politics but without the politically incorrect brutality towards a person of Afro-Caribbean descent. Whether the politician actually intends to help the poor is immaterial. It would matter, however, if the politician announced that such mythical help would be financed by tax increases. The voter must be reassured that this is a game played by the rules, but a game nonetheless; and money, especially his own, is real life. A good politician will mollify the philistine voter by promising to increase government spending without increasing either the taxes or the money supply. The voter could, of course, ask where the money is going to come from in that case, especially if the economic growth is slow, but is unlikely to do so. He is, after all, satisfied that the right glossocratic noises have been made. He is ready to consent to be governed. In other words, he is ready to accept the pre-emptive benefit as real.

If a voter regards himself as more right than left, then he will want a guarantee that his taxes will not go up. A politician seeking his vote will grab the USP opening by issuing such a guarantee in as emphatic a fashion as it takes. The elder George Bush's 'read my lips, no new taxes' was a good example of such a USP positioning. Of course, both the Modman politician and his 'conservative' supporter know that taxes will go up – they usually do. You can emulate George Bush Senior by inviting friends to read your lips: taxes will go up. If the rate of income tax remains the same or even drops (the favourite trick of 'conservative' glossocrats), then some other, less visible, taxes will make up for this generosity. One way or the other the Modman state will make us pay more because by so doing it will increase its power over us and that is what it craves. The difference between 'right-wing' and 'left-wing' glossocrats lies not in their actions, much less in their principles, but in the glossocratic response they wish to elicit from the electorate.

By the same token, a 'right-wing' or 'conservative' glossocrat is expected to make patriotic noises, be that commitment to defence (more USA than UK), to sovereignty (UK), to anti-Americanism (France) or, implicitly, to international dominance (Germany). The pitch of such noises has to be set just right: too low and the core market will not buy; too high and the market appeal will be too narrow. In any case, the real issues behind the words will never come into play. The words, proper glossocratic messages, are all that matter. The winner in the glossocratic stakes will be a politician who finds the right vocabulary to claim, in the language of advertising media buyers, both coverage and depth – keeping the loyalty of his core supporters while at the same time appealing to a broader audience. A talent for doing so requires any number of qualities: an instinctive 'gut feel' for mass moods, cynicism, the ability to identify and operate the right market 'drivers', and charisma, but preferably divorced from any set of personal beliefs. What it demonstrably does not require is morals, honour, a strong mind, good taste, loyalty or sense of high duty. Such qualities would disqualify a Modman politician from any public office worth having, for they would make it impossible for him to play the glossocratic game with sufficient conviction. If there exist any politicians in the West who possess such qualities (which is doubtful), then they must have perfected the art of not acting on their convictions. That is tantamount to not having any in the first place. In fact, it is even worse – such people ought to know better.

It is amusing how the glossocratic mendacity of successful Modman politicians, at least in the Anglophone countries, often starts from the egalitarian names they go by. There is something unglossocratic about Anthony or William. Such names bespeak obtuse traditionalism; it is as if today's Philippe Egalité were to revert to

Duc d'Orleans rather than progress to a more likely Phil. Of course, one has to be fortunate to have been given a name that can be glossocratically shortened without sounding risibly infantile. Had John Major been named Ronald, he probably would be prime minister at the time of this writing. 'Ron Major' sounds like a square-jawed warrior, a bloke next door who will go to the wall fighting for his neighbours. That is a clear election winner, especially since, as we have seen, the name can be also shortened to an egalitarian 'Ronnie' without losing any of its appeal. Not so 'Johnny' Major, who could only be a wimp with a golden chain under his shirt. No, one might as well take one's lumps as John, rather than go down in posterity as a bed-wetting Johnny. Likewise, George Bush Senior probably lost to Bill Clinton partly because his name does not lend itself to glossocratic shortening: 'Georgie' Bush would be a polo-playing layabout, not the leader of the free world. His son won his elections, but only because he is known as a cosy 'Dubya'. Even so, he still lost the popular vote to an Al, whose contracted name makes a perfect glossocratic sound.

Of such little games Modman's glossocracy is made. But, illogically, the outcome is not an aggregate of little games, one big game in which children point their index fingers at one another and squeal, 'Bang, bang, you're dead.' The big game of glossocracy is played by grown-ups who prefer real guns spewing real death. The history of the blood-soaked twentieth century is its score sheet.

THE WAR TO END ALL WARS

'They make a desert and call it peace.'

(Tacitus)

Once a society has been subjugated and Westman within it suppressed, Modmen's expansionist cravings can no longer be satisfied in their own country, for there the goal has been achieved. As the modern state is innately expansionist, the thrust of expansion has to be directed outwards. A triumphant state can only grow away from its own domain. Modmen have to strike out in the direction of other domains, a process that can take the shape of either military conquest or else the formation of seemingly peaceful political and economic alliances. 'Seemingly' is the key word here, for, irrespective of their explicit goals, Modman international alliances are always pregnant with international war.

A comparison between the Franco–Prussian and First World War provides a good illustration of this. At the heart of the former lay Germany's dissatisfaction with France that ran deeper than any expression of articulated geopolitical grievances could have possibly delved. The Germans simply could not understand why their versatile talents and industry had failed to earn the respect to which they were entitled. France, which the Germans mistakenly regarded as frivolous, had used its facile glitter to attract adulation from all over the world. And the French language ruled supreme as the lingua franca of the Western world, while German had some currency only in the low-rent part of Europe. The Germans felt aggrieved, an irrational feeling for which pseudo-rational expressions were never in short supply, what with the thorn of Alsace and Lorraine stuck in the sides of both countries. A war broke out in 1870, and the proto-socialist Prussian state, ably assisted by nihilist subversion inside France, quickly sorted France out, proving to itself that its laudatory self-assessment was true. But as the war was fought one on one, its consequences were not disastrous to anything other than France's pride and bank balance.

This was not so of the war that began in 1914. Even though the old resentments were still in place, augmented this time by France's revanchist sentiment, they were not the driving force. For neither France nor Germany was any longer alone, out to fend for itself. Having succumbed to the expansionist, supranational urges of Modmen, both were now part of inflexible alliances wherein an offence against one member would push the button for the automatic mode of universal response. Even Britain, the coolest head among the European belligerents, had for the first time in her history entered into an alliance in which she undertook to go to war automatically in the event of Germany's attack on France. The carnage that followed spelled the end of Westman, a tragedy comparable to the sacking of the Hellenic world by the ancestors of today's Germans.

The tools both sides used to push millions over the top into clouds of noxious gas were not physical but glossocratic. There was no real reason for the First World War, apart from words. It was to words that the masses responded, not to any fundamental need. Any real geopolitical problem could easily have been swept under the carpet had the consequences of solving it by violence been weighed in the balance. It was not that any of the belligerents actually had a geopolitical grievance in the traditional sense of the word. The war was fought not for geopolitical but, on that scale for the first time in history, economic gain. Plunder and greed were on the mind of the philistine Modman. Materialism was his god, markets his church and he was prepared to kill millions if this would make Messrs Krupp, Vickers and Ford happy. But even those appetites could have been satisfied at a negotiating table. Some give and take, trading rather than stealing horses, maybe a quiet bribe, a sweaty handshake and perhaps the Morgans and Thyssens could accept that killing millions just may be unnecessary.

Glossocratic vocabules, however, cannot be dismissed so easily. Their power is irrational and therefore has to be absolute to be anything. And nothing promotes absolute power as effectively as a war can, the bloodier, the better. The Great War was the first major conflict ever fought mostly for words, though regrettably not only with words. Millions had to die, taking what was left of the West with them. Neither side was averse to particularizing its claims and going from the general to the specific. They were both fighting to save civilization in a broad sense, but at the same time they were making the world safe not just for democracy (the marasmatic Wilson was welcome to that one) but also for true faith, world commerce, family, security, children, church and prosperity. Both sides were out to defend those in their own eyes and to rape them in the eyes of the other side.

Almost instantly the war acquired a character that went beyond any national grievances or indeed economic interests. The world was rife with proposals for unifying the control of global raw materials in a single body that could also administer international taxes aimed at levelling inequalities among nations. The air was dense with phrases like 'World Organization', 'The United States of the Earth', 'The Confederation of the World', 'A World Union of Free Peoples' and, finally, 'The League of Nations'. Both sides 'positioned' themselves as defenders of international law. The British, for example, eschewed self-interest as the reason for joining the conflict, opting instead to depict the war as a holy crusade for the law of the nations. Not to be outdone, the French organized a Committee for the Defence of International Law. The Germans were at first taken aback by this sudden outburst of affection for global legality, but they quickly recovered to fight back. Belgium, according to them, was not neutral in the inter-national-law sense of the word. It was conducting secret military negotiations with the British aimed against Germany. The British were not squeaky clean either. They were systematically violating the trading rights of neutrals on the high seas. Germany was really fighting for the freedom of the seas and the rights of smaller nations to engage in peaceful trade without being harassed by the dastardly Royal Navy. However, the entente would not allow Germany to claim the pre-emptive benefit of defending the small and weak. It was the allies who were after liberating the oppressed nations, by which they no longer simply meant Alsace and Lorraine. This time they meant the oppressed minorities in the Austro–Hungarian empire and the Polish minority in Germany (not to be confused with the German minority in Poland, whose plight was a *casus belli* for Germany's next war). That most of Poland was a minority in the Russian empire could be overlooked for as long as the Russians played ball on the right side. Funny you should mention oppressed minorities, replied the Germans, who hated to be outdone by anybody and especially the British. It was they, the Germans, who were fighting to liberate the small nations of the world. More specifically, I refer to such small nations as India, Ireland, Egypt and the entire African continent.

But never mind puny nations. Both sides had broader aims: they were out to save civilization. Both carried on their broad shoulders an equivalent of the white man's burden, ignoring the obvious chromatic incidental of both of them being equally white. It was only at first sight that the similarities between the warring sides were more basic than the differences. They simply would not stay in the same bracket; each side was out to save civilization, nothing less. A week after the war began the London *Evening Standard* was already carrying headlines screaming 'civilization at issue'. France was fighting a *'guerre contre les barbares'*, while Germany was laying about her for her *Kultur*. Germany, the nation of composers and philosophers, the country that had established a spiritual ascendancy over the world thanks to her industry, fecundity, wisdom and morality, was waging war against the degenerate Latins (an undegenerate Italy was to fight Germany's corner in the next one), barbaric Russians and mercantile British in whose assessment Napoleon would have been correct had he not been French. The British were usurers (a role they were to cede to the Jews before long); the Germans were Teutonic heirs to Arminius and Alaric. The British were unable to see beyond their utilitarian little noses, as demonstrated by their philosophers; the Germans had the sagacity to penetrate the meaning of life, as proved by their thinkers. The war was fought for heroic, self-sacrificing *Bildung* and against the pecuniary British.

Speak for yourself *sale Boche*, objected the French. The war was waged by one (good) race against another (bad). The Gauls of France and Belgium were fighting the Hun, and never mind *Bildung*. This argument secretly appealed to the Germans who had been beaten to the racial pre-emptive benefit that time but decided to store it for future use. Race more or less equalled God, as far as the French glossocrats were concerned. While every belligerent country claimed that God was on her side, *La Croix* in France made the case with a forthrightness not normally associated with the French: 'The story of France is the story of God. Long live Christ who loves the Franks.' '*La guerre sainte*', screamed *L'Echo de Paris*, and *La Croix* agreed in principle but wanted to expand: yes, it was 'a war of Catholic France against Protestant Germany'. But it was more than just that. It was a 'duel between the Germans and the Latins and the Slavs', a contest of 'public morals and international law'.

Hold on a minute, the British begged to differ. The French, while on the side of the angels in this one, could not claim exclusive possession of God. The Bishop of Hereford explained this succinctly:

> Such a heavy price to pay for our progress towards the realization of the Christianity of Christ, but duty calls, and the price must be paid for the good of those who are to follow us. ... Amidst all the burden of gloom and sorrow which this dreadful war lays upon us we can at least thank God that it brings that better day a long step nearer for the generations in front of us.

Which generations were to lose, conservatively, 300 million in assorted wars and purges (some estimates run much higher), but then, to be fair, the good bishop had no way of knowing this.

Never mind God, or in the case of the Germans the gods of their Valhalla. As a British musical promoter wrote at the time, this was really a war between different types of music:

> The hour has come to put aside and to veil with crêpe the scores of the men who have crystallized in so unmistakable a

manner the spirit of the modern Huns. ... The future belongs to the young hero who will have the courage to exclude from his library all the works of Handel, Mendelssohn, Wagner, Brahms and Richard Strauss ..., who will draw from the depths of his own being tone pictures of all that is beautiful in the wonderful poetry of Great Britain, and find the vigorous rhythms that will tell of the dauntless spirit of those who go to death singing 'Tipperary'.

At the risk of being known as Hun lovers, we could still argue that the Hunnish music of a Bach cantata is a long, long way from 'Tipperary', even though our preference does not come into this. The gentleman displayed a great deal of prescience, however. His future and our present indeed belong to the young hero who has courageously excluded Handel and Brahms, while including, with equal courage, Sex Pistols and Band Aid. The impresario also displayed much insight: the underlying aims of the war were not geopolitical but cultural.

The role played by America in the First World War is instructive. On the surface, this was not America's fight: her geopolitical or economic interests would not have been unduly threatened by any possible outcome. Wilson's sloganeering along the lines of 'making the world safe for democracy' would have sounded frankly ludicrous to any other than a glossocratic audience. Such an aim presupposed that the Great War was waged against democracy, and only General Pershing in shining armour was there to save it. That simply was not the case. All major combatants either already were democracies or constitutional monarchies – or else were moving in that direction with no outside help necessary. The big slogan would seem to be a big lie, but only if we insist on using words in their real meaning. Of course by then Modman glossocracy had taken over, so the word 'democracy' did not really mean political pluralism. It meant Modmen's rule.

By the time the United States entered the war, the pacifist

propaganda the Bolsheviks waged and the Germans paid for had already paralysed Russia. She had been almost knocked out of the conflict and, with her armies deserting *en masse*, was months away from falling into the grip of the worst tyranny the world had ever known. At the same time, on the Western Front supposedly civilized people were no longer fighting a war; they were engaged in mass murder for its own sake. Under such circumstances, it did not take a crystal ball to predict that any possible conclusion of the massacre would come at a cost to traditional institutions. As the flower of Westman holdouts were being mowed down, so was the habitat in which the West could possibly stagger back to life.

Woodrow Wilson did not need fortune-telling appliances to predict such an outcome. The thing was that this was precisely the outcome he craved. Alone among the wartime leaders, Wilson had clear-cut objectives that went beyond simply winning the war. Unlike, say, the Clemenceaus of this world, he heard the clarion call of Modman not as a distant echo but in every tonal detail, and responded by employing every Modman technique at his disposal. Shortly after the war began, and two years before America's entry, Wilson set up the greatest advertising agency ever seen. Called the Committee on Public Information, it included America's leading propagandists, and was headed by George Creel whose own political sympathies lay far on the left. Their task was clearly defined: America had a mission to convert the world to her way of life. The president had come to the conclusion that this mission could be fulfilled only by entering the war. Therefore the American people who, in their ignorance, opposed such a move had to be made to see the light. Anyway, the American people hardly mattered: Wilson had in mind a programme for all mankind, not just parochial interests, and if the programme could be put into action only at a cost to American lives, then so be it.

Having won the 1916 re-election on the glossocratic slogan 'He kept us out of the war', Wilson went on to demonstrate that every means was suitable for dragging America into the meat grinder. Technically neutral until April 1917, she had begun to violate the provisions of neutrality from the start. The House of Morgan, for example, floated war loans for Britain and France in 1915, while war supplies were flowing from America across the Atlantic in an uninterrupted stream. The Germans were thus provoked into unrestricted U-boat warfare (not that they needed much provoking), which in turn helped Wilson to build a slender pro-war margin in the Congress. As if to demonstrate that a good idea should never go to waste, Franklin D. Roosevelt, Wilson's spiritual heir, later used a similar stratagem to push America into the next war.

Nor was Wilson particularly bashful in putting his agenda across, when, for example, describing the blood bath as:

[T]his great war in which there is being fought out once [and] for all the irrepressible conflict between free self-government and the dictation of force ... a struggle whose object is liberation, freedom, the rights of men and nations to live their own lives and determine their own fortunes, the rights of the weak as well as of the strong, and the maintenance of justice by the irresistible force of free nations leagued together in the defence of mankind.

In his own mind, or perhaps viscera, Wilson knew exactly what he was after: the destruction of Westman's world and its replacement with a world of Modmen led by the philistine American subspecies. That is why the propaganda spewed out by the Creel Committee went beyond amateurish attacks on the bloodthirsty Hun. Every piece of promotional literature Creel put out and every speech by Wilson was an incitement to revolution, both political and social, across Europe.

Thus America had no quarrel with the industrious people of

Germany; it was the oppressive Junkers class that was the enemy. No sacrifice was too great to liberate the Germans from their own domestic tyrants. No peace, no armistice was possible until the existing social order and political arrangement were destroyed – in other words, until a revolution took place. Likewise, Wilson had no quarrel with the quirky people inhabiting the British empire; it was the empire itself he abhorred. Even though for tactical reasons that particular message could not yet be enunciated in so many words, dismantling the offending institution was clearly one of Wilson's key objectives. A fanatic of a single world government, Wilson was at the same time a great champion of national self-determination. Anticipating a possible confusion on the part of the reader, there was no contradiction there at all, at least not to a glossocratic mind. The first was the end; the second the means.

The marginal peoples of the empires, all those Czechs, Poles, Finns and Serbs, could not make good any promise of self-determination without a prior destruction of all traditional goverments – QED. It was no concern of Wilson that the dismantling of a rather jumbled but still workable Austro-Hungarian empire would lead to the creation of artificial, and ultimately untenable, states. For example, fashioning a federation out of the culturally and religiously hostile peoples of Yugoslavia was tantamount to pushing the countdown button on a time bomb. But such concerns are never a factor in glossocratic calculations; nor did it matter to Wilson on which side an un-Modman government fought. He was as hostile to the British and Russian empires as he was to the Central European ones. It stood to reason that he would welcome the demise of those institutions, even at the cost of reversal in the fortunes of war. Thus, when the tsarist regime collapsed, Wilson was ecstatic. Here was another democracy hatched out of the dark recesses of absolutism. That the new 'democracy' was so weak that it could not keep her troops at the front mattered little. For Modmen this was not about winning a war but about winning the battle for the world.

That is why Wilson, Lloyd George and their followers in the ranks of the Modman glossocratic intelligentsia constantly downplayed the risk of a Bolshevik takeover and failed to respond to it properly once it took place. Though they would have preferred a Kerensky-style democracy for an ally, they were prepared to live with the Bolsheviks as long as the quasi-Westman Whites could be kept out. Wilson, in fact, contributed to the Bolshevik revolt by facilitating the return of Trotsky from New York to Petrograd. Germany's role in providing a similar service for Lenin is well known and, after 70 years of lying Soviet denials, universally acknowledged. Out of fairness if nothing else we should similarly acknowledge the gigantic efforts of President Wilson who had to countermand his own State Department to ensure that the future leader of the Bolshevik uprising, armed with a crisp US passport, found himself aboard a transatlantic liner. The affair caused some awkwardness: as American papers had just published documented evidence of Trotsky's dependence on German funding, Wilson was in effect helping an enemy agent. But such incidentals were not allowed to interfere with his global vision.

People like Wilson and Lloyd George had much greater affinity for the Bolsheviks than for any administrators of the traditional empires. In general, Modmen of either the philistine or nihilist hue have more in common with one another than they do with Westmen. A philistine Modman state may have democracy written on its banners, but instinctively it will always be closer to a Modman totalitarian government than to true Westman autocracy or even parliamentarianism. Deep-seated cultural affinity overrides intellectual posturing whenever the going gets tough. This explains the otherwise inexplicable benevolence of many 'democratic' statesmen towards either the Bolsheviks or the Nazis or, as in the case of Lloyd George, both. Modman nihilists, for all their manifest failings, did not threaten the hidden treasures of Modman philistines' hearts in the manner in which Westmen did. A Modman nihilist could destroy millions of Modman philistines without endangering Modman philistinism, while Westmen presented such a threat without ever laying a finger on a single philistine.

In his memoirs Lloyd George implies as much: 'Personally, I would have dealt with the Soviets as the *de facto* Government of Russia. So would President Wilson. But we both agreed that we could not carry to that extent our colleagues at the Congress, nor the public opinion of our own countries which was frightened by Bolshevik violence and feared its spread.' Implicitly, neither Wilson nor Lloyd George shared that fear. They were, however, mortified by the thought of any possible restoration of a Westman-holdout government in Russia. That is why their support for the White movement in the Russian Civil War was lukewarm at best. To both Wilson and Lloyd George, the Whites were out to restore the tsarist empire that would present a greater danger to Modmen's interests than the Bolsheviks ever could. Of course, they had to mollify the public in their own countries, and the public was not yet prepared to accept the ongoing massacre of millions in Russia as the march of progress – especially since not all eyewitness accounts of it could be suppressed.

Early in 1918 Sidney Reilly, for example, pleaded from Moscow that his superiors in London shift the emphasis of their policy from the war to the Bolshevik revolution: 'This hideous cancer [is] striking at the very root of civilization,' wrote this well-known sceptic who then went on to prove that his mind was not fashionably open at all:

> Gracious heavens, will the people in England never understand? The Germans are human beings; we can afford to be even beaten by them. Here in Moscow there is growing to maturity the arch enemy of the human race. ... At any price this foul obscenity which has been born in Russia must be crushed out of existence. ...

Mankind must unite in a holy alliance against this midnight
terror.

But Reilly was a foreigner, an ex-Russian with an obvious axe to
grind and, to mix the metaphors, a pro-Westman chip on his
shoulder. He was also a Jew, born Rosenblum, of which Bruce
Lockhart, at the time the senior British official in Russia, never
stops reminding us in his memoirs. In other words, Reilly could
never be trusted. Instead, it fell upon Lloyd George to express the
dominant emotion of Modman:

> Our attitude [towards the Bolsheviks] was that of the Fox
> Whigs towards the French Revolution. ... A Bolshevik
> Russia is by no means such a danger as the old Russian
> Empire. ... Bolsheviks would not wish to maintain an army,
> as their creed is fundamentally anti-militarist. ... There must
> be no attempt to conquer Bolshevik Russia by force of arms.
> ... The anti-Bolshevik armies must not be used to restore the
> old Tsarist regime and reimpose on the peasants the old
> feudal conditions under which they held their land.

Admittedly, there was the minor matter of Lenin having betrayed
the alliance and signed a separate peace with Germany, while 'the
anti-Bolshevik armies' were committed to honouring Russia's
obligations. HMG had to be seen as providing some token support
to the Whites. But there were strings attached.

HMG was willing to supply surplus munitions if the Whites
were to agree to 'renounce class privileges' [this anticipated John
Major's brand of conservatism by a good 80 years], 'refrain from
restoring the former land system' [which, in the non-glossocratic
world, had been roughly the same as Britain's] and 'make no
attempt to reintroduce the regime which the revolution destroyed'
[that is, parliamentary democracy]. In case the Whites were
desperate enough to accept these conditions, Ernest Bevin, then a
young union leader on the rise, promised HMG that any attempt

to send help to the anti-Bolsheviks would result in a domestic revolution precipitated by a general strike from hell. Thus Westman's last defenders died in the icy steppes of Kuban and on the hill slopes of the Urals, their lifeless fingers clutching empty rifles even in death. The last chapter of the Great War was finished and no war in human history has yet had such a devastating effect on the world, an effect far out of proportion to the numbers killed.

Whether the agents of Westman's demise, the Wilsons and Lloyd Georges of this world, acted in that capacity consciously is an interesting but moot question: it is as impossible to answer as any such questions on human behaviour. One cannot second-guess others' motives; even one's own are sometimes shrouded in darkness. Human lives, indeed human spirits, seldom progress in a straight line; development is not a sequential accumulation of energy needed to make the next step. Our thoughts, beliefs, our very destinies zig and zag, they take a step forward, then two backwards, then a few sideways and forward again. Except that by then our heads are spinning and we are no longer certain where forward is. If there is any bias that determines the general direction of human meandering, it comes not from reason but from something more deep-seated. Reason alone cannot explain why great masses of humanity allowed themselves to be led to slaughter; nor can it explain why their leaders chose to do the devil's work.

It is doubtful that many of the key personages who shaped the murder of Westman were aware of what they were doing. For all we know, Wilson actually believed in making the world safe for democracy as much as Hitler believed in making the world safe for *Kultur* or Lenin in social justice for all. But underneath the epidermis of their conviction lay a murky layer of intuitive cravings, something of which they may or may not have been aware, and something into which they perhaps chose not to delve. It is in this murky substratum that evil resides, which is why it is impossible to uproot. But its presence can be surmised from known facts. That is why it is pointless to try to understand the motives of life's key players; they themselves may not have been fully aware of them. But deflection in the lives of millions influenced by evil leaders provides the evidence we seek, and perhaps a deeper insight into human nature than rational research could ever produce. Men who caused the First World War were evil because their deeds were.

That war is often described as Europe's suicide and in some ways it was just that. Above all, however, it was the murder of Westman within Europe's borders, the triumph of Modman. The inner impulse that injected murderous energy into Europe came from Modmen's desire to destroy the habitat in which Westman could return to life. Since *de facto* power had already swung to Modman, he was in a position to act as both ventriloquist and puppet master. It was his voice that sounded behind the moving lips of seemingly Western statesmen; it was he who was pulling the strings. The easiest way to demonstrate who the real perpetrator was is to apply the ancient *cui bono* principle. Indeed, the First World War knocked out the two political cornerstones of Westman: the British and Austro–Hungarian empires. These last strongholds of Westman polity were pushed into oblivion, along with the quasi-Westman Russia. In the process, whatever trust had existed between Europeans and their governments was gassed out of existence in Flanders and shot up to pieces in East Prussia. Trust was replaced by cynicism at best, hatred at worst. Since the perpetrators bore an uncanny resemblance to Westman, he was unfairly implicated in this crime. As a result, all the underlying ideas of his world were compromised, and Europe was left at the mercy of glossocratic larceny.

Emerging victorious was Modman, who somehow has been overlooked as the real driving force behind the scenes. Both subspecies were thriving: the nihilist grabbed Russia and, soon thereafter, Italy and Germany. The philistine was also doing well.

Britain and France fell under his sway. Westmen there were cowering underground, if they were alive at all. Glossocracy now reigned supreme.

ART IMITATING DEATH

The cultural anomie of Modmen was camouflaged not to appear to be the real reason for the Great War. However, in matters directly related to culture, no such disguise was possible. Shining the torch of hindsight at the decades intervening between the Franco–Prussian and First World Wars we discern anti-traditionalism. Since we already know that this proved to be the fatal infection that killed Westman, we should pay serious attention to various manifestations of the malaise. As ever, art reflects life, or it may be the other way around. In either event, they are intricately linked, and so art merits a closer look if only because such radical innovations as Braque's and Picasso's cubism, Kandinsky's abstract painting, Marinetti's futurist poetry and Schönberg's dodecaphonic music all appeared in the run-up to the Great War. It was not just in politics that Modman was running amok.

'Fascism is merely futurism in practice,' wrote Wyndham Lewis whose ear was fine-tuned to the link between contemporaneous politics and modernistic spasms. Modman art trends are all products of what was described earlier as 'conscious innovation'. The artists developed new forms not only because they felt constricted by the old ones but also because they wanted to destroy them. This is not something one can prove in any *prima facie* way, which without a doubt weakens the argument. But there are enough indications pointing in the direction of this conclusion for it to be plausible.

New art forms are not *ipso facto* destructive. Introduced for the right reasons, they resuscitate art with a breath of fresh air. Having pushed conventional forms to their limit, the artist may feel constricted by them; everything he tries comes out pale, repetitive, lifeless. Convention is no longer a useful starting point; the walls of tradition are closing in on him. So he experiments; he tries to expand the limits of his genre by pushing against the walls with both palms. If the artist belongs to the chosen few in history who had sufficient strength in their arms and shoulders, then a miracle can happen. The walls give way and even if the roof falls in the artist shakes off the fragments and emerges unscathed, proud of his Samson-like strength. This is how it would be if art were created in a social vacuum. Alas, it is not. Artists are not hermetic monks who spend their lives bundled in holes cut in walls. They are creatures of their time and place, with only the greatest among them able to transcend both history and geography. None of the artists mentioned above falls into that category, although they were all talented. There must have been a different motive behind their urgent desire to reform their arts. A comparison between Beethoven and Schönberg could prove useful in elucidating the issue.

Beethoven did have a proclivity towards conscious innovation. But it was in the background of his work, overshadowed by a genuine quest for uncharted territory. His place in history would have been assured, and his artistic mission largely fulfilled, even if he had died before composing the late quartets and the 'Hammerklavier', especially the latter. It is a brave musicologist who will state unequivocally that Beethoven's Fifth Piano Concerto is better than his Third, or that his Ninth Symphony is superior to his Seventh. Beethoven had to strike away from classicism not because he could not write classical music but because he had exhausted its possibilities. The late quartets, for which he was proclaimed insane, were thus a new vessel for Beethoven's genius, nothing more and nothing less. Against this background, his revolutionary urges appear only as minor and largely irrelevant irritants.

The same cannot be said of Schönberg. His early work, written in the same post-romantic idiom Mahler had used, showed nothing like the same greatness. Had he not written *Pierrot*

Lunaire and all his subsequent works, Schönberg would now be bracketed with a myriad of other post-romantic composers we have safely forgotten and only occasionally take off the mothballs for curiosity value. As it is, his theories are universally revered even by those who seldom listen to his music. Actually, there was nothing wrong with Schönberg's theories. His writings on harmony, dissonance and consonance, and related matters of musical theory are nothing short of brilliant. Schönberg was an exceptionally clever man, but unfortunately that is not the same as being a great composer, a great Western composer at any rate. That is why even the same Westman holdouts who find Schönberg's music interesting seldom find it moving.

One detects in Schönberg the destructive impetus so typical of Modmen, something absent in the work of his student Alban Berg who sparingly used a similar idiom but managed to weave it into genuinely moving music. One also senses in Schönberg a keen nose for what the customer wanted, a quality again missing in Berg and possibly Webern, but amply present in the likes of Picasso. Schönberg's music does not constitute organic development; it is an artificial construct. Dodecaphony did not appear as a natural continuation of the diatonic scale; Schönberg manifestly set out to destroy it. The diatonic scale itself was an organic development neatly fitting into Westman's progression of 'begats': ancient chant, possibly going back to the Temple, begat modes, modes begat polyphony, polyphony begat tonality, tonality begat tempering, and so forth. In other words, music based on the diatonic scale followed the same evolutionary pattern as other cultural possessions of Westman and, in common with them, gradually turned the tables and made Westman its own possession. Westman music imposes a discipline that is a spur to creative freedom, not a yoke around its neck. Great composers of the romantic era showed how strict harmonic and structural principles can produce untethered freedom of expression, sounding almost anarchic to the uninitiated.

Not so the 12-tone row Schönberg constructed. Like Modman politics, it pretends to be liberating but ends up being tyrannical. Indeed, adhering to strict dodecaphony imposes not so much discipline as a strangulation hold designed to stifle real artistry. And, unlike socialism, which is rooted in human nature, albeit its darker sides, the musical tyranny of Schönberg cannot claim any natural appeal to even the baser forms of humanity. For real music is within us. Even as writers of genius help us discover parts of ourselves, so do great composers delve the depths of our souls to uncover the music within. The listener is thus a passive co-creator: passive for he is not the one who wrote the music, co-creator because without him music would not exist. And since music is probably metabolized in the same part of the human soul as religious feeling, the proximity adds an almost divine aspect to this symbiosis.

A Modman, with his insatiable appetite for reducing everything to formal reason, ignores all that. He will devour books on harmony and will talk non-stop about temporal relationships, harmonic progressions, tempo rubato, inversions, diminished sevenths and double thirds. The point he misses is that all those things, essential as they are, do not make music. They are solely the means of conveying music, which is not at all the same. As long as we keep that distinction in mind, we could all profit from studying books on musical theory – including those by Schönberg. But lose sight of that distinction and music starts emanating the mildewy smell of decomposing corpses. Without its direct, suprarational appeal to a secret crevice within our souls, music becomes so much intellectual autoeroticism. It stops being music, which is to say it dies.

Obsession with musical theory at the expense of music itself also has an egalitarian effect. It drags music out of a sphere to which few have full access and into an area where anyone can succeed with a little industry and application. Musical theorizing thus answers a deep craving of a Modman by making him as successful in his own eyes as he wants to be, not as God made him capable of becoming. The results can be ludicrous: there are many people who hardly ever listen to music, opting instead for parsing and decorticating endless scores.

Just as painting is more than crusted pigment on canvas, analysable music written on a score sheet is a formal shell designed to house the soul and communicate the metaphysical provenance of man. But if we agree that faith and music share the same compartment in our souls, it will be so much easier to agree that the music residing at such lofty quarters is not atonal. As an experiment, one could find a musical virgin, someone who has never heard any classical music at all (these days, a search for such a simpleton would not take long) and drag him into a room with a piano. One could then proceed to play the basic triad first, and then simply lower a hand on random keys. Even our ignoramus would have no difficulty telling one from the other: that to him would be unmistakably music and this would be a load of something unspeakable. If one took the experiment a step further and played a quotation from, say, Haydn followed by a bit of late Schönberg, the reaction would be roughly similar.

Art may be semantically linked with artifice, but when it begins living down to its etymological origin, it stops being art, at least in the Westman sense of the word. At best it can become a sort of pseudoartistic mule, half thoroughbred half ass. And like that work-a-day beast, it is incapable of producing progeny. That is why Schönberg's innovations were short-lived. His constructs were tried by his pupils, such as Berg, perhaps a few others, and then largely dismissed by the great composers of the twentieth century. In his glorious Violin Concerto, for example, Berg, a greater talent than his master, cannot throw off the tonal under-pinnings which, combined with the surface atonality, make his music so much more moving: a reflection of a disintegrating world that provides the backdrop against which the concerto unfolds.

The strength of Western art lies in its natural symbiosis with Westman's strength. The weakness of Modman art is in its manmade artificiality. This applies to any art, including painting. Picasso, the patron saint of Modman art, did not even bother to conceal towards the end of his life that most of his work after the 'pink period' had been a hoax played on an unsuspecting public. His cynicism notwithstanding, Picasso's admissions ought to be taken seriously. Here we have a gifted artist who senses what the public wants: not art, but artifice; not beauty, but beastliness; not creation, but destruction. Picasso's cynical insight must have been true, judging by the millions he earned from it. What should concern us in the context of this chapter is that the soil during the run-up to the Great War was fertile for seeds of destruction.

Preoccupation with form, while not necessarily decadent in itself, is a sign of decadence. In post-Westman society it is also subversive: Westman, after all, became what he was precisely because of his ability to concentrate on the essence of things rather than their outer shell. There is nothing wrong in expanding the limits of tonality or harmony, nothing objectionable in dissecting and rearranging physical shapes into constituent elements – provided that the purpose of art is not lost behind all those expansions, dissections and rearrangements. The original and ultimate purpose of Western art was to express Westman's soul, stating that it exists and therefore God exists. That by the beginning of the twentieth century this purpose had been either lost or put on hold conveyed implications that went much broader than art, implications made clear by the guns of Verdun and Ypres.

Circumstantial evidence for this comes from the personal links of many twentieth-century innovators to twentieth-century politics. Pound, Severini and Marinetti became fascists; Picasso, along with others whose name is legion, was a life-long communist. Khlebnikov and Pasternak welcomed the Bolshevik revolution, while the erstwhile futurist Mayakovsky glorified its worst excesses – show trials, mass repressions, purges and the executions of hostages. And even the true geniuses of the twentieth century, Prokofiev and Shostakovich, were ambivalent about the revolution, in broad sympathy with its goals even when furtively critical of its methods.

In spite of his leftward leanings, Prokofiev's first response to the revolution was to flee abroad. Later he, along with Tsvetayeva, inspired by the GPU's exploitation of émigré nostalgia, got caught up in the Changing Signposts movement and went back with his tail between his legs. His was a tragic fate, for he found himself between the Scylla of one reference Modman country and the Charybdis of the other. He had to choose between endangered cultural survival in the United States and imperilled physical survival in Russia. Those who never have been in his position have no more right to judge him than those who have been, but made the opposite choice. This does not mean we cannot contemplate his decision, analyse its psychological and historical contexts and perhaps express selfish gratitude for it. For, had Prokofiev preferred the life of commercial composer or – marginally better – itinerant pianist in the West (for which he was less equipped both emotionally and pianistically than Rachmaninov) to that of Stalin's court composer, it is unlikely that his Seventh, Eighth and Ninth piano sonatas would be here to spellbind us. These and Prokofiev's other great works of the same period shine out of the rubbish he had to produce to stay in Stalin's good books. Shostakovich, whose quartets and Eighth Symphony, among other masterpieces, also place him in the front row of composers, fared even worse in that department, having had to bang out masses of populist trash, what the Russians call 'skating-rink music'. That is why he still sometimes suffers a bad press in the West, possibly because some commentators do not know his best music well. Such critics could do worse than remember that an artist should be judged by his best work. With the possible exception of Bach, no composer could pass the test of greatness on any randomly selected piece, as anyone who has heard Chopin's First Sonata or most of Mozart's youthful compositions will confirm.

This should apply especially to those great Westman artists who had to labour under the conditions of the worst tyranny ever imposed by Modman. That Shostakovich had to spend half his waking hours fearing imminent arrest makes his achievements so much more grandiose. Not to have sunk under the weight of such a millstone around his neck is an achievement in itself. Shostakovich found a way around political tyranny by churning out trashy cinematic scores in the way of tax on greatness. But he did not succumb to the musical tyranny of the 12-tone row, even though he may have flirted with it on a couple of occasions. Westman art is incompatible with Modman artifice. It will fight to the end and will either conquer or die in the attempt.

THE TRAILBLAZERS OF NIHILISM

For the last two centuries Russia has been a shining beacon for the nihilist subspecies of Modman. But since the philistine is closely related to the nihilist, the former has also been guided by Russia's reflected light. We already have seen that the word 'nihilist', while Latin in form, was Russian in origin. The time has come to talk about another similarly derived word: 'intelligentsia'. Though this class first made its appearance in eighteenth-century France, it took its mature shape in Russia in the nineteenth century, and it was the Russian variant that has since then inspired similar groups elsewhere. Old Russian dictionaries defined 'intelligentsia' as a group of educated people hostile to the ruling regime. Defined with the benefit of our terminology, it can be described as the intellectual vanguard of Modman's onslaught on Westman.

It was in the decades immediately preceding, and in the century following, the 1825 revolt that a new class appeared in Russia: an intelligentsia innately opposed to what their descendants in the West today call the Establishment but what in fact is Westman's world. The new class quickly became dominant in Russian culture and thought, as it is now dominant in the West. For any shouting contest will be won by the individual with the loudest voice and worst manners. The new class possessed those attributes in abundance, so it swept all before it. Interestingly, the origin of this group can be traced to the so-called Westernizers who began engaging their opponents, the Slavophiles, in the years following Catherine II's reign. As with most terminology beloved of Modman, this designation was imprecise. The Westernizers were hearing in their heads the echoes of the anti-Westman voices in France, screaming the slogans of the Enlightenment. Had they understood the essence of the contemporaneous West, they would have renounced their 'Westernness' in an instant.

As it was, they bellowed their creed from the pages of magazines and newspapers, the media that, before the advent of broadcasting, were more conducive to making loud noises than any other. Journalism, unless it is used simply as a means of communicating factual information, is at best useless and at worst harmful. It is useless when it vulgarizes a complex issue by pretending to elucidate it in a thousand or fewer words; it is harmful when trying to exert an intellectual and social influence on the basis of such pretence. For an article, no matter how well written, cannot throw light on a serious problem. Such issues are invariably impossible to clarify one by one. Things are interconnected in life, and 1000 words would be barely adequate even to state a problem, never mind delve deep into it. The format of an article allows the writer merely to slide along the surface of a thought, not to penetrate its core. Sufficient only to express opinions, it can seldom help an intelligent reader to work out an important point. This limitation makes journalism ideal for Modman, what with his disdain for the substance of things and their interconnection. That is why journalism grew in proportion to Modman's power, and as Modman became the absolute ruler in the West, so did the press.

Philosophically, the press promotes Modman's empiricism. Weaned on the belief that real knowledge can only come from the senses, Modman is ready to accept an eyewitness report as the truth simply because of its first-hand verisimilitude. However, when used to make a serious point, 'I saw it with my own eyes' is inadequate because the eye sees only the surface of things, and that is not where the truth usually lies. We can cut a man open, but our eye will see only a few internal organs in a puddle of blood – not the essence of man. A cranial trepanation will reveal a pulsating brain, but it will not uncover a mind.

Journalism has only a limited usefulness even when reporters operate in their own countries. A devious enough government can always ration information in such a way that the press will report what the government wants. Courtesy of Tony Blair's government in Britain, this activity has even acquired a name: spin. But philistine Modman states are babes in the woods compared with their nihilist cousins, such as Russia. There spin, or 'disinformation' in Latinized Russian, is more than just a by-product of governmental business. It is the business itself. When Western reporters weaned on the unimpeachable sanctity of eyewitness reports arrive in Russia, the Russian *speen doktors* open their arms with come-to-papa conviviality: easy prey is begging to be gobbled up. For generations, Western reporters, further hampered by their almost universal inability to converse in Russian, were made to see what the Soviets wanted them to see and write what the Soviets wanted them to write. Modman readership swallowed those useless dispatches hook, line and sinker – and do let us not forget that in philistine countries *vox populi* can be influential. Thus, at a key period in history, policy making in the West was compromised by journalism biting off more than it could chew.

Until the nineteenth century the Russians had fared better: there were hardly any newspapers. However, once it appeared, the press grew in influence rapidly, outstripping the great literature burgeoning at the same time. Before too long the voices of such journalists as Belinsky and Chernyshevsky began to be heard more clearly than the whispers of the literary giants. The latter had to resort to journalism to get their share of voice, a situation not unique to Russia. Tolstoy's silly article 'I Cannot Remain Silent' had a greater social resonance than his sublime *War and Peace*; Emile Zola made a bigger splash with his article 'J'accuse' than with his novel *Nana*, which admittedly was not quite in the *Anna Karenina* class. Now, a century later, many of the same people who have heard of 'J'accuse' would be unable to name a single novel by Zola.

The press in its present form is a Modman invention and, as such, it reflects all his foibles, being shallow, materialistic, cruel, arrogant, ghoulish and voyeuristic. And even when a publication does not start out as a mouthpiece of hatred for Westman culture, it often ends up as such. For it is the press that creates, or helps to create, an intellectual atmosphere in which Westman cannot survive. In nineteenth-century Russia this process took 50 years or so; in the West, much longer. But the parallels are easily observable: in both places it became impossible to question Modmen's animadversions. In Russia this was achieved in part by hijacking the cause of supporting the weak and the downtrodden, which evoked the Gospels. By transference, the journalists tended to describe themselves and their friends as the actual downtrodden, rather than merely their champions. This was a lie typical of Modmen: in fact, as they began to shape what today is called public opinion, Modman hacks began to acquire the power and riches none of their Westman, as opposed to Westernizing, contemporaries could even imagine.

Professing hatred for the rich and powerful quickly became a lucrative and influential occupation, yet another example of Russia showing the shape of things to come elsewhere. While the Slavophile thinker Leontiev led what the philosopher Rozanov described as a 'miserable quasi-life of grief and sorrow', and while the conservative critic Strakhov often could not even afford to offer a cup of tea to his visiting friend Dostoyevsky (who himself subsisted in a bedsit favoured by cabbies and prostitutes), their inferiors Dobrolyubov, Mikhailovsky and Chernyshevsky were parlaying progressivism into a life of renown and power. Contrary to Bolshevik-inspired falsifiers of history, those clamouring for the destruction of Westman's civilization became 'the Establishment'; while the loyal, church-going conservatives were the real rebels.

Anyone familiar with the world of journalism in the West today will confirm that the course first charted by the Russians is being faithfully followed. Deviations occur only because some mainstream publications in Europe have a conservative genealogy that continues to attract, by force of inertia if nothing else, the Westman-holdout readership in numbers sufficient to justify an occasional bow in the direction of Westman principles. For that purpose the odd conservative columnist is kept on tap. In America, the reference Modman country of today, even such quasi-conservative publications no longer exist in the mainstream. Every major American newspaper and magazine is devoted to promoting the destructive agenda of Modman. As far as broadcast journalism is concerned, here both American and European channels operate in unison, acting as enthusiastic mouthpieces of Modman's glossocratic power. What Burke described as the fourth estate now dominates the other three.

In parallel with nihilist Soviet Russia, where Westman holdouts had to find outlets for their bile in samizdat publications, Westman holdouts in philistine Modman countries flock to semi-samizdat magazines with minuscule circulations. Soviet authorities tended to stamp out samizdat when they could not infiltrate it. Philistine authorities could do the same, but there is no need: they know that Westman-holdout, also known as 'conservative', publications have no influence. They can buy influence only by changing their spots, usually in favour of what in America is called 'neo-conservatism'. In other words, they must convert to a philosophy that reflects faithfully the aspirations of the philistine Modman: surreptitiously destroying everything Western, while keeping enough private enterprise to satisfy philistine cravings – the cultural answer to the NEP. 'Liberals mugged by reality' is a witty but insufficient description of the neo-conservatives. 'Nihilists gone philistine, while remaining Modmen' would be more precise.

It is refreshing to observe the extent to which today's news-papers and television channels abandon even the pretence of free speech. For speech to be free opposing views and philosophies must have an airing; it is as simple as that. Freedom from govern-mental interference alone does not make free speech: a government for and by cannibals, for example, would not have to put its foot down to ensure that every newspaper in the land promotes the interests of cannibals. That would go without saying. Their pluralistic subterfuge notwithstanding, all television channels and major newspapers in the West promote the cause of Modman with the same lack of remorse with which the press in Soviet Russia promoted communism. The only differences are stylistic: the philistines have learned how not to sound like their nihilist brothers. But the X-ray vision of a Westman holdout can still get under the skin of both subspecies to see the similar innards.

What the Russian intelligentsia achieved in the nineteenth century closely parallels the accomplishments of the Anglo-American intelligentsia in the twentieth, and the mechanisms involved are identical. Fashion based on conformism was the principal one. Paradoxically, though the intelligentsia loves to portray itself as courageously iconoclastic, it is a conformist group. If it is sensitive to anything, it is to that magic moment when fashion becomes orthodoxy; and it will jump on the bandwagon with alacrity. Even as 'rights activists' like to portray their appetites as rights, intelligentsia tends to depict its turgid musings as an intellectual *fait accompli*, which soon becomes a self-fulfilling prophecy. When a new orthodoxy is hatched, conformism kicks in; and suddenly it becomes impossible to voice any view that goes against the grain of the new consensus. While the new orthodoxy still remains in a touch-and-go phase, it lashes out at infidels with violence. Once it feels it has reached the point of no return, it adds new weapons to its arsenal: jeering, mockery, derision. The weapons were tested in the eighteenth century, so our inchoate orthodoxies know that they work; blast by blast the weapons go off, scattering Westman holdouts and driving them underground.

The Russians showed the way, demonstrating that a gossamer social fabric filled with hot air will blow up sooner or later. Like the Russian intelligentsia of yesteryear, the glossocratic intelligentsia of today's West is busily uprooting the last remaining vestiges of Westernness. The press is one gardening implement they use; education is another.

EDUCATING PHILISTINE EMILES

'Much learning does not teach understanding.'

(Heraclitus)

A one-eyed man can become king, but to effect such an ascent he has to blind everyone else. Modman tyrants of both subspecies should be credited with understanding this logic well. That is why they have always paid particular attention to the young. Leon Trotsky is a case in point. Like other nihilist Modmen, Trotsky loved the young because they were less anchored in the Westman past, less likely than their fathers to fall back on pre-Modman tradition. He echoed Confucius and pronounced that 'the young are the barometer of a nation'. Tersely put, although his Chinese counterpart, unencumbered by the availability of meteorological instruments, expressed the same thought more poetically: 'A youth is to be regarded with respect. How do you know that his future will not be equal to our present?'

The critical significance of the young is precisely why education is a burden the Modman state, in its endless beneficence, has chosen to place on its meaty shoulders. For Modman to live Westman has to die – that is basic; and the most important step in subduing Westmen is kicking sand into the eyes of the young. There is some logic behind this, for the prime concern of an organism is survival. Modern states are like any other organisms. Survival is their biological imperative, and this holds true regardless of whether or not the people who make up the institutions of Modman states are aware of it. Modman governments are not only corruptible, but they are inevitably corruptible; and that is why sage men of the Western past regarded governing least as the *sine qua non* of governing best. Modman, however, is a totalitarian by nature. He will not accept governing least; his rule has to be both wide, covering as many people as possible, and deep, reaching into the subjects' minds. Exactly how this is achieved varies from state to state, but the underlying principle is easy to discern. Of the two types of Modman statecraft, it is the philistine variety that is more interesting for being less obtrusive.

Explicitly, the glossocratic philistine state regards 'pursuit of happiness' as both its main promise and its claim to redemption. At the same time it can never forget its implicit goal, the destruction of Westman. The implicit and explicit can in this case coexist happily, but caution must be exercised to make sure they do. One wrong step and the positive end of happiness can get too close to the negative end of cultural mayhem, sending sparks flying all over the place. The need to tread carefully determines both the educational and the economic strategies adopted by the Modman state. On the one hand, it has to make both voters and consumers as ignorant, or at least as gullible, as they must be to snatch happily at anything glossocracy dangles in front of them. On the other hand, the Modman state has to watch its step, for, in making people so ignorant that they can meekly accept glossocratic tyranny, the state can inadvertently render them unable to make a living in a modern economy. This might jeopardize the social balance by making the state renege on its blanket promise of happiness, thus swinging the pendulum away from the philistine and towards the nihilist.

It is Modmen's big achievement to have been able to implement a dual strategy that gets around this potential conundrum. This has been done by a high-tech revolution that has reduced most economic activity to virtual-reality computer games. As a result, education can be safely reduced to training youngsters to play such games with nothing short of whiz-kid dexterity – at the expense of anything that resembles Westman culture. Modmen have the will and have found the way. Children can now be trained to succeed in Modmen's world, while a uniform educational system can ensure that nothing of Westman can ever grow in their souls. And the ablest children can become effective glossocrats, Modman's answer to the aristocracy of yesteryear.

Like any tyranny, glossocracy can succeed only by creating a new ruling class and a new way of controlling minds. The former comes from forging an alliance between politicians, corporations and 'the fourth estate'. The latter is facilitated by creating an educational system designed not to educate people but to brainwash them into taking glossocratic make-believe on faith. Of the two, the latter is more invidious, for the power of glossocratic wordmongers is conditional on the receptiveness of the masses they tyrannize. However, in promoting this receptivity, Modmen again have to avoid a few pitfalls. Unlike the violence of the nihilist, philistine glossocracy has to be a subtle form of control for it has to preserve the illusion that the masses are still free to shake off the bondage. Such an illusion can be maintained only at the cost of leaving some potential for resistance intact.

This potential could conceivably realize itself only through an education encompassing Westman values, as was demonstrated even in the nihilist kingdom of Soviet Russia. The state there could induce the half-starving scientists to keep cranking out missiles only by preserving Westman culture, in however perverted a form. This quaint policy was successful for a while, but eventually it backfired as the vestigial Westman culture, preserved in Russia to compensate for the lack of worldly goods, immunized the populace against the glossocratic aspect of Bolshevism, leaving the regime with no fall-back position when it lost the spunk to do mass murder. At the time of this writing, it is still struggling, though one can be certain it will ultimately succeed. After all, resistance to Modman could only come from Westman, and he is dead. But in the short term, the Soviets probably came to rue having kept some remnants of Westman culture extant.

The philistine Modmen know that for them such a mistake could prove fatal: glossocratic mechanisms of power are all they have at their disposal; mass violence, at least within their own borders, is not a realistic option yet. An occasional bloodletting still comes in handy, but philistine rulers tend to masquerade the need for it as a noble foreign expedition. However, in the interbellum periods, made more protracted by the apocalyptic power of new weapons, violence is not a technique on which they can rely for everyday population control. That leaves them potentially vulnerable to the anti-glossocratic, which is to say Westman, elements in education and makes them particularly eager to expurgate any such elements. Though applied to education, the technique they have developed to achieve this goal comes straight from agriculture.

Farmers have learned to protect themselves from blights without having to slaughter the offending insects. They simply catch as many males of the species as they possibly can, sterilize them with radiation and then release them. Come mating season, the sterilized males copulate with their females, but without producing offspring. This breaks the reproduction cycle by creating a chain reaction of infertility that removes several generations from circulation. Educational glossocrats have used this technique to push Westman to the brink of extinction. In this undertaking they have proved so successful that we should stop talking about the 'failure of our educational system', a frequent lament in the conservative press all over the Western world. For, if success means achieving the desired result, then education in philistine glossocracies has been hugely successful. At least two generations have been taken out of the cultural reproductive cycle, and more will follow. As a result, Westman holdouts find themselves not at the pinnacle of the cultural pyramid, but on the receiving end of universal ridicule.

In a democracy, and more so in a glossocracy, an enlightened electorate is the only possible counterbalance to a mushrooming Modman state: a responsible government can be elected only by responsible citizens and producing those has since Socrates been the real purpose of real education in real democracies. That is why, for a start, Modmen had to turn the very word 'education' into a glossocratic misnomer used to describe the acquisition of skills with which a citizen can fend for himself in the marketplace. This tore the word away from its Westman meaning, and quite rightly too. There is no link between economic success and Westman education: the qualities required to pursue happiness can be picked up in street fights, the skills learned on the job or, these days, by playing computer games. Today's advertising industry is a prime example. If we take its most successful practitioners, we find that precious few have ever studied advertising academically, which does not prevent them from owning cute villas in Spain.

Every educational system has a desired product in its sights, the ideal towards which to strive. In Athens, it was the citizen responsible enough to vote. In aristocratic, which is to say Westman, times, it was the paladin who wrote madrigals in his spare time and then did battle outside the city walls while the town folk cowered inside. In early Western democracies, it was the gentleman, a link with the traditional Westman past. Glossocracies, be they philistine-liberal or nihilist-totalitarian, will not be outdone: they have educational targets too. And since they like to claim God-like powers of planning, they work towards their goals with consistency.

The Modman state promotes egalitarianism. Because Westman

culture was hierarchical, Modman educational institutions have to be levelling. That was the animus behind the otherwise inexplicable destruction of British grammar schools, which in less than a generation turned British state education from the envy of the world into its laughing stock. And this is the animus behind the present efforts of the British government to blackmail universities into admitting more students from the working class, regardless of academic qualifications – a practice that was eventually abandoned even in Stalin's Russia for its sheer impracticality but one that is widely used in the West. This, as well as the other pet idea of providing university degrees for half the population, is impossible to comprehend without our methodology. It should be clear to anyone that any scheme even approaching this scale is bound to devalue higher education so much as to render it meaningless. The USA, for example, now has roughly ten times as many universities as it had in the 1950s, and only the naïve believe they all provide the same quality of higher education as before. But Modmen want all students to be equally ignorant, not some of them well educated and the rest merely competent. From this it is easy to deduce which qualities the Modman state will discourage in its young. They are the same qualities and the same type of learning Westman families used to encourage. The curricula of today's state schools in Britain and America are designed with this goal in mind. In a two-sector arrangement of any kind, be it health or education, it is the numerically dominant sector that sets the tone. That is why, although private education in the West is still marginally better than anything the state provides, this margin is getting narrower by the day.

Using such tools as centralized school curricula, the state makes sure the academic subjects that half a century ago were regarded as indispensable now often find themselves surplus to requirements. And those that cannot be done away with are routinely turned into a grotesque parody of their former selves. Political philosophy, for example, is outright seditious as far as Modmen are concerned. What if a youth reads Plato or Burke and gets ideas beyond his station? Let us replace it, if we must study politics at all, with 'citizenship classes', or some such. The content of those is similar to the citizenship requirements of the US Immigration and Naturalization Service, along the lines of 'how many states are there?' and 'who was the first president?' Aristotle's *Politics* or Plato's *Republic* simply do not come into it.

Classical music is too elitist. Let us offer it to as few students as we can, and even for those irrepressible overachievers do let us reduce music to a purely mechanical ability to read scores and play simple pieces. Better still, let us expand the concept of music so that all those Teutonic composers begging for talented renditions are flooded by MTV. We are all democrats, are we not? Majority tastes should rule in musical education just as they govern in politics. Everyone in favour of Bach's chorales, please raise your hand. Now, who is in favour of Eminem? Eminem has it a million to one.

Naturally, the same logic applies to the literature created by the Dead White Males. Shakespeare, for example, is too hung up on heterosexuality and gang warfare, so he has to be scaled down or, ideally, expurgated and replaced with Salman Rushdie, Philip Roth, Martin Amis and other 'modern classics'. Actually, children should not read at all, for television provides all the information they need. If they are in a highbrow mood, then that is what we have BBC or PBS costume dramas for, ones we subsidize with our taxes. Rhetoric, logic? Forget those, or else people old enough to elect yet another glossocracy will realize that our leaders can commit every known fallacy in a short speech. Economics? Really. A student reads Adam Smith or, God forbid, von Mises, and before you know it will grow up resentful of feeding Modman's Leviathan to the tune of half of what he earns. History? Perhaps, but let us make it modern history, say, the last couple of years; on second thoughts, let us do current events instead. And, if we do choose to discuss the dull events of the past, we should make them more 'relevant' by putting a Modman twist on them. Thus 'the plight of women in Athens' is more relevant than knowing who Pericles was; and 'what the common foot soldier felt in battle' is more important than what the battle was about or when it was fought.

LANGUAGE AND OTHER VICTIMS OF MODERNITY

Foreign languages are ridiculous; it is about time we all spoke the same tongue anyway, preferably some grammarless form of monosyllabic Euro-type English that is spoken universally in Northern Europe and elsewhere. Incidentally, those Anglophone people who wax enthusiastic about the ability of all northern Europeans to speak English are being either too generous or too Modman. In fact, of the two statements 'everybody in northern Europe speaks English' and 'nobody in northern Europe speaks English', the second is nearer the truth. Or rather it would be if we still persisted in defining language as an instrument for conveying the subtlety of the mind. Understood in Modmen's way, language is but a means of commercial discourse; in common with Westman's other unmaterial possessions, it has been allowed to keep its formal shell but not its essence. Anglophone glosso-crats are happy to know that their German or Danish counter-parts can converse with them in a lifeless patois only a step removed from the perversion of English they themselves favour.

Every pre-Modman lingua franca, such as Greek, Latin or French, was more fortunate with its foreign users than English is today. (Naipaul, Nabokov or Brodsky – along with others of supreme talent – are obviously exempt from this observation.) Seeking proof of this sweeping statement, French-speaking readers could do worse than read a modern French translation of *War and Peace*, where the author's original French used liberally throughout the book is italicized. Such a reader will find that Tolstoy's French, his second language, was better than that of his native-speaking translators. Another profitable exercise would be to compare Nabokov's English with that of his homegrown US contemporaries. Josephus wrote beautiful Latin and Greek, Gibbon a rich Latin (he even toyed with the idea of writing *Decline and Fall* in that language), and Joseph Conrad did not exactly butcher the language he had borrowed.

Of course, foreigners should only be blamed for linguistic sabotage if the natives themselves are blameless, which they are not. Amazingly, these days many people, including some who write for a living, believe that the freely flowing solecisms one takes such delight in lampooning spring from some sort of educational bungling in the past. They write names like John Dewey or Shirley Williams, Wilson or Heath on posters, pin them to the wall and let the darts fly. But there was no bungling; the people responsible for the young have produced exactly what they desired, exactly the result for which their Modman loins ached. Language had to be denatured before it could become a universally applicable glossocratic tool. It had to shed every vestige of semantic, stylistic and grammatical rigour before it could become moulding clay lending itself to Modmen's kneading. That Modmen have succeeded in this educational undertaking is demonstrated clearly by the advent of political correctness. This would have been impossible had two generations not been conditioned to respond with Pavlovian gusto to glossocratic vocabules conveying implicit marching orders.

The culture of political correctness has to span this chapter and the next, for the wheels of PC would stop turning unless they were greased by some collusion between education and law. Collusion in this case does not mean a conspiracy, a dozen desperados meeting in a smoke-filled cellar to plot the downfall of whatever it is they fancy to bring down. Something like that would have been necessary had Modmen not destroyed reason by pushing it beyond its level of competence. Made to fill the vacuum formed by the demise of the soul, reason could not handle the stress and went off the rails. In the past, when reason was used to perform its proper function, that of bringing up the cognitive rear, it could be dislodged only by conscious conspiratorial activity. In the world extruded by Modmen, no clandestine villainy is necessary. It is enough to encourage people to act according to their newly acquired instincts. They will be even more successful than the Roman soldiers whose sandals were treading the fields of Carthage as they sprayed them metronomically with coarse-grained salt so as to kill fertility for ever.

Glossocracy depends on such a long-term investment in ignorance. Reliant on words not used in their real meaning, it can only welcome a situation where most students do not know what the real meaning is. It will be easier to convince Johnny when he grows up that British sovereignty will be much more secure when vested in Brussels or that American budget deficits do not matter if, as a student, he is allowed to use 'enormity' for 'immensity', 'willy-nilly' for 'at will', 'continual' for 'continuous' or 'expectancy' for 'expectation'. Also, egalitarianism in all walks of life can advance more briskly if any usage is acceptable, if a hierarchy of language is not there to reflect a hierarchy of culture. And a hierarchy is indispensable not only within a culture, but also in its relation to other cultures. If most people living in the West accepted that Westman culture was not simply different from others but superior to them, they could likewise accept that it was superior to the culture of the internal barbarian. For even as no athlete can defeat an opponent without self-confidence, neither can a culture succeed if it sees itself as merely one of many equally valid options.

The same goes for religion. Belief has to be based on a sense of rightness, and if one's way of worshipping God is right then all other ways must be wrong. They may be regarded with curiosity, respect or even admiration. But the moment they assume parity, one's own faith becomes a formality at best. When the heir to the British throne pronounces himself to be the defender of all faiths, or when Britain's top public schools begin to allocate the same amount of time to each of the five most widespread religions, let us not applaud their even-handedness. It is the kiss of death for things Western.

Without a hierarchy, anything worth keeping, including language, is doomed to death by vulgarization. That is why throughout history the English language has been beautifully stratified. Some people have only used it to communicate simple concepts, whereas others, while also capable of expressing simple concepts, wrote *Canterbury Tales*, *Hamlet* and *Paradise Lost*. Regardless of what we think of the social aspects of this stratification, it has worked linguistically by creating arguably the richest language in Europe. Then, some time in the twentieth century, the two strata came together, accompanied by a big bang of glossocratic rhetoric. Language has shed the shackles of class parochialism! One language for all! Progress! Curiously, however, English has not become bigger. In fact, apart from four-letter words having entered the mainstream of English discourse, it is getting smaller by the minute.

Language reflects the part of human activity that Darwin somehow forgot to explain. The life of the mind thrives on precise definitions, each crying out for a name. The longer one takes to ponder a concept, the more of its aspects will be broken off as separate words. And the closer two or more concepts are, the more critical does distinction become, for without it they could come together into one amorphous blob. How the purity of a language can be protected from Modman vandalism is open to debate. The French have relied on their Academy for quite some time, latterly with little success.* No institution can protect linguistic rectitude in the face of the enfeeblement of Westman and the concomitant burgeoning of Modman. Sure enough, once

---

* During a recent tennis match shown on French television, the commentator described a high-bouncing second serve as '*le service bien kické*', probably not a usage of which the Academy would approve.

the Modman masses were able to exert influence upon language, their crudity began to take its toll.

People break what they do not understand. Internal barbarians do not understand language, so they break it. And in our glossocratic times there is an additional incentive for encouraging linguistic vandalism: quest for power. Modmen correctly identify the provenance of proper usage as hiding in the coffers of West-man heritage; so they single it out for the usual treatment reserved for this heritage. In doing so, Modmen also practise a safety procedure. After all, language, real language that is, could easily become the cosh with which to clobber glossocrats on the head. Thus no effort should be spared to break it up into innocuous little pieces. The warning signals are ringing throughout the English-speaking world. Kevin says 'masterful' when he means 'masterly' – beware! A good word is on its way to perdition. Jill is 'disinterested' in classical music – woebetide 'uninterested' (not to mention classical music). Gavin thinks 'simplistic' is a more elegant way of saying 'simple', 'fulsome' is a sophisticated version of 'full' or 'naturalistic' of 'natural' – English is coming down to a size where Modmen can handle it comfortably. Trish thinks 'innocuous' means 'innocent' – in a few years it will. And it is not just words; whole grammatical categories bite the dust. Present Indefinite, where is your brother Subjunctive? Trampled underfoot by Modman and the education he has spawned.

Once words are deprived of their substance, Modmen can perpetuate their glossocracy by enforcing the formal aspect of any word. That is precisely the impulse behind political correctness that has succeeded only because resistance to it was softened by Modman education. A semi-literate population is a soft touch for glossocratic Humpty Dumpties insisting that words mean whatever they want them to mean. Who cares about nuances of meaning if a lexicon of a thousand words is sufficient to get one through modern life? When a dictate is issued that some stylisti-cally neutral word is now taboo, people just shrug with equanimity. We cannot say Negro any longer? That is fine, we will say black. 'You prefer African-American?' yawns the New Yorker – splendid. 'Afro-Caribbean?' echoes the Londoner – right you are, gov! Words do not matter.

And, in fact they do not – as such. It should not really matter to anybody, including Negroes themselves, what they are called, as long as the word is not pejorative. What does matter, however, is the glossocratic impetus behind the words, the Humpty-Dumpty power to enforce the arbitrary meaning of words at the expense of their real meaning. This matters because the united glossocrats of the world know that they assume a greater power every time they win a linguistic skirmish. Thus, when a New York public official is made to apologize in the press for having used the word 'niggardly', yet another triumphal chariot rolls through Modman's world.

Modmen know that when they pretend to be sanctimonious their power grows. Self-righteousness is a means of enforcing glossocratic laws, such as political correctness. Modmen have to register and enforce their disapproval whenever someone dares to defy their laws by using a term that has been declared a non-word by Modman glossocracy. Let us say, the term is 'Red Indian', a non-pejorative way of describing the aboriginal population of America. No offence meant, none taken? Not at all. Upon hearing the term, a Modman glossocrat will contort his features in a semiotic message of opprobrium and say something as humourless as 'You mean a native American?' At least one can understand, if not sympathize with, his concern if he is an American. But there are precious few, if any, Red Indians in Britain, so one would think that an English glossocrat would let such an offence go unpunished, saving his strength to fight similar battles over more relevant concerns, such as replacing the word 'chairman' with the noun normally used to denote a piece of furniture. One would think he would let Americans fight their own battle, but one would be wrong for glossocracy knows no nationality. American concerns are our concerns; American fashions, such as sugary drinks and baseball caps worn backwards, are our fashions. And American glossocratic dictates have to become ours as well.

LAW VERSUS JUSTICE

'Wrong must not win by technicalities.'

(Aeschylus)

Jurists used to distinguish between *malum in se* and *malum prohibitum*, the former reflecting an immutable injunction against attacks on life, liberty and property; the latter encompassing transgressions like not wearing a seat belt. It has always been understood that the two are in a morally hierarchical relationship. For example, stealing a man's horse is a worse crime than parking it on a double yellow line, and killing one's wife is more reprehensible than making love to her without permission. But no *malum* is really *in se*; evil and good are meaningless in the absence of a detached moral arbiter whose rulings can sometimes be interpreted but never questioned. Take that arbiter away, and we have erased the absolute line of demarcation, making moral distinctions relative, which is to say inoperative. Indeed, we find ourselves beyond good and evil, in a space where things are distorted to a point at which *malum prohibitum* can be punished more surely and often more severely than *malum in se*.

When God died, law in the West suffered the fate of a clock smashed to pieces: all the bits are still there, but they do not add up to much any longer. Gone is the fundamental premise of Westman legality: the primacy of the individual derived from the ultimate primacy of God. When there is no God, the secular state will enforce its own primacy, and the law will sooner or later become its pliant servant rather than a martinet called upon to restrain its excesses. Without God laws are arbitrary and can fall prey either to evil design or to ill-conceived political expediency,

264

which is another way of saying that without God law is tyranny. That is precisely what law in the West is becoming. More specifically, it is now the tyranny of Modmen, who have played the same trick with law as they have with other possessions of Westman: the same word is being used to describe something different. Of course, 'law' has a fine glossocratic tradition in such nihilist countries as Soviet Russia and Nazi Germany. Capitalizing on the people's habit of obeying law, more pronounced in Germany than in Russia, the rulers of those countries self-righteously demanded the same obedience to their own laws as to those their predecessors had enjoyed.

Westman laws indeed ought to have been obeyed, as they were a reflection of higher laws, their secular expression. Westman jurisprudence was lovingly put together by sage men over scores of generations, and its ability to protect both society and the individual was tested over time. Whenever a law could not pass such tests, the ruler and the ruled alike realized it was enforceable only by arbitrary force. When such a realization sank in, the transgressor was in trouble sooner or later and even Charles I could not save the Earl of Strafford. Modman laws, by contrast, are tyrannical because Modman's political state has usurped the power to decide which of the ancient laws should and which should not be enforced. The law has thus stopped being a complex bilateral agreement between the people and the state, becoming instead something the state can grant or withdraw at its discretion. Most links between generations past and present have been severed, and the law no longer has the authority of millennia behind it. Intuitively aware of this, people treat laws as mere statements of intent, and break them without much fuss about morality. There is no morality in law any longer, only expediency as defined by the state. And it does not matter whether its regulations are good or bad; in any event they cannot function as the rule of law. Even some of the regulations that passed for laws in Nazi Germany or Soviet Russia were unobjectionable by any

Western standards. But they were not Westman laws in spirit, which made them instruments of tyranny.

Whenever contemporary laws in Western countries are described as tyrannical, there is no shortage of those springing to their defence. The widespread defence strategy is based on drawing direct comparisons with those Modman countries we now know to have been despotic, usually Soviet Russia and Nazi Germany. The advocate will then point out that there are no concentration camps in the north of Scotland or in Alaska and smile in that particular QED way so characteristic of champions of modernity. As far as he is concerned, his case has been made. Well, not quite. It is true that, while Westman's rule of law was based on absolute principles, despotism is relative. There is a difference between a regime that unlawfully imprisons ten million and one that makes do with a mere million. But this is a difference of degree, not principle. The two countries have more in common with each other than either has with a country in which an unlawful imprisonment of even one citizen can result only from a mistake.

The rule of law presupposes a set of constitutional guarantees that are equally binding for the state and for the individual. These guarantees may be written down in an a priori document, as they were in America. Or they can be based on centuries of tradition and an intricate system of legal precedent, as in Britain. But the real difference between a constitutional state and a tyranny is in (a) whether such guarantees exist and (b) how binding they are. When a government takes it upon itself to violate such guarantees, the number and degree of violations are unimportant as they depend only on variable political expediency. A state capable of prosecuting one person for his thoughts is equally capable of prosecuting thousands, and will predictably do so when it has consolidated its power enough to get away with any outrage.

Moreover, the most horrendous regimes in history provide an inadequate frame of reference. And, at the other end of the spectrum, so does any abstract ideal of justice. A much more useful yardstick with which to measure the constitutionality of a country is her historical experience and that of her neighbours, especially those that resemble her in many essential respects. Thus the guardians of, say, British legality should not feel smugly complacent because their country is governed by regulations that are fairer than the Nuremberg laws or the Stalin constitution. Instead, they should grieve for the demise of certain constitutional principles that Englishmen took for granted a mere century ago. The letter of the law has not changed much, but the spirit has largely evaporated. In its absence, the letter is but a collection of hieroglyphics.

By exempting themselves from obeying the spirit of the law, Modman political states find it increasingly more difficult to make their subjects obey even the letter. Crime statistics in just about every major modern country of Europe bear this out, with a traditionally law-abiding Britain having overtaken even the United States in most crime categories, except murder where Americans are still protecting their lead. Citizens no longer venerate laws because they know the state does not. And the state, somewhat naively, gives them more and more demonstrations of this.

Protection of life? Thou shalt not kill? What nonsense. An 'abused' wife mutilates her husband and the law is silent. A husband cripples his wife because he suspects her of infidelity and the law nods understandingly. A criminal murders a man who is trying to protect his property and the law explains to the bereaved widow it was an act of self-defence by the poor youngster who felt threatened by the exaggerated wrath of the victim. While killing is still frowned upon, other violent crimes, including assault and even attempted murder, often go not only unpunished but even unprosecuted in many Western countries. Unless, of course, they are committed in self-defence, something the state abhors as this diminishes its control over the life and property of its subjects.

Protection of property? Thou shalt not steal? Let us not be silly.

A couple of drunks steal a car to go on a 'joy ride' and the law does not see that as a crime because there was no profit motive involved. A car radio is stolen and the owner's first call goes to an insurance agent rather than to a policeman, who he knows is unlikely even to turn up. Burglary is more likely to elicit a visit from police officers, but they will probably evince yawning uninterest. They will then go through the motions of solving the crime, failing unregretfully in approximately 95 per cent of the cases. And why should a servant of the state be concerned about private property if his master is in the business of extorting it? Few taxpayers seem to regard it as strange that, in peacetime, Modman states should confiscate almost half of what citizens earn or bequeath, or that a (Conservative!) government can pass an abomination like the confiscatory leasehold law. People do not find this detestable because they have been trained not to worry about such trivia. But the message gets through to their intuition even if it bypasses their reason. They sense that private property is no longer off-limits and act accordingly.

Has the law atrophied? Is it beginning to die away? Not at all. Law enforcement is funded at unprecedented levels, what with about 30,000 policemen keeping vigil in London alone, which is roughly the strength of three peacetime divisions – more than the Germans needed to police most of France during their earlier attempt to unite Europe. And we know from our everyday experience just how vigilant police officers are: you can be slapped with a £100 fine for not wearing a seat belt. If we look around us we shall see innumerable signs of police activity: thousands of speed cameras on our roads (in France and Britain these are supplemented with millions of surveillance cameras, about one per thirty citizens), and tax services getting instant access to every detail of our financial lives.

It is not just law enforcement, but also law-giving that is growing apace. Parliaments all over the world are churning out laws by the bucketful. Yet they fail to protect citizens so spectacularly that one is tempted to think this is not their real purpose. Indeed, vigilant concern about public safety is not what makes MPs keep long hours. Their diligence is directed at promoting the interests of their master, and only the naïve among us still believe they are servants of the people. Judiciary activism so prevalent in Western countries is also easy to explain from another angle: Since legality now replaces, rather than translates, morality, the judiciary process has to take on overtime work. But legal casuistry is a poor substitute for what Kant described as the moral law within us: the stronger the former, the weaker the latter and vice versa.

As a result, policing and crime tend to grow in parallel. Though England, for one, is being policed at a level that would make Robert Peel spin like a top in his grave, an Englishman's person is increasingly unsafe in the streets, and his property is at the mercy of any derelict who can smash a window and shove his tattooed arms inside. Contradiction? None whatsoever. The state functions not as a man endowed with free will but as an animal brought into this world to perform only one or two tasks but to perform them well. The lion, for example, is adept at chasing the antelope, which is a real wizard at running away from the lion, with neither able to ponder *malum in se*. The political state's genetic code compels it to expand its power over individuals *ad infinitum*, regardless of such incidentals as the will of its subjects. That is why when it destroys the legal foundations of the West, the state is acting in character. Governments are no longer there to protect society and the individuals within it. They are out to protect the sacred cow of statism from whose udders they have sucked out what passes for their conscience. For that reason a crime committed by one individual against another is of little consequence to them, and yet petty crimes against the state, such as driving after a sip of wine too many or neglecting to pay duty on a watch, take on an almost religious significance, eliciting swift and sure punishment.

While failing to protect us, Modman laws also deny us the right to self-defence (the USA being one notable exception, but only in some states). If a burglar breaks in, we are not allowed to defend our property with anything other than our bare hands, useless against the murderous hammy palms of yet another 'victim of social injustice' who is unlikely to be overburdened with concerns about the sanctity of human life. Yet a citizen has a God-given duty to protect himself, his family and his property against criminal intrusion. This always was an unshakeable certitude in Westman times. But now we live in Modman times and old certitudes no longer apply. Western countries are now run not by constitutional governments but by Modman glossocracies, wielding political correctness like a club. The glossocratic logic they apply runs roughly as follows:

❑ A criminal, say a burglar breaking into a house, is not really to blame for his actions. He is plying his trade, like anybody else. Of course, his trade is slightly naughty when compared with that of a butcher, a baker or a candlestick-maker. But the poor man is not to blame for plying it. He grew up needy and down-trodden, and it is we, society at large, who are to blame for his plight. The house he breaks into belongs to a person who has amassed greater wealth because he was privileged. And anyway, though we should not talk about this out loud, the burglar is in the same business as the state: redistributing wealth. Burglary is a form of income tax, and the burglar merely collects the excess that has evaded the tax collectors' net. Naturally, he has not been authorized to act in this capacity, so he deserves to have his wrists slapped. If he is caught, and we should not go out of our way to catch him, he should be tried, perhaps even convicted. But, even if this is not his first offence, he should not spend more than a few months in prison, if any.

❑ The owner of the house does not have much to complain about. His possessions are insured, so he can always buy another stereo and replace the smashed window without suffering a great fiscal loss. Therefore he should not resist the poor man breaking into his house. If he does, the burglar may have to defend himself, as he is entitled to do, and the whole thing can escalate into nastiness.

□ If it is the burglar who initiates or threatens violence, unlikely as it may sound, then the owner has the right to defend himself too. But this right is not a licence to kill. The force used by the owner must be exactly commensurate with the force he is trying to repel. Thus, if the burglar brandishes a baseball bat (shops selling those are doing brisk business in the UK even though nobody plays baseball), the owner is allowed to use a baseball bat in self-defence. If the burglar pulls a knife, the owner is allowed to use a knife. If the burglar brandishes a gun, the owner – well, let us not get carried away. The owner still is not allowed to have a loaded gun handy anywhere in Western Europe except Switzerland, so he should not have provoked the poor young man into resorting to such egregious extremes. If the owner uses force that exceeds that with which he is threatened, then he is the criminal and the burglar is the victim. If the owner panics and kills the burglar with a meat cleaver when none is found in the burglar's possession, then the owner shall be convicted of manslaughter.

There goes another certitude according to which a criminal violating a citizen's property is not entitled to the benefit of the doubt. He may have broken in 'just' to steal a TV set, not to rape and murder. But the burden of proof should be on him. However, a frightened, confused owner of the house, awakened in the middle of the night to find a gorilla-like stranger in his bedroom, has no time to grant the intruder to produce such proof. He has to assume the worst. The owner's duty to himself and his family is to assume that the intruder has come to do murder. Even if murderous intent is unlikely, the risk is always there and that is not a risk a law-abiding citizen should be expected to take with his life. This ancient certitude, however, flies in the face of modern times by negating the three-step logic above. In our time, the state has to have monopoly on violence, so armed citizenry is off limits. A Westman holdout who thinks otherwise presents a greater threat to Modman than even a murderer. The former assails the glossocratic premise of Modman's government; the latter merely attacks individuals.

That is why it is useless to quote reams of evidence, demonstrating that places that do not restrict gun ownership enjoy lower crime rates than those that do. Washington DC and New York City, where guns are outlawed, have two of the highest murder rates in the USA; Vermont and New Hampshire, with the highest gun ownership in the country, two of the lowest. Burglaries are almost unheard of in those places where most households are armed. Switzerland, with the heaviest-armed population in the world, has practically no crime, while Britain and Holland, with their strict gun laws, are crime-ridden. And in the first two years after a complete ban on handguns was introduced in Britain, gun crime went up by 50 per cent and it is still growing. A Modman does not want to hear any of this, and, if he is made to anyhow, he will not be swayed. All he needs to know is who is more likely to threaten his rule – the criminal or the victim. Seen in that light, the criminal is a safer bet. He may be naughty as an individual towards other individuals, but, as far as the state is concerned, he is no threat whatsoever.

In this, as in many other aspects of his life, the philistine Modman has taken some profitable lessons from his nihilist brother. Both the Nazis and the Bolsheviks treated enemies of the state with murderous efficiency, while petty criminals often got away with no more than avuncular admonition. The Soviets, for example, developed the concept of 'the socially close' to describe criminals of proletarian or peasant descent. The concept was expounded in detail by A. Makarenko, manager of the first Soviet colony for juvenile delinquents. The underlying assumption was that, because they were 'socially close' to the state, young criminals, many of them murderers, were not beyond redemption. They ought to be rehabilitated, not punished. 'It is only the intelligentsia, children of the upper classes, priests and landowners who are beyond redemption,' wrote Makarenko. While today's Modman bureaucrats are unlikely to have read this, they proceed from similar assumptions. An illiterate criminal in no way jeopardizes Modman's power. The lout's victim, especially if he is a Westman holdout, may. Therefore, every law devised by Modmen will favour the criminal over the victim. Even if an ancient law remains on the books and an attempt at enforcement is made, the state will make sure that whenever possible an arrest will not result in a conviction or a conviction in imprisonment. In Britain, the proportion of convicted criminals going to prison is in a steady decline. At 38 per cent in the early 1950s, it was at a mere 15 per cent 40 years later.

Presumably, the ideal that the state sees in its mind's eye is prisons exclusively populated with clubbable, tweedy gentlemen who should not have had that last port before driving home. Westman holdouts can scream appeals to the English common law, its American offshoot or the Napoleonic Code till the judges come home: the very basic assumptions are no longer assumed. For example, all the state needs to do these days to deprive an Englishman of the ancient right of refusing to provide self-incriminating evidence is to pronounce him a terrorist (incidentally, another piece of Conservative legislation). Again, a terrorist differs from a common-or-garden murderer in that he often has in his sights not an individual but the state, and that just will not do. That is why in New York State only the murder of a policeman is classified as first-degree: as far as the Modman state is concerned there exists a broad divide between murdering a private citizen and a state official. Westman, to whom murder was murder, regardless of the victim's CV, must have been terribly misguided.

We could easily continue this martyrology of Westman laws. At some point we would probably come to the conclusion that, even under most of the kings who ruled and not merely reigned, the legal framework of society was made of much sterner stuff than in putative Western democracies that have in reality become glossocratic states. Witness, for instance, the death penalty, which was never regarded as a cruel and unusual punishment in the ultimate moral code of the West, the Scripture. When society and community were more than just figures of speech, the moral validity of the death penalty was not in doubt. It was understood that murder sent shock waves throughout the community, and the amplitude of those destructive waves could be attenuated only by a punishment commensurate with the crime. Without it, the agitated community would run the risk of never recovering its eirenic order. That is one salient point in favour of the death penalty; deterrence is another. While the deterrent value of the death penalty is often disputed, it undoubtedly deters the executed criminal. This is no mean achievement considering that in the 40 years since the death penalty for murder was abolished in Britain in 1965 more people have been killed by recidivist murderers released from prison than the number of murderers executed in the 40 years before the abolition.

However, even a Westman holdout may argue against the death penalty, citing, for example, the corrupting effect it has on the executioner – or else doubting the right of mortal and therefore fallible men to pass irreversible judgement. Such arguments are noble, but they are not Modman's arguments. For it is not just the death penalty with which Modmen are uncomfortable, but the very idea of punishment. More and more, the philistine subspecies betrays its Enlightenment genealogy by insisting that people are all innately good and, if some behave badly, they must be victims of correctable social injustice. More and more one detects a belief that justice is an antiquated notion and that law is only an aspect of the social services. And so it now is, for it appears to be subject to the same inner logic as welfare, whereby a government activity invariably promotes the very mode of behaviour it is designed to curb. If the single-mother benefit encourages single motherhood and the unemployment benefit promotes unemployment, then by the same token it is the crime-fighting activity of the Modman state that makes crime worse.

SPEAK NO EVIL – OR ELSE

While Modman states are conspicuously lax in enforcing ancient laws designed to protect the individual, they are getting downright frantic in their attempts to protect glossocracy, in which undertaking political correctness is an effective instrument of power. Take, for example, laws against racism, a subject on which Modman glossocrats will wax more sanctimonious than on any other. Conditioned to accept meaningless words without demurring, few citizens will cast a critical eye over these laws to see what it is that is actually being proscribed.

Let us cast such an eye and ask yet another subversive question: so what exactly is racism? The word used to describe a belief that one race is innately superior to all others, which conviction became unfashionable when philistine glossocracies sided with Stalin rather than Hitler. Now it has been expanded to include the belief that races are different in any other than the purely chromatic respect. In both instances, we are talking about a belief, not something traditionally criminalized in Western countries. For old times' sake we should recall distant history, say 50 years ago, when a holder of any belief, no matter how reprehensible, was not treated as a criminal unless he committed a criminal act. It was only the Soviets and Nazis who persecuted people for their thoughts. People in the West were scathing about the thought police of totalitarian states.

Now let us wave a magic wand and imagine we still live in a Western country where freedom of conscience is guaranteed by law, and citizens are free to think whatever they please. Of course,

275

allowing people to think what they want becomes a valid test of liberty only if we disagree with their thoughts. If we agree, then it is no hardship to be permissive. Let us take it as read that we all find racism, in every possible and impossible meaning of the word, reprehensible. In fact, we find it as revolting as pushing an old woman out of the way in a bus queue or tossing a rusty nut into a blind beggar's cup. Nonetheless, we do not suggest that the ill-mannered brute or sadistic mocker should be punished by law, even though we may think it a good idea. What makes racism so special then? Why must we have a law against it? We already have laws against criminal acts inspired by racism or any other pet hatred. Racially motivated murder is a criminal offence simply because it is murder; ditto, racially motivated assault; ditto, racially motivated terrorist threats; ditto, incitement to racially motivated violence. None of these offences requires any more laws for an offender to be prosecuted, which should render any specific legal injunction against racism superfluous – provided it is the government's aim to stop criminal acts.

But we have already seen that it is not. The business of a Modman government is to make sure that the cogs of its power mechanism are meshing smoothly. Since Modman governments are glossocratic, the most important cogs are the desemanticized vocabules that lie at the foundation of the glossocratic state. Laws against racism are therefore not even meant to punish criminal acts. They are on the books to reassert the power of the state to control not just the citizens' actions but, more important, their thoughts and the words they use to get these across.

One could object that any legal code should have a certain number of unenforced laws designed simply to express society's disapproval of behaviour it deems unacceptable, and that laws against racism are among those. But that is not the case. Far from being unenforced or unenforceable, racism laws have already been invoked in European countries to imprison people with whose views the state disagrees. A Dutch journalist, for example, was sentenced to 12 months in prison in 1998 for publishing an article in which he argued that Holland was not designed to be a multiracial society. We may be willing to give the Dutch courts the benefit of the doubt and assume that the article was criminally bad. But in a supposedly free society there should exist an uncrossable line between criminally bad and criminal. A country that imprisons people for speaking their minds is a tyranny different from the likes of Nazi Germany only in the frequency of such occurrences, not in the principle behind them.

Modman governments do not act in this manner just because they want to enforce their glossocracy, although that is an important reason. Even as a military dictatorship can survive only if it keeps a tight rein on the military, a glossocracy will die unless it controls the use of language. But in the case of racism, glossocracy is not the whole story in Modman countries waging a war against any survivals of Westman. Like a frenzied killer who continues to pump round after round into an already lifeless body, Modmen keep fighting someone already dead. However, suspecting that there may be life after death after all, they have to make sure that in this case no resurrection will ensue. Since Western culture is the centrepiece of Westman, it is anathema to his conquerors. Modmen have to drag in every means at their disposal to ensure that Westman culture stays smashed, to which end it is useful to dilute Western societies with large numbers of people who are not Western culturally. Racism laws are thus the state's way of telling its citizens, especially those suspected of pro-Westman sympathies, that no challenge to the state's authority will be tolerated. Implicitly, the coloured or Muslim segments of the population enjoy special protection because they are expected to act as a battering ram of modernity. The normal protection the law is supposed to extend to all citizens, regardless of colour or religion, is thus seen to be inadequate not because traditional laws are biased but specifically because they are impartial.

Alienating the races more than they are alienated naturally is one important aim of Modman's law. Alienating the sexes is another. Sexual abuse, rape – 'date', 'marriage' or otherwise – and paedophilia have all become permanent features in even the so-called 'quality' press, where every lugubrious detail is lovingly described for the panting readers. This would have been impossible without the tyrannical miscarriage of justice that passes for law in Western countries now they are all in the hands of Modmen. Westmen traditionally saw sex in the context of marital, or at least romantic, love. Sex to them had to be a physical expression of a metaphysical emotion for it to be condoned. It was also the only means for man to act upon the biblical prescription to multiply. That God chose to associate the act of physical love with pleasure used to be regarded by many as a tacit blessing for the symbiosis of the profane and ideal in love. Marriage gave a proper setting not just to sex but also to the sexes, creating an environment where men and women could perform their different, but equally important, roles. At various times in history Westmen were more or less prepared to stray outside a familial setup in search of sexual gratification. But that was relatively unimportant as long as profligacy was indeed seen as straying away from a universally accepted moral standard. These days Modmen no longer see loveless, mechanical sex with strangers as straying. To them it is a laudable standard, one to uphold vigilantly and to pass on to the next generation unfailingly. This destroys the traditional frame of reference, which is exactly the desired end: since family was the core unit of Westman society, Modmen had to smash it to emerge victorious. Sex thus had to be yanked out of the marital, or even extramarital, bed and placed at a street corner where 'liberated' men and women were to turn Westman ritual into Modman sleaze.

Having taken sex out of the naturally egalitarian context of the Westman family, Modmen placed it into their own vision of trumped-up equality, where men and women have to be regarded not just as equal but as identical. This was a purely glossocratic vision; something communicated but never really felt. The idea was to produce a sexual mechanism of glossocratic power by creating an environment in which the sexes looked upon each other as enemies. Thus divided, they could never present a united, familial front in the face of the glossocratic megalomania of Modmen. The testosteronal aggressiveness of males had to be portrayed as specifically directed against women and even a consensual sexual act was being likened to rape. Feminists of our own generation have been straightforward about this, although subterfuge would have served their cause even better. As it was, their assertions that even married sex is crypto rape sounded ridiculous even to the kind of people who would normally applaud any attack on Westman. Such people failed to realize that 'sex equals rape' was not designed as a statement of fact or even of faith. It was a battle plan of Modmen, pure and simple.

And follow the plan they did, using both legal and glossocratic means of locomotion. Glossocratically, they saturated the press with lurid descriptions of rape and sexual abuse, creating a climate where the words 'rape' and 'sex' were intermingled in the minds of the public. A quick scan of, say, the *Daily Telegraph* or *The Times* these days, compared with the same London papers of even 20, never mind 50, years ago, will show the staggering increase in their coverage of sex crimes. It is as if at a time when even kissing a woman on the lips instead of the proffered cheek could land the offender in gaol, men, with reckless disregard for their own liberty, have suddenly begun to force themselves into chaste females on an unprecedented scale.

Legally, Modmen have expanded the meaning of rape in the same way in which they have expanded the meaning of racism, and for the same reason. The aim is not to protect the more vulnerable groups of people but to impose the power of the Modman state on the people in general. Suddenly, certain types of behaviour became not just frowned upon but outlawed. A man who compliments a female colleague on her appearance risks dismissal if he is lucky or a lawsuit if he is not; a man who assumes that a woman who takes her clothes off and engages in an hour-long foreplay has consented to sex and confuses her panting 'no' with a cry of passion, is courting a long prison sentence – as demonstrated by the case of a City lawyer who a few years ago found himself in that situation with a woman colleague, only to find himself in prison for the next 12 months. Even marriage is no longer regarded as blanket consent to hanky-panky. The state insists on squeezing its body of laws into every nuptial bed in some kind of monstrous threesome. From now on it is the state that will decide what really went on there and whether it is to be allowed – and as with any other rape, the definition of marriage rape has become much broader than ever before.

Riding roughshod over traditional laws and indeed over simple arithmetic, Modmen have declared women to be not just a minority, but an oppressed minority at that, one in need of protection. This goes hand in hand with the legal assault upon the family undertaken by the Modman state. Since in a philistine-Modman world money is the principal lever at the state's disposal, this assault is waged by using taxes as the heaviest, though not the only, weapon. Taxation and benefits systems in Western countries have gradually shifted from encouraging families to penalizing them. In today's Britain, for example, a family of two adults and two children living on one average wage would be at least a third better off if they were not married. In parallel, unmarried couples, of the same or opposite sex, are given the recognition that in the past was reserved for couples united in marriage. In Europe it is Holland that is leading the way, but Britain and other Protestant countries are only a step behind, and the Catholic countries perhaps two steps.

Sex is yet another area where law and education converge in pursuit of a common goal. Sex-education classes have become compulsory in most schools, and sensible parents find themselves unable to keep their children away no matter how hard they try.

The official justification is the supposedly morbid effect sexual repression and ignorance used to have in the past. Contrasted to that is the state's ideal of pubescent youngsters joyously re-enacting sex manuals in the safety provided by easily available contraception. Sex, in other words, is too vital to be left to individual choice and parental guidance. Yet again it is important to realize that governments are not acting on their conception of public good, however misguided we may think this conception is; otherwise, government officials would see in an instant that the sex policy started at schools and continued by various social services is producing a social and moral catastrophe. A pandemic of teenage and, increasingly, pre-teenage pregnancies, rampant VD, more than half of all marriages ending in divorce, a quarter of all pregnancies ending in abortion, a third of all children born out of wedlock all testify to the failure of the state's policy even on its own terms.

One would find it difficult not to come to the conclusion that perhaps some sexual naivety is good for children. That even though the traditional standards of sexual behaviour may be hard to enforce, we should still keep those standards for they act as the frame of reference for moral judgement. *Romeo and Juliet* provides a better guide to sex than a graphic depiction of certain ballistic possibilities; youngsters are better off being guided by their emotions, in however bungling a way those may be expressed initially, than by a mechanistic, cold-blooded description of sexual variants. They would be better off not just sexually but also, more important, aesthetically, morally and socially.

Children's well-being is, of course, much less critical to a Modman state than its own power to control every aspect of people's lives, including the most intimate ones. If sex education alone does not do the job, then laws will have to lend a helping hand. The cringe-making word 'partner' has replaced the traditional English vocabulary not only legally but colloquially as well. The underlying assumption is that there must be no valid distinction, legal, ethical, moral or otherwise, in the status of a married heterosexual couple and a cohabiting hetero- or homosexual one. The last semblance of resistance is being mopped up at the time of this writing, but within a year or two unmarried 'partners' will have the same legal rights as families in adopting children, division of property in case of a breakup, pension and inheritance.

At the same time toleration of 'alternative' sexual behaviour has become a new orthodoxy. Homosexuality is being equalized in status with normal sex not because Modman states have become more tolerant but specifically because they are no longer prepared to tolerate even vestigial manifestations of Westman ethics. Homosexuals are allocated the same role as racial minorities: that of a battering ram of modernity. And like race, homosexuality leaves its obvious domain and becomes a form of political expression, a sort of cross between sexual democracy and homo-socialism. Yet again the state is prepared to ignore the innermost convictions of the very demos in whose name it allegedly governs. Observation suggests that most people intuitively regard homo-sexuality as wrong, even though they may have submitted to glossocratic tyranny that is prepared to punish any expression of anti-homosexual distaste more severely than burglary. But, as they often are, people's instincts are truer than their pronouncements. Homosexuality is ill-advised any way we look at it: ethically, aesthetically or, if we insist on worshipping at the altar of *ratio*, demographically. After all, if expanded indefinitely, homo-sexuality can spell the end of our species.

Modmen are, of course, deaf to any such arguments. If told that the Bible describes homosexual acts as 'abomination', they will deny that the Scripture has had any lasting effect on the ethical standards by which we live. If told that most people are repelled by homosexual activity, they will either deny the validity of this statement or aver that people's instincts have nothing to do with the high moral purpose with which modernity is imbued. Homo-sexuals, they will say in that smug way of theirs, are not to blame for the way they are born. That much is true: homosexuals should not be blamed, much less prosecuted, for their proclivity. Nor, for that matter, should a murderer be blamed for his innate propensity for violence until he actually kills, or a kleptomaniac punished for his desire to steal until he actually does so. People must not be blamed for what they are; it is for what they do that they should be held accountable. In Western societies homosexuality was criminalized not because it went against Leviticus but because it contravened the universally accepted standards of allowable behaviour. Homosexuals were not expected to reform; they were expected to stay celibate, thus sacrificing their sexuality for the sake of decency. This is a great sacrifice to expect from anybody and a person willing to make it is worthy of greater respect than a normal heterosexual for whom abstinence from homosexuality entails no hardship. Indeed, recognizing one's own instincts as shameful and making an effort not to act upon them should rank with other acts of moral heroism, those that reassert man's ability to make a free choice between right and wrong. Heroes, however, have never been thick on the ground. Most people are weak and incapable of resisting temptation, a recognition that lies at the foundation of our religion. Those who are generally tolerant of human nature will agree that a discreet homosexual cannot be expected to become celibate any more than an average Christian can be expected to develop stigmata. Moral heroism cannot become a moral norm, but neither should indiscreet, demonstrative homosexuals expect society to accept them on their own terms.

As an argument in favour of homosexuality its advocates often point out the prevalence of that practice in antiquity, mentioning such macho institutions as the Roman army. Caesar is cited *ad nauseam* as 'the husband to every woman and the wife to every man'. Without going into this issue on those terms (though it would be interesting to see the supporting statistical data), we should stick to the terms of this book, according to which many aspects of Hellenic civilization are alien to Westmen. What was laudable to Hellenic man may well be reprehensible to Westmen and, as the example of catacomb Christianity will illustrate, vice versa. Plato, for instance, regarded the healthy male body to be a thing of divine beauty; most men now prefer the sight of a female nude. References to the private lives of Greek philosophers or Roman generals may well enliven a conversation, but as serious arguments they do not cut much ice, and certainly not when they are used as justification for moral lassitude.

The key consideration here is that 'gay rights' is a form of political and glossocratic aggression. Straight advocates of this movement do not care about homoeroticism in itself. 'Gay rights' is part of the struggle to stick yet another knife into Westman's back. And as any other struggle, it must have its heroes and martyrs. Western governments are reluctant to oblige by putting homosexuals in prison and, until the advent of AIDS, the movement had lacked icons. AIDS changed all that. Suddenly, glossocratic peashooters were reinforced by a howitzer. The targets were all those empirically trained people who could not help noticing that the disease had a homosexual bias. This observation was ever so more infuriating for being obviously true. The howitzer began to spew out the usual grapeshot at the usual suspects. AIDS stopped being strictly a medical problem and became a focus of glossocratic hysteria. Saving lives never came into it, except as a glossocratic slogan. In fact, by diverting to AIDS a great deal of the research funds that until then had been devoted to the treatment of numerically greater killers, such as cancer and heart disease, the AIDS glossocrats must have had a detrimental net effect on death statistics. No matter; glossocrats are not about saving lives. The red ribbons they proudly wear on their lapels play precisely the same role as did the straw worn by supporters of the *Fronde* on their hats in the seventeenth century.

That saving lives is not the issue here is proved by the way philistine Modman governments are responding to the real epidemic of AIDS in sub-Saharan Africa. With 1500 afflicted by

HIV every day, hundreds of thousands dying and millions soon to die, one would think this would be a perfect outlet for Modmen's charitable impulses. After all, it is pharmaceutical companies in Western countries that have developed the antiretroviral drugs capable of keeping AIDS at bay. Yet these drugs have not been given free to dying Africans. The problem is that antiretroviral drugs are expensive. It is not that they are all that expensive to produce, not really. It is simply that the political overtones of this therapeutic area have removed any restrictions on the demand in philistine Modman countries. Drug companies would be silly not to milk the marketing opportunity for all it is worth. Why should a company upset its shareholders by giving its product away to people who cannot afford it? Of course, Modman governments could easily make it worthwhile for the companies to airlift vast quantities of antiretroviral drugs to the stricken continent. When it suits them, these governments know perfectly well how to bend corporations to their will. Using tax incentives, large government contracts, government-secured loans, straight subsidies and so forth as either the carrot or the stick is a technique Modman states have drilled to automatic fluency. If they really cared about saving millions of lives, they would find a way. That they are doing little along these lines goes to show yet again where their real interests lie.

Modman governments will couch their actions in the language of glossocracy, but their real aim is destruction of everything that stands in the way of greater power. Thus, for example, the 'fairness' of having different races proportionately represented in a workplace matters to them much less than their power to dictate employment policy to 'free' enterprise. If, on the other hand, they felt that their power could be secured only by keeping the coloured races out, then every office in every country would display a 'whites only' sign. The same goes for Modmen's laws against 'sexism', 'homophobia' and other atrocities they have committed against language and common sense.

What we are witnessing at the moment is only a beginning. All of those politically incorrect 'isms' will be outlawed before long, if they are not already. Until now, mock-legal opprobrium has been extended only to acts that may conceivably offend the delicate sensibilities of glossocratic slaves, such as discrimination against women in the workplace. That law followed a similar injunction against discrimination on racial grounds. Like its predecessor, it is bound sooner or later to leave the domain of proscribing actions and join the realm of prosecuting words. Then, simply stating that women may not be as good as men at some jobs, such as digging ditches, will in itself become an imprisonable offence.

Remembering Cassandra's fate, it is perilous to make predictions. However it is relatively safe to predict that, over the next ten years, more and more people in Western Europe and North America will be sent to prison not for something they have done, but for something they have said. That stands to reason: a dictator whose power is based on the bullet is most scared of bullets; a glossocrat whose power is based on words is most scared of words. At the same time, real crime is going to increase, all to the accompaniment of governmental bleating about giant advances in law enforcement. In fact, no government can fight crime effectively if it proceeds from Enlightenment principles. The more unassailable those principles are, the greater the crime rate. Enlightenment-style 'fairness' is the exact opposite of Westman's justice.

PART 4
CODA

THE MOPPING UP

'I have seen the future and it works.'
(Lincoln Steffens on visiting Lenin's Russia)
'I saw the Dome and it works.'
(Tony 'Anthony' Blair on visiting Greenwich)

In the twentieth century Modman reached maturity, which enabled him to finish off Westman and mop up his remains. It is fortunate that by now the cognitive methodology used in this book, along with some essential assumptions, has been tested enough to take on the task of looking at the major upheavals of this period in some detail.

I began this book by singling out the mass murders of modernity as the most indisputable proof of Modman nastiness. The hundreds of millions of corpses are a fact, difficult even for the most ardent advocates of modernity to deny, impossible for them to dismiss. Modmen would construe as a matter of opinion any other aspect of modern life held up as evidence. The cultural decline, nay catastrophe, brought about by Modmen, is to them a mere replacement of one culture with another. The collapse of morals and civility is the arrival of a new set of standards. Spiritual poverty is offset by material riches. The disintegration of any social balance is compensated for by the general absence of physical pain. Non-existent education is obviously no obstacle to 'happiness'. Yes, but the murders, Mr Modman? What about the skeletal victims at Auschwitz and Vorkuta; the millions blown to smithereens in assorted wars? Murdered in internal strife? Starved to death in the name of progress? Tortured in the cellars? Their souls demand an answer, yet they receive none, at least none that can be regarded as adequate by a Westman holdout.

The arrival of the new millennium has inspired many an author to cast a retrospective look at the century just past. By and large, their efforts fall on either side of the demarcation line between left or right. Those on the left, assisted by rightist rationalists, admire modernity for its dentistry, for its widespread prosperity, absence of pain, longer life expectancy and the generally benign nature of its philistine governments. Those on the right by and large agree, but still remind us of some of the outrages mentioned in the previous paragraph, regretting that modernity delivered all those fabulous things at a terrible cost. We should not argue the point at such a low level. Yes, we all like analgesics, cars, CD players and clean food. But even mentioning those things in the same breath as the catastrophic collapse of Westman religion, culture and civilization, never mind holding up the former as compensation for the latter, puts the discussion side by side with the infantile American joke: 'Yes, but apart from that, Mrs Lincoln, how did you enjoy the play?'

Where the left and right agree to disagree is in assigning a relative weight to the gains and losses, so their scales go up and down, tottering on their fulcrums. But what weight is it really possible to assign to the pile of corpses produced by Modmen? And before we venture a guess, let us not forget that every human being is an atom with a high valence. Destroy a man in the prime of his life and what have you done to his parents or his fiancée?

Kill a father and what happens to his wife and their children? Torture a woman in front of her husband or a child in front of his mother and who suffers more? Do let us multiply those actually killed by, conservatively, three to get a cool billion of lives destroyed in a single century. Then, for good measure, let us throw in all those who were not killed but merely crippled, all those emerging from camps or battlefields as shadows of themselves. Notice how our scales have gone haywire?

Even if Westman had not died and his heritage were still intact, if his great culture continued to flourish, if honour and civility still counted for more than a thick wallet and loud voice, then the twentieth century would still be by far the worst in history. The newsreels of Verdun, Buchenwald, Kolyma and Hiroshima would not let any other assessment sound credible. Except that, had Westman not been killed first, none of the sadistic orgy would have happened. It is debatable whether painless root-canal work is wholly ascribable to Modmen's achievements, but there can be no doubt that the murders are. That is why it is worth talking about everything that goes into the making of Modman: his morals, education, law, history, instincts and origin. While talking about those things, do let us remember that we are discussing the worst criminal in history. If a murderer's proficiency at his job cannot be used as a mitigating circumstance at his trial, then Modmen cannot get off simply because they have learned how to stuff arsenic into dental cavities.

The twentieth century was characterized by what looked like an irreconcilable conflict between, in our terminology, the nihilist and philistine subspecies of Modman, but what was in fact their joint fight against the remnants of Westman's world. This the two subspecies proved by affecting an accelerated convergence directly the West had been scrubbed clean of everything Western. At the time of this writing, the convergence is by no means complete, and more bloodshed will probably be needed to provide enough adhesive to bind the two subspecies together. This century will shake the mixture vigorously, and it would be sheer guesswork trying to predict its ultimate flavour. But there can be little doubt that a mixing process is under way.

After the Great War, Modman spent the rest of the twentieth century trying to work out a *modus vivendi* that would allow the two subspecies, the nihilist and the philistine, to live in peace and move closer together. Such a *rapprochement* became a priority because the war adumbrated the arrival of an aggressively messianic nihilist state: Soviet Russia. A long-term counterbalance to the nihilist upstart could have come only from an equally messianic philistine state, America, which alone among the countries of the West was able to match Russia not only in proselytizing fervour but also in physical bulk. Russia assumed the championship of the nihilist, which she shared for a decade or so with Nazi Germany; whereas the United States slowly but surely took over the captaincy of the philistine team that also stars western Europe. The twentieth century has been defined by interplay between these different but not irreconcilable subspecies of Modman.

The game did not proceed as smoothly as it could have done. Largely to blame for the uneven progress was temporary failure on the part of the nihilist to acknowledge the commonality between him and the philistine. Blinded by the red mist in front of his eyes, the nihilist went for the philistine's throat, which, as subsequent events demonstrated, was a mistake. The nihilist would have been much better served by pursuing the path of what Lenin called 'legalism': a gradual takeover of philistine Modman states by exploiting their own institutions, using them to uproot Westman's heritage and to allow weeds to suffocate the field in which a great culture once had grown so luxuriantly. But such an elaborate approach would have required patience and sagacity, qualities not to be found readily among the nihilists. Dedicated materialists, they were keenly aware of the inbuilt limitations imposed by their own mortality: it was all good and well to lay the foundation for the future success of their creed, but what about their own success? Impatience is inevitable for people who live only in the present, severing, or perhaps not even seeing, any links with the past and future. They want their own slice of the pie (or in this case of Westman's heart) and they want it now.

Thus, shortly after the Bolsheviks grabbed Russia and while still mopping up pockets of resistance in their own country, they sent their cavalry in the general direction of the Channel: Germany and France were the targets but, unfortunately for the impatient Soviet youngster, Poland lay in the way. The West generally misunderstood the far-reaching ambitions animating the so-called Russo–Polish war. Even now historians sometimes describe it as a local conflict, ignoring the famous Order No. 1423 the Red Army commander M. Tukhachevsky issued: 'Soldiers of the proletarian revolution! Direct your eyes towards the west. It is in the west that the fate of the world revolution is being decided. The way towards a world fire lies through the corpse of White Poland. On our bayonets we are taking happiness and peace to workers of the world. Westwards – march!' Poland thus was a step along the way, not the final destination. Alas, the impetuous conquerors found the Polish army of 1920 to be quite a different proposition from the unarmed Russian peasants the Bolsheviks had been culling *en masse* and from the soft-handed *contra*s (aristocrats, priests, teachers, writers, scientists and administrators) they had been mutilating in all sorts of imaginative ways.

Melgunov's *The Red Terror in Russia*, published in the West while Lenin was still alive, documents thousands of instances of such niceties as skinning people alive, rolling them around in nail-studded barrels, driving nails into people's skulls, quartering, burning alive, crucifying priests, stuffing officers alive into locomotive furnaces and pouring molten pitch or liquefied lead down people's throats. All this went on against the background of mass shootings that in the first three years of Soviet rule dispatched almost two million in a quasi-judicial way and millions on top of that without even a travesty of justice.

The Poles were not quite ready to proffer their crania to Bolshevik carpentry. Unaware that the Red steeds had winds of progress behind them, they routed a Red Army ineptly led by the subsequent idol-martyr Tukhachevsky. But for the Poles' remarkable fight-back at Warsaw, the Soviets might indeed have gone all the way, as no viable military force existed to the west of Poland in the wake of the demob-happy pacifism in Germany, France and Britain. As it was, the Red hordes had to flee home, venting their frustration along the way in a series of murderous anti-Semitic pogroms in the Ukraine.

Other Bolshevik rape attempts, namely in Hungary and Germany, were equally unsuccessful, though in Hungary the Cheka-inspired regime of Bela Kuhn and Tibor Szamuely did hang on long enough to spill a most satisfying amount of blood. The backlash was severe enough for the Bolsheviks to see the writing on the wall: the world was not quite ripe for a world revolution. That the message was received and understood was due to Lenin and Stalin who, alone among the early Bolsheviks, were realistic enough to mitigate sanguinary impatience. Temporarily forced into a modicum of good behaviour, the Soviets set out to consolidate their gains in Russia, while trying to subvert the West in ways less straightforward than a cavalry charge. So the first nihilist state after the French Revolution managed to survive. Trotsky and Bukharin who, amazingly, still enjoy some posthumous fame as innocent victims of Stalinism, were pushing hysterically for what Trotsky described as 'permanent revolution': non-stop military aggression waged all over the globe, as a result of which the Red steeds would drink from the English Channel and the Indian Ocean. However, cooler heads, those of Lenin and Stalin, prevailed. It was then that a split occurred between romantic and glossocratic communists. The romantics, whose roster is more or less coextensive with the list of the defendants in the show trials of the 1930s, were driven by the Marxist dogma calling for world revolution. They were prepared to march against the whole world and either vanquish or die in the attempt. Internally, they were guided by a literal reading of the *Communist Manifesto*, on the basis of which Trotsky, for example, called for the complete militarization of labour.

Lenin and Stalin represented the pragmatic strain of nihilist modernity, which made them more dangerous in the long run. They were driven by evil that was more deep-seated than even the recess in which straightforward Bolshevism lurked. Their aim was to exterminate Westman. Communism, in a single country or worldwide, was for them the means, not the end. They, and their ideological heirs, relied on communist verbiage glossocratically for as long as it was useful. Internally, they used it to vindicate violence and deprivation, while externally they used it to prepare the world for the advent of more violence and deprivation. Being pragmatic, rather than romantic, monsters, they were at all times prepared to abandon communist rhetoric, or at least to temper its use if that would put them in a stronger strategic position.

Western observers were invariably taken in by the varying pitch of intensity with which the Soviets used glossocracy. Themselves slaves of glossocracies, philistine Modmen equated power with words, and this pandemic of cognitive dissonance prevented them from realizing that others may not be quite like them, which was why they were so ready to hail the NEP as the end of Bolshevism and were so shocked when Stalin signed the pact with Hitler. Lenin and Stalin, the first glossocratic Bolsheviks, which is to say the first nihilist Modmen who used Bolshevism as a glossocratic lever only, would have declared themselves God-fearing monarchists had they felt that such an about-face would enable them to achieve their objectives more quickly. Once the infantile impetuosity of the Bolshevik state settled down, Lenin and later Stalin began to weigh the pros and cons of this or that action with detachment and a thoroughly utilitarian objectivity. Both realized that philistine Modman states would fight, however reluctantly, if they felt their comforts were being threatened. Otherwise, they

could be counted on to remain affably neutral and generally sup-
portive. Shrewder men than the contemporaneous politicians in the
West, Lenin and Stalin must have sensed that, deep down, philistine states differed from the Soviets only in the means preferred to
achieve the anti-Westman ends, not in the ends themselves.

Quoted above were Lloyd George and Wilson whose pronouncements on the nascent Soviet state vindicated, and must
have helped shape, this Bolshevik vision. Both those philistine
Modmen felt kinship with their nihilist brethren – provided the
latter did not jump at their throats. The weight of 'public opinion'
in both Britain and the USA was solidly behind appeasement, as it
was to be 20 years later in relation to Hitler. Few Westerners
shared Sidney Reilly's understanding of the threat Bolshevism
posed to the West, and many of those who did were Modmen
and, as such, broadly sympathetic to the idea of destroying
Westman, but preferably without the stomach-churning business
of stuffing people alive into locomotive furnaces. Being philistines,
they tended to favour bloodless annihilation and hoped that the
Russians would play along.

Sensing the deep need of Modman philistines to love their
nihilist brethren, Lenin and Stalin responded to their adversaries'
spoken and unspoken requests to make such love possible. To that
end the Bolsheviks devised, over protests from Trotsky and his
followers, a two-pronged policy that, with variations, Russia has
been following ever since. The two prongs were at the time of
their origination called Military Communism and New Economic
Policy. The former illustrated the difference between the means
favoured by the nihilist and philistine, while the latter showed the
similarity of the ends. The two policies, if under different names,
have been alternating ever since. The Russians would first scare
the living daylight out of Western philistines by perpetrating
unspeakable atrocities (Military Communism), then allay their
worst fears by softening their brutality and emphasizing the commonality of their heritage and aspirations with the philistines (NEP).

The purpose of Military Communism was to force first the country and then the world into submission; the chief objectives of NEP were to mitigate the effects of Military Communism, back-pedal, let off some steam, and then set up the next round by attempting to present to the world a picture of 'change', 'liberalization', Stalin's *'perestroika'*, Khrushchev's 'thaw', Brezhnev's *'détente'*, Andropov's 'communism with a human face', Gorbachev's *'glasnost'*, Yeltsin's *'perestroika'*, Putin's 'reform' and so forth. Sudden shifts in Russian policy can never surprise anyone who is familiar with this alternating pattern: the blood-thirsty collectivization followed by Stalin's caution against 'vertigo from success'; postwar witches' Sabbath followed by 'the thaw', which was bound to adumbrate Brezhnev's reaction, which in turn set the stage for the ongoing NEP-like binge underpinned by post-communist criminality.

Just as the Romans who, during the senescence of their civilization, managed to survive a few centuries longer by paying off the surrounding barbarians, the philistine West, now bereft of its erstwhile moral fibre, has been trying to keep the nihilist at bay by massive infusions of money and technology. This process has been proceeding in an uninterrupted fashion since the Bolshevik takeover and is now at its height. Not all this support has been offered out of fear. Some of it is attributable to the broad sympathy philistine Modmen felt for 'the first state of workers and peasants'; the first state, in other words, that was manifestly, as opposed to implicitly, dedicated to the elimination of Westman. Western politicians envied the forthrightness with which the Bolsheviks expressed their aspirations. The Lloyd Georges, Ramsey McDonalds, Woodrow Wilsons and FDRs of this world had to couch a similar sentiment in polite words so as not to scare off their philistine constituencies. Their tactics were predetermined to be attrition, not a rusty nail hammered into a recalcitrant cranium. This they realized, but that realization did not prevent them admiring the robustness of the Bolsheviks, much as an unpopular nerd admires the monosyllabic seduction technique practised by the campus athlete. At heart, the flabby philistine always wanted to emulate the muscular nihilist. That is partly why Berthold Brecht, habitually clad in black paramilitary uniform criss-crossed by leather thongs, became such a darling in the philistine West.

The Bolsheviks sensed this secret longing and did their utmost to cater to it. Their own power was only partly glossocratic, what with the old nails still clanking in their tool box, ready to see the light of day at a moment's notice. But the glossocratic element was important, and they did not mind fashioning it to suit Western glossocratic cravings. While the Cheka, the most murderous organization in history, was established just six weeks after the Bolshevik coup, a worldwide propaganda service followed immediately. Equipped with powerful radio transmitters and manned by poets, artists and musicians, this service hastily created the masculine ideal of leather-jerkined modernity, missing in the ethos of an effeminate philistine West. Power seduces; absolute power seduces absolutely: Before long Western champions of modernity began to flock to Russia much in the way of Muslims going on those hadj pilgrimages to Mecca. The new pilgrims were not all uncritical Fabians in the vein of the Webbs, Shaw or Wells. They also included businessmen bearing investment capital, scientists and engineers offering their expertise, administrators seeking to organize famine relief, what with famine being an automatic by-product of universal social justice, communist-style.

The Soviets would have had to be deaf not to hear the plaintive voices of their foreign admirers begging to be loved, offering love in return and imploring those 'dreamers in the Kremlin' not to do anything so vile as to make it difficult to love them. Deaf the Soviets were not and neither were they dumb. The Comintern propaganda machine never left high gear and the glossocratic messages of nihilist modernity filled the airwaves with subversive venom. At the same time the Soviets transferred their entire economy onto a war footing to prepare themselves for future conquests. The aim was to create the mightiest military force in history, which meant first developing heavy industry beyond any level that ever had existed in Russia. Given the inherent ineptitude of socialism, augmented by the Russians' understated work ethic, this could not have been achieved without sacrificing every civilian sector of the economy, including agriculture. As there was not enough to go around, the fruits of agricultural production had to be taken away from the producers and channelled into the cities where they could keep industrial workers strong enough to do daily 16-hour shifts for a few years and then keel over, only to be replaced by new slaves. The enslavement of the peasantry, glossocratically called collectivization, was thus not just an extension of orthodox Marxism but an economic necessity. Without it the Soviets would never have been able to industrialize fast or thoroughly enough. Thus Stalin's savagery against his own people was different from the violence of the French Revolution: it was utilitarian rather than principled. Later myths of Stalin's insanity could have been spread only by naïve philistines who had to regard as madness any behaviour different from their own. Not only was Stalin in full command of his faculties, but he was perhaps the most astute and self-controlled villain in history. His life was dedicated to the execution of a master plan for world conquest.

While creating the most formidable military machine in the world, Stalin aimed his foreign policy at sowing discord among Western philistine states. The exact mechanism was first suggested by Lenin who presciently realized that Germany would never accept for long the supine status imposed on her by Versailles. Sooner or later, the Germans would seek revenge on the countries that had so humiliated them. Following the treacherous separate peace Lenin had made with Germany at Brest-Litovsk, Russia was not one of the victors, which made her the only possible ally as far as Germany was concerned. For Russia, on the other hand,

Germany was a potential 'icebreaker for the revolution', in Lenin's apt phrase, as Germany's desire for revenge was exploitable. The makings of a mutually profitable alliance were thus in place and the deal that sealed it, the Rapallo Treaty, had a more enduring impact on the world than even Versailles did. Following Rapallo, the two rogue states came together on the basis of mutual interest: Germany could use Russian territory for training and Russian factories for equipping the new German army. The Russians, apart from the secret long-term benefit of rearming Germany and setting her loose on the West, had many short-term benefits as well: German technology could help them build their factories, while German *Freikorps* officers could whip some *ordnung* into a Red Army that still resembled a loose association of gangs more than a regular fighting force.

Like the subsequent Non-Aggression Pact, the Rapallo Treaty had secret clauses. Unlike those of the later deal, these clauses never have been made public, but we can surmise their existence from much of the ensuing activity that was not based on the published document. The Germans built a number of armament factories in Russia, with the proviso that the Soviets would keep half the output and all the technology for themselves. One such factory was the Junkers aircraft plant at Fili, near (now in) Moscow, whose buildings formed a giant 'A' shape legible from above. The corollary benefit for the Germans was that this tongue-in-cheek advertisement made it easy for the Luftwaffe to hit the plant once the Rapallo process went sour. The Soviets established training bases in Lipetsk, Riazan and elsewhere, enabling the Germans to create an illegal panzer force, and Reichswehr officers to share expertise with their Russian counterparts. Concurrently with the post-Rapallo bliss, the Soviets stepped up their subversive activities in Weimar Germany. They were far from sure that Stresemann's weak-kneed government would ever conjure up the will to seek revenge on the West, even if Russia provided the means. Though the Reichswehr still had the gumption to do what was necessary, Germany's Weimar government was at odds with its armed forces. It was singing from a different hymn sheet and the tune smacked of *Mein Lieber Augustine* more than of a military march.

This would not do, and so the Soviets began to cultivate those groups within Germany that were more Stahlhelm than Weimar in spirit. Thus they formed a close relationship with the Nazi party even before it acquired its name. There is plenty of circumstantial evidence for the existence of this special relationship, mostly uncovered by post-*perestroika* Russian historians but, by and large, still kept under wraps in the West. The reason for this reticence is not an elaborate conspiracy but the fact that in the light of such revelations too many glittering academic careers would appear ill-deserved, based as they are on a spurious view of modern history. Nihilist glossocracy has misled too many Western academics into basing their learned deductions on an imaginary political spectrum demarcated by communists on the left and Nazis on the right.

In fact, if one disregarded the glossocratic fog spread by both nihilist subgroups and looked merely at their actions and aspirations, the striking similarity between them would become obvious. They were united in their post-Westman, which is to say post-Christian, insistence on looking upon humanity in purely utilitarian terms. To Westmen, the individual represented a finite quality, an end in itself. To Modmen, the individual is part of a quantity, a means towards an end. Some groups were acceptable to the nihilists; some were not. That the Nazis based this division primarily on race and the Soviets mostly on class was insignificant when juxtaposed with their overriding similarity: hatred of Westman. Soviet class struggle and Nazi racial purity were merely glossocratic stratagems leading to the same implicit goal: a world purged of Westmen. The upper classes were statistically more likely to cultivate Westman's pre-Enlightenment recalcitrance, and, being consummate Modmen, the Soviets were firm believers in statistics. So the upper classes had to be wiped out.

Likewise, the Jews, while perhaps more pre-Westman than wholly Westman, were nevertheless resolutely anti-Modman in their values and practices. The importance of family, a patriarchal organization of society, religiosity governing every aspect of behaviour, a set of religious laws seen to have primacy over any secular regulations – all these characteristics made the Jews unacceptable to Modmen. While anti-Semitism in the West is roughly coextensive with Christianity, there is a difference between Christian and Modman varieties of Judophobia. The Christians sought to convert the Jews; the Modman nihilists sought to exterminate them. As far as the Christians were concerned, they had seen the revelatory light, whereas the Jews had not. People generally hate to see their pet ideas scorned; when the pet idea is so grandiose that it overshadows life itself, they can become violent towards the infidels. From the time of the Crucifixion, Christians have been obsessed with bending the Jews to their way of thinking and, for those who would not bend, the consequences could be as dire as those suffered by the Jews at the hands of Modman. But in Westman times a Jew usually could save his life and property by uttering five simple words: I believe in Jesus Christ. Once those words were uttered, Westmen experienced the satisfaction of someone who had just won an argument. The Jew still was not entirely trusted, but he was usually left alone.

Deliverance from prosecution was thus so easy that many Jews resorted to ostensible conversion while remaining religious Jews in secret. Using this stratagem, the Marrano community in Spain managed to escape not only death but even the 1492 expulsion. It was as if Westmen, now they had won their argument, were not in the least offended by the intellectual and behavioural patterns of the Jews: these did not differ quite as dramatically from his own as Judaism differed from their religion. Even in old Russia, which was more anti-Semitic than any Western country, a Jew was accepted at any level of society once he renounced his Judaism. If a Shapiro was prepared to become a Shafirov, he could become deputy first minister to the tsar (in this case, Peter I) with the same ease with which Joseph rose to a similar post at the court of his pharaoh. Hundreds of baptized Jews practised law, medicine and – as for instance Lenin's maternal grandfather – commerce in Moscow, Petersburg and elsewhere outside the Pale of Settlement. Four of the seven authors of *Landmarks* (1909), the influential collection of conservative essays, were ethnic Jews.

For Modmen, on the other hand, it is not what the Jews profess but what they are that is repugnant. What offends Modmen is not Jewish or any other religion, what with all of them having been successfully marginalized in the modern world, but the staunch denial of the post-Enlightenment secularism that many Jews carry in their breasts regardless of their religiosity. Hatred of the Jew is thus consistent, and largely coextensive, with hatred of Westman. The difference between the Nazis and the Soviets in this respect was merely a matter of priority. Stalin was getting around to the launch of his own extermination programme in the late 1940s and early 1950s, and only his death prevented the Soviet Final Solution; Hitler placed anti-Semitism at the top of his agenda. And their common intellectual ancestor Karl Marx also used the Jew as the focus of his hatred of Westmen. That he was a Jew himself did not matter: Marx was satisfied that he was a fully paid-up Modman. His credentials were thus impeccable, which was more than he could say for the Jews who had not seen the light of modernity.

Given half a chance, the Soviets indulged in anti-Semitic atrocities even before they became part of an enunciated policy. When the Soviet Union entered the Second World War by stabbing Poland in the back, Polish Jews would run away from the Nazis to the Soviet zone – only to flee right back, having suffered even worse persecutions. On that issue the two champions of nihilist modernity yet again differed not so much in substance as in glossocratic technique. In most other aspects, the differences were as slight. Economically, both sides were socialist: Hitler's four-year plan was patterned after Stalin's five-year precursor. The organizers of the Gestapo owed much to the advice of NKVD experts; even Hitler's rallies, both before and after Goebbels elevated them to monumental theatrical productions, bore much resemblance to similar Soviet rites. Speer's architecture would have fitted seamlessly into the plans of Soviet cities; Nazi paintings were stylistically indistinguishable from Stalin's 'socialist realism'; Nazi obsession with paramilitary uniforms was the same as in Stalin's Russia. The organizational aspect of the NSDAP, and its interaction with the government, were patterned after the CPSU and the people's commissariats. Nazi people's courts were dead ringers for Bolshevik *troika*s and the very style of Nazi politics was remarkably similar to its Bolshevik antecedents. Even the colour of their flags was the same revolutionary red, though with different superimposed symbols. Ribbentrop was not just paying his hosts a compliment when he said at the post-pact banquet in the Kremlin: 'I feel as if I were with my party comrades in Berlin.' If *le style c'est l'homme même*, then the style of politics should provide a clue to its substance. It is the brazenly pagan style of both Soviet and Nazi politics that should have tipped off any intelligent observer that, while proclaiming his devotion to class struggle, Stalin was really after the hide of Westman, a prize Hitler craved as well, even though his glossocratic goal was the preservation of the racial purity of the German *volk*.

Hitler had an unwitting role to play as well, that of the 'icebreaker for the revolution'. For that reason he had been cultivated by the Soviets even before his abortive *putsch*, and that is why he was allowed to win the 1933 election in Germany. Hitler's own silence on the *putsch* speaks volumes. Indeed, sitting in gaol after the collapse of his first revolution, which until then had been the epitome of Hitler's struggle for power, he wrote *Mein Kampf*, a book appropriately dedicated to Hitler's comrades killed when the Weimar police dispersed the *putsch*. Yet this is the first and last reference to the culmination of the eponymous *kampf* the book was about. This reticence is hard to explain in an author not usually known for that quality. The Hitler we all know would have been much more likely to devote the longest chapter in his book to the *putsch*, and then the second longest to the degenerate crypto-Yid traitors who contributed to its failure. However, had Hitler chosen to elucidate that event, he would have had to explain many other mysteries, including the choice of the date on which he had marched. And the date is remarkable.

The Soviets at that time had not yet come round to the idea of biding their time, and a secret Central Committee meeting had decreed that a world revolution should begin with a simultaneous violent outburst by the radical left-wing parties everywhere. The date on which they were all set to march was dictated by the Soviets' love of symbolic pageantry: 8 and 9 November 1923 – immediately after the celebration of their revolution's anniversary on 7 November. At the last moment, however, the Bolshevik ring-masters changed their minds and tried to call the dogs off. Most they caught in the nick of time, but a few extreme parties, including several German ones, missed the second signal and marched – straight into police guns. One of the parties thus punished for that break in communications was the NSDAP. Understandably, in a book filled with glossocratic anti-Bolshevik puffery, Hitler could not talk about a *putsch* that might have been ordered by the Soviets.

Just as understandable is the Nazis' silence on the 1933 election. In his diaries Goebbels writes about the gloom at NSDAP headquarters after the disastrous 1932 election that left the Nazis on the brink of collapse, with not a pfennig in the party coffers and the party leaders feeling suicidal. Then his narrative fast-forwards to the 1933 election the Nazis won. How did they replenish their treasury? Surely not all their funding came from Fritz Thyssen, the anti-Bolshevik industrialist whom grateful Nazis later shipped to Dachau. How did they regroup for the victorious campaign? How did they bring the German people around? Goebbels, a veritable chatterbox on any subject under the sun, here keeps silent. We can sympathize with his taciturnity, for the victor of that election was determined by Stalin, not by the German electorate. The electorate voted in the Popular Front coalition of the Social Democrats and the Communists. Though the two parties did not run as a bloc, years of Popular Front propaganda, expertly whipped up by the Soviets, had conditioned the German voters to think that the minute differences between the social democrats and the communists would be swept aside in the face of a Nazi threat. Most voters were casting their ballots for one or the other party almost interchangeably, not bothering about what they saw as the technical differences between them.

Those differences went, of course, much deeper than technicalities. The Social Democrats were variously sympathetic to the Soviets, but they were not their puppets. The communists were. The puppet master in the Kremlin pulled a few relevant wires, and his German dummies dutifully refused to form a winning bloc with the Social Democrats and other anti-Nazi forces, thus delivering the election to Hitler who had nowhere near enough votes for an overall majority if faced with a bloc of left-wing parties. We probably shall never know how exactly that transaction was handled and what the preconditions were: the answer is buried somewhere in the Soviet archives and so far the Russians have been selective in what they have allowed to make public. But the 1933 election was, at least as far as the Soviets were concerned, a natural continuation of the Rapallo process. It culminated in the 1939 pact effectively dividing Europe between Hitler and Stalin and pushing the button for the Second World War that began a fortnight after the pact had been signed.

It would have been natural for the Western allies to feel apprehensive about the strengthening bonds between the nihilist forces in Russia and Germany, but a reader looking for any signs of such apprehension in the contemporaneous press is likely to come a cropper. Then as now, philistine Modmen were unable to overcome their cognitive dissonance and realize that, although they were not conspirators, others were capable of plotting against him. Granted, people in Britain, France and the USA were sensitive to the glossocratic elements of Bolshevism and resented communist propaganda. Likewise, they resented and generally discouraged old-fashioned Soviet espionage of the type they themselves would occasionally practise against their adversaries. But the isolated seers who were pointing out the aggressive, as opposed to merely glossocratic, nature of the secret cooperation between the Soviets and Nazis were branded as alarmists, conspiracy theorists and so forth. Not only the general public, but even the intelligence services, which ought to have known better, were ignorant of the growing threat, much to the Soviet defectors' consternation. For example, Boris Bazhanov, the defecting secretary to Stalin, was astounded to find that his US interrogators considered him highly eccentric for maintaining that it was the Communist Party, not the Soviet government, that ran Russia and the Soviets who ran the Comintern, not the other way around. Against the background of such ignorance it was hardly surprising that when Walter Krivitsky, the first ranking GRU defector, predicted early in 1939 that Germany and the Soviet Union would soon sign a pact ringing the bell for Germany's westward push, he was treated as an amusing madman.

The Nazis and Soviets were united in their shared thirst for Westmen's blood, and the pact enabled them to slake some of this thirst. The purges the Soviets conducted in the Baltic states they had received as their share of the spoils were directed against groups containing the greatest number of Westman holdouts: priests, teachers, writers, officers and all other usual suspects. As a result, those countries suffered genetic catastrophes from which they still have not fully recovered. Having lost between 20 and 30 per cent of their total populations (mostly picked off the top), Latvia, Lithuania and Estonia became a cultural wasteland providing little sustenance for Westman. Now they are free of their

Soviet masters, the Balts are fighting an uphill battle to rejoin the Western world, unaware that it is no longer there. One hopes they will eventually find their own way, but one fears it will not be any time soon.

The Georgians, who had the misfortune to be Stalin's compatriots, suffered a similar fate. Georgia, along with Armenia, had more of a claim to being a third Rome than Russia had. It was there that the fire of Byzantine Christianity had been burning bright until it was brutally put down by their Russophile countryman. But, having lost their cultural elite to purges, the Georgians have become something of a broad ethnic joke in Russia, cast in the same role as the Irish in Britain, the Poles in America or the Belgians in both France and Holland. Westman holdouts everywhere should mourn the cultural demise at the periphery of the Western world and light an occasional candle for those who died trying to preserve our soul in the face of the nihilist onslaught.

Poland provides another example. This long-suffering land caught it coming and going: crushed in the jaws of the Nazi–Soviet vice, the Poles suffered greatly at the hands of two powers pursuing the same cultural agenda. An aristocratic society with a proud elitist tradition, the land of Chopin was the only country in history to have been led by a classical pianist. Alas, Paderewski was a better musician than statesman. Militarily, the Poland of 1939 was different from the victor in the Russo–Polish war, or rather not different enough. Still largely relying on cold steel, the Polish army was no match for Nazi and Soviet armour; after a heroic struggle the country was partitioned yet again. That the Soviets instantly began to exterminate the educated classes in their occupation zone, a programme of which Katyn was a culmination not the sum total, was predictable. After all, the glossocratic aspect of Bolshevism called for just such extermination the world over. That is why, according to the glossocratic nomenclature in the West, the Soviets were left-wing. Hitler, on the other hand, was supposed to be right-wing. Did he not rant against the

Bolsheviks in *Mein Kampf*? He was an anti-Bolshevik; the Bolsheviks were left-wing; therefore, Hitler had to be right-wing.

This spurious logic did not prepare philistine Modman labellers for the Nazis' behaviour in Poland. For, far from justifying their position at the opposite end of the imaginary political spectrum, the Germans set out to exterminate exactly the same groups as the Soviets did: officers, priests, intellectuals, artists, merchants, industrialists, government officials and, of course, Jews; in other words, the very same groups where the proportion of Westman holdouts was presumably higher than among the workers and peasants. So, while Poland was being squashed in the pincers of nihilist modernity, it was Westman who was feeling the pinch.

THE SPANISH DETOUR

The only European war in the twentieth century in which Westman holdouts took up arms against Modmen and won was the Civil War in Spain. Spain thus became the only European country that managed to reverse the initial success of Modmen and delay their full advent by almost half a century. The amount of vitriol still being sputtered at the victors by every hue of Modman goes a long way towards vindicating the main point of this book.

Stalin's Comintern mistakenly identified Spain as the weakest link in the West. The mistake was caused by the false Marxist methodology Stalin tended to apply to his analysis of societies he did not know first-hand. The latently feudal Spain was the least 'bourgeois' of the western European countries, which to a Marxist was a sign of weakness. In fact, Spain was at the time Europe's most aristocratic country, which made it the most Western in the sense in which the term is used here.

Not having had the benefit of a pre-Enlightenment cognitive methodology, Stalin singled Spain out for a greater dose of Popular Front subversion than any other country in the West, except possibly France. At first his strategy seemed to be succeeding spectacularly. Having destabilized the transitional regime of Primo de Rivera, the Popular Front, inspired by the Comintern, installed its own government that was eventually taken over by the 'Spanish Lenin' Largo Caballero. In short order, Spain sank into anarchy, with every traditional Westman institution being destroyed and even the army disintegrating into chaos. In Stalin's eyes, that made the country ripe for a Bolshevik takeover: the 'revolutionary situation' seemed to be in place. What Stalin did not realize was that Spain was perhaps the only place where Westman was not yet extinct as a social force. That the Soviet chieftain did not get away with this misapprehension was owed to the invisible hand of historical serendipity that plucked the right man out of relative obscurity and put him in the right place at the right time.

Francisco Franco was not a political general. He was a man who loved his country, saw it being destroyed by the chatterboxes and grasped the opportunity to do something about it. Simple in his theoretical constructs, Franco thought along the lines of God and country and probably was uncertain where one ended and the other began. He succeeded because his country had not had to endure a century of Modman erosion. Comintern subversion had had merely a decade – enough time to plunge the country into anarchy, but not enough to corrupt it to the core. There was enough Westman spunk left in Spain, and all Franco had to do was channel it into the right conduits. This he proceeded to do, armed not only with patriotism but, fortunately for Spain, also with pragmatism. The second quality enabled him to look for help anywhere he could find it. Internally that led to an alliance with the Falange, externally to one with Mussolini and Hitler. Perhaps an alliance is an inadequate word to describe an essentially one-sided arrangement. Franco accepted Hitler's help, having scored the diplomatic coup of promising nothing except money in return. Not only did Spain under Franco fail to enter the Second World

War on Germany's side, but his government even denied Hitler the right of passage to Gibraltar. Franco joyously traded salutes with the Nazis, but balked at trading favours. It was by design that he was so unreceptive to Hitler's overtures that the latter likened talking to Franco to having one's teeth pulled out.

Even as Paris was worth a mass to Henri IV, Madrid was worth an outstretched right arm to Franco. But he was far from being the fascist of Modman's mythology. He was the last Westman among the great leaders of the world, which earned him the undying enmity of the nihilist and philistine alike. Westmen are detestable to Modmen above anything else. For that reason the International Brigades, Stalin's Comintern army, could boast roughly 200 times the number of British volunteers that Franco could attract (the score, according to the Carlist volunteer Peter Kemp, was about 2500 to a meagre 12). Stalin was a Modman, Franco a Westman: in the face of that difference the relatively insignificant disagreements between the two subspecies of Modman were swept aside. Notwithstanding his subsequent *Homage to Catalonia*, in which he criticized the Loyalists more from the left than from the right, someone like George Orwell had more in common with Stalin than he did with Franco. For Modmen, the choice was clear – and still is.

Now, almost 70 years after the Civil War and 30 since Franco died, Modmen still have not relented. To them it is immaterial that, but for Franco, Spain would have fallen to Stalin and today would be like Romania or, perhaps, Yugoslavia. Franco was the first statesman who stopped Modmen by force of arms. So Modmen will never give him the benefit of the doubt. Even Stalin and (in France especially) Trotsky, Modmen through and through, are still seen as having possessed redeeming qualities, much as they are begrudgingly admitted to have been offset by their brutality. Franco, Pinochet and a few other men who saved their countries from the rack of modernity, rate nothing but visceral hatred.

THE PARTITION OF THE WORLD

Modman's great champions were poised to blow up the world. After all, even though Westman was in his last throes, the agony was taking too long. The scale of his achievements was growing smaller, but some great music was still being composed, a few good books were still being written, European countries still had cultured elites, although rapidly dwindling ones. It is not that those things were intolerable in themselves; Modmen were not that unforgiving. But they were all indications that Modmen's rule was not quite absolute. Resistance was still persevering.

Modmen knew from recent experience that palliatives took too long. A world war was much better, or at any rate quicker. Take the only surviving European empire, for example. Admittedly, it had been dealt a deadly blow the first time Modmen went all out in the twentieth century. But in symbolism, if not already in substance, it was still hanging on. Who knows, perhaps given breathing space, the wily Brits would be able to resuscitate their moribund empire and set a rotten example for other Europeans to follow. This hatred of the British empire, while shared by Modmen everywhere, including in Britain, was not the reason for the Second World War. It was, however, a thorn in Modmen's side, a reminder that they still had work to do.

Of the three key players, two – America and Russia – were pursuing a waiting strategy. The third, Germany, could not wait. The long-term pack was stacked against her, what with Russia's endless human resources and America's inexhaustible industrial might. The philistines entrenched in the United States were waiting for their chestnuts to be roasted in the fire of a European war. They knew that the last vestiges of Westman's heritage, such as the British Empire, would vanish regardless of who the nominal winner would be. But it was important to American Modmen that the empire should not fold too quickly without first sapping the German nihilist's strength. With all the key participants having been desanguinated, a full-blooded American economy would rule the world, and the American Modmen would generously share the crumbs of their happiness with the Europeans – but at a price. The price would be Westman's head on a cultural platter. Modman expansionism was thus alive and well in the United States, but it was somewhat held in check by the philistine's distaste for the sight of blood, mostly his own. So the American philistines had to wait.

The Russian nihilists also had a long-term expansionist strategy, but theirs was more bloodthirsty. They would continue their militarization, the scale of which was unprecedented in history. Then they would use every imaginable alliance to protect their rear and buy more time, build a military machine rivalling that of the rest of the world put together, drive it to his Western border – and wait. Sooner or later, the battering icebreaker, also known as Germany, would win its victory and then run aground from sheer exhaustion. The Soviet Modmen would then ease their military machine into a high gear and roll over Europe. The blood of Westman would flow into the earth, and no lilies would grow on the spot this time.

Only Hitler did not have a strategy worthy of the name: he simply could not afford one. A strategy needs time to be carried out, and time was not something Germany had at her disposal. Her population was nihilist for the time being, but at heart it was philistine. Talk of guns before butter did not sit well with the Germans; so it had to remain just that, talk. Germany did not transfer her economy onto a total war footing until her failure to take Moscow in the dying days of 1941, when it was already too late. By contrast, the Soviet economy had been operating in a war mode since the summer of 1939, two years before the Soviets actually had to fight in earnest. The expansionist cravings of the German Modmen had to be satisfied by tactical, not strategic means. This they proceeded to do, knocking European combatants out one by one with a series of lightning strikes.

The British, who had been dragged into the war kicking and

screaming, were ill-prepared for it both strategically and tactically. Their armament programme, such as it was, had not started in earnest until a few months before the war. Moreover, Britain, as ineptly led in the run-up to the Second World War as she was in the First, had not learned from her mistakes. Yet again she had entered a treaty that left her no room for manoeuvre: if Germany invaded Poland, Britain would fight no matter what. While French intellectuals, corrupted by Stalin's Popular Front, were smirking '*mourir pour Danzig?*' in Left Bank cafés, the British and French governments had undertaken to do just that.

For a while the war was unfolding in a way that would seem to vindicate every strategic aspiration involved. Germany was not bleeding profusely, but she was bleeding. At the same time she had conquered most of continental Europe, cutting down most Westman holdouts still standing. Britain was hanging on by the skin of her teeth, growing more dependent by the minute on American handouts. These were proffered surreptitiously, what with America still being technically neutral. Roosevelt knew he would have to get into the European war sooner or later to pick up those roasted chestnuts. Faced with the same public distaste for war as Wilson had to contend with 20-odd years earlier, Roosevelt chose the same tactics. In general, as far as any Modman politician is concerned, the clarion call of his inner agenda easily muffles the rumble of an electorate. The people do not want to fight? OK, let us present them with a *fait accompli*. So America kept violating the provisions of neutrality by keeping up a steady flow of supplies across the Atlantic. But military and economic assistance came with an implicit price tag attached: for supplies to come, Westman had to go.

Meanwhile, Russia was quietly oiling her juggernaut poised at the German border. Soviet tanks, exceeding both in number and quality anything the rest of the world combined had to offer, were ready to roll. (Hitler attacked the USSR with 3350 light tanks. The Red Army, as of 21 June 1941, had 24,000 tanks. In quality, most of these were at least a match for anything Hitler had, while Stalin's 1363 T-34s, 677 KVs and 731 BT7Ms, equipped with the same B2 diesels as the other two, by far exceeded in every characteristic – speed, weight, armour, fire power, overall layout and engine quality – all German tanks until the introduction of the Tigers and Panthers in the run-up to Stalingrad. At the same time, the Soviets unveiled the IS-3, again superior to the German innovations.) Had Hitler really been the halfwit satirized in the comic films of the time, everything would have proceeded according to plan. Stalin's thrust across Europe sooner or later would have steamrolled over an exhausted Germany. America's economy would have come to the rescue of a devastated Europe, and the two subspecies of Modman would have danced together on Westman's grave. But though Hitler was many odious things, a fool he was not. Even if he took too long to realize what role he was playing and who had written the lines, in the end he did realize it and tore up the script. Hitler did the only thing he could do under the circumstances: launch a pre-emptive strike against the crowded millions of the Soviet troops waiting for their marching orders in east Poland. The Führer knew, of course, as did any German schoolboy, that his country could not fight a two-front war without suffering dire consequences. But he also realized she no longer had a choice. Germany's only flicker of hope lay in landing a quick knockout punch, so Hitler closed his eyes and took the hardest swing he could.

Germany could not win a war against Russia, certainly not with an undefeated Britain still in her rear. Paradoxically, because she could not win she almost did. Stalin, the patient fencer, did not anticipate that his opponent would grab an axe and bludgeon him with it. This move was not part of the game, so Stalin was unprepared for it. His armies, equipped and trained for launching a surprise attack and deployed in a strictly offensive mode, had to learn as they went along how to dig in and defend. Stalin's tank crews had been trained to operate at depth on good roads behind the enemy lines, not to waddle through the swamps of Russia. His pilots had been trained first to obtain air superiority by hitting enemy airfields, then to support the advancing troops by strafing ground targets – not to win dogfights. By striking first, the Germans rendered Stalin's preparations useless and his troops confused. The old strategy no longer applied and the Soviet hordes were routed yet again. In the end, they did emerge victorious, but it was not the scale of victory Stalin had planned.

America's scenario did not quite unfold according to plan either. Pearl Harbor distracted her from the anti-Westman strategy and eventually delayed her victory, but only for a while. Once the shock waves of the nihilist outburst were attenuated in Europe, America was ready to claim her philistine spoils. What made things more cumbersome was that Hitler's tactical astuteness had prevented a total strategic victory of the Soviet nihilist. America's postwar proposition was thus less straightforward than it would have been otherwise. She now had more than one customer to deal with, quite a few ends to play against the same middle. Dealing with a single customer was what America had always wanted and still does, which is why the United States has for the last 100 years been a passionate, if not always open, advocate of world government or its near approximations. The motives behind this passion are often misunderstood, especially by people who think simplistically that America pursues nothing but commercial interests. From that standpoint, it is indeed hard to understand why the United States has always been a supporter of the manifestly anti-American United Nations, or, for that matter, of the cause of European federalism. After all, the express purpose of the European Union is to create a protectionist bloc aimed against non-Europeans in general and Americans in particular. Is America cutting off her nose to spite her face? Not at all.

The United States is more than just a giant commercial concern with an uncertain cultural background. It is the messianic flag bearer for the philistine subspecies of Modman. And Modmen love uniformity of any kind. At the heart of their beliefs lies the smug certainty that underneath it all everybody either is, or desperately wants to become, just like them. All that is missing is the right set of conditions, and who better than the old US of A to create them? The American philistine is thus not just an international trader but also an international proselytizer. As such, he knows that a single government would probably be easier and definitely quicker to convert to his way of life than many separate governments. For a single European government today can never be a Westman body. It can only be a Modman Leviathan grown out of all proportion. Its links with any culture, be that local European or general Western, are severed (as being proved at the time of this writing by attempts to admit Turkey to the EU). Its traditional patriotic loyalties are non-existent. Its only loyalty is pledged to the international political elite that is distinctly Modman in genealogy and character. If this elite is not already Americanized, it can be trained to be. If training proves difficult, it can be bought.

Moreover, a single world government can be achieved only by an irreversible destruction of the traditional political and legal institutions. These institutions are, of course, traditional in form only. Their substance has long since been perverted by Modmen. Still, even if they are nothing but a skeleton, there is always the danger that some unexpected upheaval may put new flesh on the old bones. That is a remote possibility to be sure, but Modmen like to play for keeps. They will welcome any political development that will push traditional Westman institutions closer to extinction. It goes without saying that the American Modman is a Modman first and an American a distant second. 'The proletariat knows no motherland,' and neither does Modman.

That is why a decisive victory in the Second World War for either Hitler or Stalin would have been preferable as far as America was concerned. The Americans could do business with an unabashedly Modman state, either brown or red, especially if it took the shape of a United States of Europe. Stalin's half-victory, on the other hand, was neither fish nor fowl. It neither destroyed diversity in Europe nor eliminated tensions. America now had to invest billions in house-training Western Europe – on top of the billions she also had to invest to arm herself against the expansionism of a still-hungry Soviet Union. Still, the vigorous American economy, weaned on the pursuit of happiness, could deliver the billions.

ALL YOU NEED IS LOVE

The Second World War did not produce a clear-cut winner, but it did produce a clear-cut loser. The war effectively mopped up the last vestiges of Westman's resistance. The First World War had eliminated him as a serious geopolitical player. The Second finished him off as a cultural force. Culture was, of course, the very essence of Westman, the organic link between his religion and civilization. Destroying it had always been high on Modmen's agenda. Now this goal moved to the top, even though Westman was no longer a threat at present or in any foreseeable future. However, simply uprooting Westman's culture was not enough. The cultural field had to be sown with coarse-grained salt so that nothing would ever grow again should a particle of Western pollen be inadvertently dropped on the barren earth. Modmen needed the salt and also something with which to replace Westman culture, something that would express Modman's inner self as exhaustively as his predecessor had managed to express his soul. The problem was that Modmen did not know how to create anything but 'happiness'. Not to worry: yet again Modmen switched into their copycat mode. Westmen's inventions were all in the public domain and stealing them was no problem. The trick was to adapt them to Modmen's ends.

For example, Westmen were deeply introspective, constantly searching for the God within them. Modmen could do self-digging with the best of them, but what was there to excavate? God was dead, and good riddance to bad rubbish. Modman did not need a deity; he was his own God. But where did this auto-deity reside, what with the soul having been scientifically proved not to exist? The answer came from the Modman prophet Freud. The old Austrian held one index finger to his lips and discreetly pointed at Modman's lower regions with the other. This is where the truth was. Modmen liked what they heard, 'heard' being the operative word as Modmen had no time to read Freud, what with his language being more complicated than that of the how-to books Modmen favoured. Fortunately, there was no need, what with a small army of interpreters sprouting everywhere. All Modmen had to do was unplug their ears and listen. And listen they did, with the smile on their faces growing wider and wider.

Man was no longer responsible for his actions, for human behaviour was not, as used to be believed, a matter of free choice. It was as good as predetermined by factors beyond our control. Most of those factors were deliciously naughty and a good job too. Modmen had always suspected that their genitals were more important than a nebulous soul, and they had been right all along. If a Modman despised his parents, it was not because they had tried to cram him full of the old stuff about morality and culture but because he secretly wanted to copulate with his mum and kill his dad. Conversely, if he loved his mother it was because subconsciously he wanted to return to her womb, penis first. If he loved his father, it was latent homosexuality, which was fine too. If he felt violent, it was because he had within his loins an ocean of bubbling, unsublimated libido. If he had trouble reading and writing, it was because his teachers had failed to divert his sexual energy into a productive channel.

Sex was his true self; the trick was to find an all-encompassing means of expression. Yet again it was Westman who showed the way by pointing, out of his grave, at a score sheet. Music and only music could wholly contain Westman's inner cravings and steer them along the foggy road leading to eternity. Well then, what was good enough for Westmen will have to be good enough for Modmen; even better, as a matter of fact, for Modmen had no need for Westmen's effete, elitist nonsense. Their music would be as young, robust and happily egalitarian as they were. The problem was that a typical Modman did not really know how to compose or for that matter to play music. If his inner self were as complex as Westman's was, he would have been at a loss, spending nights to stare blankly at an empty score sheet. But it was not, so he went straight to work.

First he reminded himself of his true Freudian self by swinging his hips back and forth. Those metronomic sexual gyrations had a rhythm all their own and Modman began to beat it on the table. One-two, one-two, and one-two-three; fast, slow, long, short – just like the sex manuals said. It felt great and Modman was getting carried away, yet he still felt that something was missing. He had got the beat spot on, but what about the words? Westman could make do with sheer sounds, all those sonatas and songs without words, but Modman felt an irresistible urge to communicate verbally. So he took stock of his lexicon, somewhat reduced on account of his reading habits. Modman then pulled the most prominent words out and, still snapping his hips to the beat imploding his head, arranged the words on the table in plausible binary combinations. Baby–bitch; love–hate; you–me; do–don't; I wanna–I don't wanna; no–yes, or rather yeah. Better still, yeah-yeah-yeah. Modman beheld the jumble on his table and saw that it was good. Yeah, he said; yeah, yeah, yeah. New music was born. The rest was marketing, a skill that comes to Modmen more naturally than any other. Overnight, pop music exploded into an unprecedented phenomenon. And even as Westman's music had been more than just music, Modman's pop excretions spilled out into the world of the spirit and became its master. Pop went the weasel of Westman's heritage. Pop music became coextensive with life itself. Generations of Modman's young have been defining themselves on the basis of the pop groups they liked; pop 'musicians' have attained a social, cultural and mythological status above that of any biblical prophet and only perhaps just short of Christ's erstwhile fame.

The very provenance of pop music made it a youth phenomenon, for the relative importance of sex tends to diminish with age. That was fine with the purveyors of the new cult. Catch the young early, when they are just beginning to feel those strange stirrings down there, long before they can be exposed to higher concerns, and they are yours for life. A youth spent in ecstatic convulsions clouded by the fog of narcotic haze is an ideal training ground for a Modman in the making. If a youngster cannot emerge from it all ready to pursue happiness, he will either die or go to prison. If he can, as most are able to, then the transition to a lifetime of philistine bliss will be so seamless as to leave no room for real contemplation, real thought, real feelings. In either case, nothing of Westman will ever take hold. Nothing will ever challenge Modmen's rule.

With its stress on the young, the pop culture of the philistine Modmen followed a well-trodden path. Soviet *komsomol*, Nazi *Hitler Jugend*, Mao's Red Guards all provided useful models to follow. Modmen of the philistine variety had the same totalitarian cravings as their nihilist brothers, so it stood to reason that they would look for similar techniques. The only technique not at their disposal was mass murder, but thankfully there was no need for it. Serious opposition could have come only from Westman, but he was already either dead or thoroughly marginalized. If some older people still had vague memories of Westman culture, it was a simple enough matter to shout them down and shut them up. Mind you, it may have been simple, but it still needed to be done.

First, a rift between parents and children needed to be widened. Turgenev showed in *Fathers and Sons* that such a rift is a natural accompaniment to a radical onslaught, and Modmen's offensive was nothing if not radical. Somehow it became fashionable to regard one's parents as 'uncool' or 'square' and to hate them if they as much as hinted at their disapproval of pop modernity. The purveyors of the 'youth culture' encouraged such commendable feelings, enlisting Freudian mumbo-jumbo for support. The young were urged to hate their families and, in the United States especially, to run away from them. The nomadic nature of American society, which goes back to its origin, now came to full fruition. The moment youngsters went through puberty, they would look for ways to sprout their pop wings and fly away from home. Nobody who was anybody went to college in his home-town, and few even considered finding a job within swearing distance of their parents. In the past, it was economic necessity that forced young Americans to regard the world as their oyster and the entire country as their market. Now it was alienation.

Pop music was the first all-encompassing mass phonomania, but it was not the first mass sound. Jazz had been that and whence came many of the behavioural patterns later to be associated with pop. Jazz too was an anti-Westman art and its practitioners could also attain a cult status. As the quasi-biblical figures they had become, jazzmen were identified by either their first names or nicknames: Oscar, Miles, Dizzy, Bird, King, Count and Duke. Had pop music not come along, jazz would have tried to take up the slack, but it would have been a poor substitute. The trouble with jazz was that it still required some musical attainment from its practitioners. The best of them, such as Art ('Tatum'), Bird ('Parker'), Dizzy ('Gillespie') and Miles ('Davies') possessed first-rate talents. As far as Modmen were concerned, this was a disqualifying circumstance. That sort of thing smacked of elitism, one of Modmen's most frightening bogeymen. It may have been fine for Parisian café goers, and jazz for a while enjoyed a greater fame in France than in its place of origin. But for the reference country of philistine modernity, jazz was found wanting. Musically, however, jazz was in many ways the precursor of pop. Traces of swing or rhythm and blues are prominent in the output of the early pop stars, such as Elvis Presley or Chuck Berry. After all, unoriginal innovators have to start somewhere, and imitation is as good a starting point as any. But even in those salad days of rock 'n roll, music played second fiddle to the cult. Presley in particular became a Christ-like figure, even acquiring aspects of resurrection after his death.

This religious surrogate aspect of pop became particularly prominent with the Beatles who started out as singers of cute little songs and ended up as false prophets, cult leaders of Modman's world. Somewhere along the way they acquired the help of musically trained assistants, so their later records display competent harmonies and even direct quotes from real composers, including Bach and Beethoven. Paradoxically, it is precisely in their late albums that music, even at its most primitive, no longer mattered. No one listened to it any longer anyway. Instead, hysterical audiences of youngsters were hanging onto every garbled word of the semiotic message they discerned behind the expertly harmonized pulse. Unlike Westman music, the Beatles had no spiritual content as such. Theirs was a glossocratic appeal, the marching orders screamed by a victorious Modman. In some extreme cases, the orders were literally understood and faithfully followed. Charles Manson and his 'family' went on a rampage of horrific murders partly as a result of the message they had perceived in the songs of *The White Album*. Charles, also known as 'Jesus Christ', claimed he was in extrasensory communication with his gods John and Paul. Perhaps he was, for he had heard nothing in the music of the Beatles that was not there. Pop music exists to express the true nature of Modmen, which is more or less circumscribed by their hatred of Westmen. Pushed to its extreme, hatred can take on a life of its own, bubble up and spill out indiscriminately. Once out in the open, it can drown everyone in its path, not just the original targets.

While the Beatles still tried to preserve a semblance of musicality, their followers have abandoned any such attempts. More and more, pop began to acquire overtly Satanist characteristics. More and more, it began to appeal not just to the darker side of human nature but to the sulphuric swamp concealed underneath it. The appeal continued to be quasi-religious, in the same sense in which the antichrist is the negative image of Christ. While Jesus redeemed his followers by dying on the cross, the messengers of the new god would commit suicide or else die of alcoholism, drug overdose or in due course of AIDS. Improbably, they were all portrayed as innocent victims of some unidentified enemy who, contextually, could only be Westman. So all those Freddie Mercurys gave their lives for a good cause. They are martyrs at the altar of hatred.

In the process, pop has become a big business, perhaps the biggest of all. Illiterate, tone-deaf adolescents can become billionaires overnight provided they can tickle the naughty bits of their mass audiences in a particularly effective way. They belch their anti-capitalist invective all the way to the capitalist bank and many critics sneer at the alleged paradox. There is none. The drug-crazed pop stars simply demonstrate the insignificant difference between the nihilist and the philistine in Modman. Walking embodiments of convergence, they emphasize the synthetic nature of Modman's business activity. Unlike Westmen, Modmen do not make products. They create markets and sell brands. They slap together subcultures. They fuse the markets and the subcultures into a uniform whole. In this case, pop music is only a part, although the most important one, of what passes for Modman culture. It is the heart of the new glossocratic Leviathan whose tentacles are numerous and ever-reaching. Pornography, fashion, show business, a great part of the publishing and record industries, electronic media including the Internet, drugs – all reach for the immature hearts and minds of Modmen's young.

It was Professor Allan Bloom who in his book *The Closing of the American Mind* commented on the unprecedented importance music had assumed in modern times. All his students seemed to define their personality in terms of music. Music was ever present in the background of people's lives; it was their philosophy, their love, their secret, their true essence. However, music has always been just as important, if not as invasive, ever since those early Christian polyphonists. But until Modman's victorious advent, music had been there to express the essence of Westman, a small island engulfed by a sea of internal barbarians. When Westman became extinct, the internal barbarian effected yet another larcenous shift by continuing with spiritual reliance on what he calls music.

DRUGS AND ROCK 'N ROLL

Fundamentalist Christians depict sex, drugs and rock 'n roll as the trident that has pierced God. As ever, their view of the world is a tad simplistic, but, if we disregard this for the moment, perhaps we shall acknowledge that their instincts are good even if their minds are not first-rate. The triumph of reason, in general, has had a curious effect on Modman's world. Reason is his professed shining path, and yet he hardly ever treads it. Even as Westmen used to stay in the 'ultra' range above reason, Modmen are at their most comfortable in the 'infra' range below it. So their arguments for or, if such is their wont, against drugs usually fall into the category of meaningless glossocratic verbiage. Yet if we ignore for the time being the glossocratic aspect of drugs, there seems to be little rational reason to object to their use.

After all, psychotropic drugs, used for medical or other purposes, have passed the test of time. The *Therapeutic Papyrus of Thebes* of 1552 BC lists opium among other recommended medicines. Even further back, Sumerian ideograms of about 4000 BC describe poppy as the 'plant of joy'. Helen passed illegal substances on to Telemachus and Menelaus and, if she lived today, would have been nicked faster than you can say 'let's see what's in your amphora, sunshine.' And Avicenna, shortly after revitalizing Christianity with a dose of Aristotle, died from an overdose of opium. Nor can even a conservative plausibly object to drugs on political grounds: not all drug users are left-wing. For example, though Byron and Shelley were a bit pink, Coleridge, who popped opium and drank laudanum like nobody's business, was as conservative as one can get. Freud, who snorted cocaine like a suction pump, was indeed politically unsavoury, but surely Queen Victoria was no subversive, and yet laudanum figured prominently in her diet.

A reasonable person of any political persuasion would find it difficult to object to the medical use of drugs. One doubts that even a Christian Scientist would submit to surgery without anaesthetics. As a true Westman rejects the primacy of matter, he should not advocate the use of morphine derivatives to deaden an aching tooth while at the same time stigmatizing reliance on similar compounds to relieve an aching soul. And if the agony of a cold in the head justifies the use of codeine, how can one decry using a greater dose of the same drug to deal with the spiritual agony produced by the cold world? One may say that, unlike recreational drugs, anaesthesia lacks an element of pleasure, to which a reasonable reply would be a resounding 'so what?' Many cases of drug addiction are iatrogenic to begin with, which is to say that medical use eventually leads to recreational abuse.

What about the moral argument? Are mind-altering drugs sinful *in se*? Every time we pour ourselves a cup of strong Lavazza to start the day or a glass of stiff Gordon's to end it, we forfeit the right to argue against drugs on that basis. And if our right foot ever gets heavy on a motorway, we are not entitled to say drugs are wrong simply because they are illegal. In any event, drug use in Britain was unrestricted until the 1868 Pharmacy Act and decriminalized until the 1920 Dangerous Drugs Act, and we cannot seriously believe that what was moral in 1919 all of a sudden became a sin in 1920. The outer edge of the moral argument reaches only as far as *malum prohibitum*, which puts dropping acid into the same category as dropping a seat belt. One would be on equally shaky grounds with a utilitarian argument. Taken in moderation, drugs are no more objectionable than alcohol. Taken in excess, some drugs, such as amphetamines, can indeed have undesirable social consequences, but anyone who has ever been attacked or vomited on by a drunk will agree that speed is not unique in that respect.

And let us not forget the positive effects of drugs. For example, a pill called 'West Coast Turnaround' improves the efficiency of long-distance transportation in the United States by allegedly enabling a trucker to go coast to coast and then immediately turn around and go all the way back. A similar concoction kept Falklands pilots flying more numerous sorties than was prudent, which was not the first time in history that the martial utility of drugs had come into play. Remember, for instance, the Viking berserks who gave rise to a good English word by munching magic mushrooms before battle, the Saracens who went on cannabis-inspired suicide missions behind the Crusaders' lines, or the Soviet soldiers in the penalty battalions who, under the influence of 96 per cent pure ethanol, would charge tanks with bayonets.

Of course, drugs have some medically undesirable effects as well, but we cannot build a rational argument on such a shaky foundation. Again, there is no proof that moderate use of drugs is medically harmful; and there is evidence that immoderate use of anything from tap water to puy lentils can kill you. Admittedly, however, if ever people do stop taking drugs, it will be a result of health fascism rather than moral absolutism, but this is immaterial to a rational argument.

Drug addiction is not a clear-cut problem either. True, frequent and extended use of some drugs can elevate the user's tolerance threshold, thus necessitating an ever-increasing dose to achieve the same effect. But, at a certain level, as a rule rather moderate one, most addicts find their own plateau dose beyond which they do not go. More often, the degree of addiction is linked to the severity of potential withdrawal symptoms but, on the purely physical level, they are usually not so bad. Qualifiers, such as 'usually', are important here, because cold turkey can peck some addicts to death. But in most cases, someone trying to come off opiates, such as heroin, is unlikely to experience physical withdrawal symptoms worse than flu, while there is no medical evidence that either cocaine or cannabis produces any physical withdrawal symptoms whatsoever. Naturally, addicts, especially those reluctant to stop, tend to picture withdrawal the way Goya pictured war, but then they would. In fact, the most dangerous withdrawal symptoms are associated with alcohol and barbiturates. Yet, though the latter have lost some of their erstwhile street cred, we can still score the former in any high street.

In the absence of physical addiction, we can talk about something no worse than a bad habit, and indeed 'drug habit' is ousting 'drug addiction' from the mantras of social workers. Being an expensive habit, drug taking can be financially ruinous ('cocaine is God's way of letting you know you're making too much money', as New Yorkers say), but, at £40 or so a gram, even a heavy user is unlikely to snort away more than say £100 a day, an amount a gambler would consider trifling and a commodity trader would not consider at all.

According to the old wisdom, what cannot be forbidden ought to be allowed: do we seriously believe that Modman states can remedy the drug problem, if it is indeed a problem to anyone but the addict himself? The 13 years between 1920, when the Eighteenth Amendment to the US Constitution put Prohibition into effect, and 1933, when the Twenty-First Amendment repealed the Eighteenth, ought to have been enough time to hammer the point home yet again: large-scale state interference does not solve problems. It either makes them worse or creates new ones. A war on poverty makes more people poor; an attempt to redistribute wealth destroys it; an overhaul of education promotes ignorance; an all-out effort to end all wars leads to more and bloodier ones.

326

At the end of all that bungling nothing beckons but an even greater expansion of the state, a further reduction of liberty. In this instance too, the price America paid for a marginal fall in cirrhosis cases during Prohibition was too high. The first organized black market was created to fill the void – predictably enough because a ban on the supply of a traditional commodity will not eliminate the demand. More damaging was the expansion of the existing services, especially those involved in law enforcement and tax collection, and also the birth of new baby Leviathans, such as the Bureau of Alcohol, Tobacco, Firearms and Explosives. Worst of all was the moral damage of criminalizing large numbers of people, many of whom had never before regarded the law as an enemy. A society where most citizens are seen, and see themselves, as criminals, is a criminal society.

While there is not a government in the world that does not pay lip service to the drug 'problem', none has solved it. The experience of countries like Thailand, where even the speedily enforced death penalty has failed to stem the flow of drugs, shows that policing cannot do the job even in conditions of dubious liberty. The inability of Western governments to stop drugs in prisons demonstrates that even absolute unfreedom enforced by the state is no panacea. The history of Britain and especially the USA, where every postwar president has waged 'war on drugs', suggests that a relatively free country cannot stop drugs no matter how much it desires such an outcome. That at least four of those presidential warriors had been drug users themselves proves the point further.

Americans are even less capable than the British of learning the lessons of history. After the dismal failure of their first prohibition, they started another one, much more fearsome than the first. The immediate casualties of the drug war were not addicts, but patients suffering from unbearable pain. Opiates remain the most, often the only, effective way to combat severe pain; yet physicians in America are under growing pressure from medical and non-medical authorities alike to curtail the use of painkillers even in cases of terminal cancer. Faced with the real danger of losing their licences, doctors often prefer to let patients writhe their way through the vicious PC circle of acupuncture, massage, hypnosis and, invariably, counselling. At least the patients can then go to meet their maker in the serene knowledge that the last weeks of their lives were not tainted by a risk of addiction. As with all such nonsense, the American experience is a taste of things to come in Britain and the rest of Modman's world, so let us pray we are not in too much pain five years from now.

To sum it all up, the rational case against drugs is weak. Then why do Westman holdouts tend to turn drugs down at parties? Why do we wince squeamishly whenever drugs are mentioned? Why do we override reason and, unless we are out-and-out libertarians, keep insisting that drugs should stay banned? Yet again, intuition goes beyond reason and, often, aesthetics beyond ethics. Acting as the trigger is the convoluted rituals drug users feel called upon to go through. At a party where no one would object to cocaine, the snorters would wink at one another, get up and, in mock secrecy, go to the bathroom where the ubiquitous paraphernalia lie upon the marble top: tiny bags of cocaine, a gold razor blade for cutting lines, plastic straws and paper handkerchiefs. Suddenly we realize it is not drugs that determine the way we feel. It is the ritual.

Any ritual is a semiotic system, not a philosophy but a way of communicating one. As a quick parallel, clothes are a semiotic system as well. A middle-class gentleman does not leave the bottom button of his waistcoat undone because he is more comfortable that way, and he does not have his jackets made with three buttons because two would not do the job – he only uses one anyway. No, what he is doing is communicating to the outside world subcutaneous signals, in this instance those related to class. What do the drug-related rituals, as distinct from drugs *qua* drugs, communicate? Why, they transmit the signals of sex-drugs-and-rock 'n roll modernity, a disease even more communicative than bad taste. And in doing so, they reflect many other dynamics of the collapse of Westman's world.

A relativist, empiricist society preaches that absolute truth is not only unknowable but non-existent, and one can discover puny half-truths by experimentation – so why not flood one's brain with drugs to see what will come up in the wash? A youth is taught that his own self is not only important but uniquely important – so why not give it a boost? A self-indulgent girl grows up never having encountered real beauty, be that art or religion – so why not create a surrogate by doing coke? Instead of St John's Passion, people are exposed to the sound bites of psychobabble harmonized with the mind-numbing beat of pop in the background. As their senses rival their minds for hopeless ignorance, they feel not happy but high, not sad but depressed – so why not use psychochemicals? Somewhere in their viscera, Modman champions are proud that the ethos they represent is at odds with what they call the 'establishment' but what is in fact the scattered fragments of an imploded Westman world. Unskilled in semantics, they have to use semiotics to scream defiance, to spit in the face of the moribund beauty they despise. It is the dead face of Westman that they are spitting in.

Drugs have not always had this hidden semiotic agenda. But semiotics change with age, so what was good enough for Messrs Coleridge, de Quincey, Collins or Conan Doyle cannot be good enough for Westman holdouts. We know that Modman lurks not only behind the belching football supporter but also, regardless of his other endearing characteristics, behind the perfectly amiable gentleman who has just offered us cocaine. *Vade retro* is the only possible response.

OPPOSITES ATTRACTING

Legal pop music, illegal drugs and semi-legal pornography show yet again that the gap between the nihilist and philistine is possible to bridge. A drug-crazed 'musician' who has become rich purveying 'I'll-slash-you-bitch' nihilism feels at ease discussing tax shelters and offshore investments with his banker. The latter lets his hair down in the after hours, goes to a football match, gets drunk and yells 'If it wasn't for England, you'd all be krauts' at the visiting fans. Convergence can thus work within a nominally philistine society, but what about geopolitical convergence between philistine and nihilist societies?

We have seen on several occasions that these have much in common: they are first cousins if not exactly identical twins. But such kinship does not preclude internecine conflicts. Cain and Abel were even more closely related than that, and yet they could not resolve their differences without violence. Yes, the philistine and nihilist have the same list of desiderata, but they arrange them in a different sequence. The philistine has the positive objectives, namely universal equality and prosperity, much closer to the top than obliteration of Westman; whereas for the nihilist it is the other way around. And priorities matter to exponents of broadly similar creeds. In fact, one can go so far as to say they matter more than any differences of core principle, at least as a potential trigger of murderous animosity.

The main difference between the USA, spearheading philistine Modman's aspirations, and Russia, the nihilist's champion, is that the former has been more successful in achieving the entire spectrum of Modman goals. At the violet, positive end the philistines have managed to spread comfort more widely and evenly. While only a tiny proportion of their people are either very rich or abysmally poor, the rest fall within a band that is possibly the widest this side of Sparta. The philistines have passed many laws designed to smooth out the natural peaks in human character so as to bring them closer to the troughs. Their people are more or less equal before the law, in that most of them accept that levelling is its essential part. The philistines' education is also successful in making the populace universally and equally ignorant. The cultural, political and economic differences among philistine states are fast disappearing.

Witness the seemingly inexorable march of the European Union, blessed by the laying on of American hands. If everything proceeds as planned, then in a few years an English visitor to Greece will not know he is not in, say, Scotland until he realizes that people around him are somewhat darker and speak grammarless Euro-English with more of a foreign accent. As a matter of fact, American tourists already are finding various European places difficult to tell apart. A gentleman who runs an English-language bookshop in Florence says that hardly a day goes by that he is not asked for directions to the Coliseum, Rialto Bridge, the Bridge of Sighs or even the Parthenon.

In Russia today universal prosperity is further away than perhaps at any time in her history. The same communist-KGB-criminal elite that has ruled Russia since the Bolshevik takeover is still ruling it. But while before it seldom bothered to express its towering social superiority in cold cash, now it is finding it more expedient to think in monetary terms. As a result, about 100,000 Russians probably have more liquidity stashed away than the richest 100,000 Americans, but the rest of the population are starving. So in neither prosperity nor equality can the Russians boast parity with the Americans. In legal matters the elite rules Russia as lawlessly and ruthlessly as it always has done, except it prefers regular to judicial murders. This exacerbates inequality among the people by dividing them into a small group of shooters and a large mass of shootees.

The philistine is also leading the way at the red-hot negative end of the spectrum. The last vestiges of Westman's heritage have been uprooted in the United States, at least among the masses, and the rest of the philistine countries are busily trying to catch up. Nothing of Westman's cultural past is seen as worth keeping and the philistine Modmen sneer at it openly. As an experiment, the reader might scan some travel books, especially those published in

America. In their historical notes, events of the past and the men who produced Westman's proudest achievements are routinely treated with ironic condescension. The authors of such booklets are either saying outright or strongly implying that all those dusty trinkets have some curiosity value, so by all means, Wayne and Sharon, take a look at them when you have nothing better to do. But please do not lose sight of the fact that it is not cathedrals and canvases that constitute the highest point of history but – well, it is you, Wayne and Sharon. Real life is made up of things like the price of land in Lincoln, Nebraska, not all those Lepantos and the dead white males who took part in them. One of them may have written *Don Quixote*, but who ever reads it anyway? The philistine in America has grown to be so smug that he no longer honours Westmen with hatred. Derisory laughter is all he can spare. In Europe, where Westmen used to live, they left a deeper imprint. Some of their symbols, such as royal paraphernalia, are sometimes taken off the mothballs and paraded in front of Modmen, thus reminding them of potential danger and stoking up their darker feelings. Hatred is more widespread here, but the essence is the same. Westman is either a risible or a hateful relic of the past.

Glossocratically, philistine Modmen are also doing better. In a way this is understandable, for glossocracy is the main power mechanism they have at their disposal. So they have refined its use and created a situation in which glossocratic messages are accepted as the truth the world over. For example, they have been broadcasting to the world the panegyrics for free enterprise, as championed by the government of the United States – in other words, the same government that plunged the world into the worst economic catastrophe ever through its staggering incompetence in handling the 1929 recession. And the same government that in the wake of the resulting depression has become a corporatist quasi-socialist Leviathan whose links with real free enterprise are growing more and more tenuous. But where reality fails, glossocracy succeeds.

The nihilistic Modmen in Russia have other weapons in their armoury and so they therefore have not had to rely exclusively on glossocracy. Unfortunately for them, having had to retain aspects of Westman's cultural heritage, they now must deal with a large group of people who, while not exactly fully-fledged Westmen, are immune to Modmen's glossocratic propaganda. In the past, once a holdout's recalcitrance was diagnosed as a terminal condition, the nihilist no longer wasted his breath on glossocratic persuasion. A quick bullet in the nape of the neck or a lifetime, mercifully short, at a Siberian resort used to be more effective. These days, a long-term starvation diet coupled with the odd surreptitious murder can do a similar job. In any case, the nihilists' glossocracy has always worked better internationally than in their own countries. After all: Westman was no longer a threat in the West and it was easy to convince the philistines that all men were created not just equal but more or less the same. People like to look for factual support of their preconceptions. They are prepared to accept the flimsiest lies if those prove them right in their own eyes. That made the philistines a soft touch and the nihilists' glossocracy has had a relatively easy ride in the West. At every point in Russia's modern history, manifestly including today, Western philistines believed about Russia what the Russians wanted them to believe.

At first they wanted to be seen as agrarian socialists out to improve the lot of the peasants, and the West obliged. The glossocratic potential of slogans based on universal equality is huge, what with philistine Modmen sharing such ideals and believing that everybody else does. Then the Russians wanted the West to believe that Lenin's NEP was a return to a semblance of constitutional government, and the assorted Shaws, Webbs, Steffenses, Feuchtwangers, Barbusses and Wellses jumped as ordered. What the Russians want the West to believe about them now is that they are genuinely committed to civilized behaviour, philistine-style. The West obliges with alacrity. After all, the

Russians appear more eager than ever to play the glossocratic game by the philistine rules. Western governments are at pains to stress the similarities between themselves and Russia, which contributes to their becoming frightfully similar. Witness the fact that Westman holdouts who managed to survive the worst excesses of Stalinism in Russia are now beginning to be marginalized in the same way as in the West. If 30 years ago a professor was a highly respected figure, then today he is an object of derision or, which is worse, pity. Convergence of any kind is possible only at the lowest possible level.

IS THERE LIFE AFTER DEATH?

'It is not, nor it cannot come to good.'

(W. Shakespeare)

Westman is dead. This much is clear, and so a quiet prayer is in order for his turbulent, tragic, talented soul. But, if our prayers include a plea for resurrection, they will go unanswered until we prove that we are worthy of special consideration. What can we, the few remaining Westman holdouts, do to qualify? Or, barring divine interference, is there any worldly hope for us? The two questions may seem unrelated. In fact, given the origin of Westman, they are one and the same. It is his soul that made Westman what he was; it is the preservation of his soul that holds a glimmer of hope for his coming back from the dead. This is our task, and one we must achieve even as Modman's cultural noose is tightening on our throats.

Unlike God, man is not eternal and neither is any human type. Sooner or later they all die, just as individuals do. Hellenic man died, though some of him went on living in Westman. Westman died and nothing of him went on living in Modman. This is the congenital defect Modman carries, for his behaviour is unchecked by traditional ethics or morals. Utilitarian 'happiness' is his only

God, hatred for Westmen his greatest passion. These may suffice when the world is in cruising mode, but not when it skids and swerves, which it doubtless will do sooner or later. Man is mortal; in violent times violent man is more mortal than any other. Modmen, with their smugness, may think they have reversed this simple law of history, but of course they have not. They may feel that their newly developed ability to clone human beings is the key to immortality, but since they can clone only the likes of themselves it is in fact a shortcut to the final catastrophe. Modman will perish one day and with him the soulless world he has hatched. Nor will he be in any position to pray for a revival, for he does not know how.

Modman was brought into existence by hatred of the kind described by Friedrich Reck-Malleczewen, whose testimony of Modman Germany is exceptionally moving. He recalls Ludendorff ordering the destruction of the castle of Coucy, a priceless treasure of Westman's past and one that had no military significance to either side. And yet Ludendorff, a nihilist Modman in our taxonomy, ordered the castle razed. 'He hated Coucy,' writes Reck, 'because he hated everything which lay outside his barracks view of life – spirit, taste, elegance, everything that gives distinction to life'. This kind of hatred must be capable of releasing immense energy, for it produced Modman and weaned him to maturity on the congealing red liquor that is his favoured sustenance. But the liquor has poison mixed in, and Modman will die by the same hatred by which he lives.

How exactly this will happen is of no interest, and gazing into the crystal ball is a tedious pastime anyway. One could, however, venture a guess, and here the pre-Enlightenment methodology of this book can come in handy. The philistine Modman tries to impose, and the nihilist feigns to accept, the materialist, mercantile idea of happiness. Many a time throughout the blood-soaked twentieth century, the philistine showed eagerness to kill untold millions in defence of his right to be happy in that tastelessly comfortable way of his. And, as he proved in the skies over Serbia a few years ago, he does not mind slaking his thirst for power with innocent blood. Moreover, so deeply is he attached to his overheated paradise that he is even prepared to die for it – the only thing worth dying for because, to the philistine, comfort is the only thing worth living for.

Therein lurks the danger. The heat generated by his central boiler has steamed up the philistine's glasses and he cannot see the perils clearly. Enveloped in wet fog, the figure at a distance appears to be a fellow philistine, whereas in fact it is the disguised nihilist. He may be converging with the philistine, but he has not yet. Even when they are close to convergence, the two subspecies of Modman can still be at each other's throats, for they will be reaching for the same prize in their soulless world. Be that as it may, the nihilist is still very much with us, and this fellow craves either the philistine's money or his life, preferably both. Money he cannot have, at least not enough of it to make a real difference. Money for the philistine is what hair was for Samson: his source of strength. Shorn of money, the philistine is easy prey to any Delilah, and he knows it. He does not mind slicing his zero-sum pie this way and that, tossing the crumbs to the nihilist, but he will not want the pie to become much smaller.

And yet there is enough of the nihilist in him to be ready to walk the knife's edge. This is not just an exercise in the cheap thrills of brinkmanship, but a dire necessity. For the philistine too is a Modman first and foremost. As such, he is driven by his hatred of Westman, not just by affection for scented loo paper. And to push hatred to its logical conclusion, he needs more than just money. He needs power, and the more absolute, the better. So when he feigns ignorance of the nihilist threat, he is not being stupid any more than a leopard is stupid when stalking a rhino. Wittingly or unwittingly, he is trying to prod the nihilist into action, for the philistine hopes that his power will be annealed in the resulting fire. States make war and war makes states, the saying goes. That partly was the motivation behind Wilson trying to drag America into the First World War and Roosevelt into the Second, or behind the British and the French ignoring the Nazi threat in the 1930s, or behind today's West feeling safe – with some foolishly claiming that history has ended simply because the Soviets call themselves something else now. And the stratagem has worked, after a fashion.

But fashions change, and God only knows what mayhem Modmen will trigger off next. One thing for sure, neither they nor their deified happiness will survive it. The architectural monstrosities they have plonked in the middle of what used to be Westman's world will collapse like a house of cards. When that happens, nothing of Modman will be left standing except the nastiness he has so diligently cultivated. The same fire will consume Modmen's non-music, non-paintings and non-books. Modmen have produced nothing of lasting value but 'happiness' and we know from the example of the last century how perishable this commodity can be. When happiness turns to misery, as history teaches it is sooner or later bound to, Modman will have nothing to fall back on. And so he will die as he has lived.

Westman, on the other hand, was not scared of suffering because it was to a large extent suffering that had made him what he was. He created real beauty because he knew he himself was created. That beauty is dead now but, like its originator, it may still rise. For, whatever the intensity of the fire to be fanned by Modman's dying breath, somewhere somehow there will be found a charred score sheet with the notes of a Bach fugue still legible, a half-burned collection of still-readable Shakespeare sonnets, a torn, but restorable Rembrandt canvas and, one hopes, the Bible. Then someone will be able to piece the glorious whole together and out will come a revived and rejuvenated Westman, a Lazarus brought back from the dead, a light reignited to blind the infidels yet again with the glory of transcendent beauty. But will there be such able restorers around at that vital moment? For if there are not, the wind will pick up the pieces and scatter them over the smouldering ashes, and they themselves will turn to ash.

If we accept that such a danger exists, then we know what we must do: keep vigil over Westman's treasure. It is in this vigil that the future of Westman lies, if there is to be a future. And readers who have got this far and agreed with at least something of what they have read will know exactly how this vigil is to be kept. Passive resistance to every unpalatable morsel Modmen try to shove down our throats is the only avenue still open. Active resistance is no longer possible, for it will be squashed with disdainful ease. Successful resistance can only come from a position of strength, and Westman's strength is in his soul, which is a place for contemplation, not physical action.

Those who seek salvation in conservative politics are likely to be disappointed, and most of them know it. Conservatism is meaningless unless there is something left that is worth conserving. Thus one can conserve the trees of today's Amazon jungle but not the trees that burnt in the stoves of years ago. If a Westman holdout thinks his conservative aspirations are best achieved through the championship of a party that uses the name 'Conservative', 'Republican', 'Christian Democrat' or some such, he is making a big mistake. 'Conservative' these days means philistine, as opposed to nihilist, Modman. Ascribing any other meaning to it is self-deception at best. By all means, we should continue to vote for the lesser of two evils as we see it, even though we may suspect that we are in fact voting for the evil of two lessers. But the pleasure one derives from such a voting pattern has more to do with aesthetics than with any realistic hope.

The cause of European integration is a case in point. Many people dislike it; some are fighting it in the political trenches. This is all good and well as long as we remember that Europe was pretty much integrated at the time when Westmen were building their great cathedrals, many of the same cathedrals that Modman nation states have blown up. So when a gentleman describing himself as a conservative insists on preserving (conserving) the nation states of Europe, he would do well to decide what it is exactly that he wishes to conserve. Our taxonomy would help by arming him with the right reasons for opposing European federalism in its present form. For the European Union, while it may loosely resemble the shape of the Holy Roman Empire, has none of its content. Today's European superstate is designed as a mixing bowl in which the philistine and the nihilist can be vigorously whisked together. The philistine wrongly believes that the mixture will have his kind of bland taste, while the nihilist knows that his is the stronger ingredient. One way or the other, the prospects are bleak for Westman holdouts.

Yet opposing Modmen politically on this or any other issue is useless – Westman holdouts simply no longer have any institutions through which such an opposition could exert telling pressure. However, there is still much we can do. We can resist Modmen's glossocratic vocabules by insisting that words be used in their real meaning. We can reject what passes for music in Modmen's world, including the atrocities they perpetrate on what used to be Westman music. We can patronize only concerts of real musicians playing real music, buy only real books written by real writers and attend only exhibitions of real art produced by real artists. We can avoid Modmen's pastimes, ignore their cajoling and openly scorn their tastes. We can try to counter the pernicious effect of Modmen's schools on our children by teaching them Westman truths. We can keep our churches going even if they are falling into the hands of happy-clappy Modmen, as most have done already. We can continue to hone our minds and tastes to a point where they become worthy of Westman's heritage. We can continue to plant seeds of doubt into the heads of borderline Modmen by mocking their ethical, spiritual and aesthetic paucity. We can set, as best we can, an example of a life of honour, beauty and charity. And we can pray.

On this note the story ends. And is it the dying echo of forlorn hope reverberating through the years to come?

London, Cortona, St Fargeau

INDEX